The
EVERYTHING.
Buddhism Book

Dear Reader:

    Like many Westerners, I was not raised a Buddhist but came to Buddhism on my own. My family did not practice any organized religion, though spirituality was strong in my home. I was introduced to Buddhism while working in publishing. Many books were coming across my desk that spoke of emptiness, suffering, and awakening to truth. My interest was piqued and Buddhism warranted further investigation.

    I discovered the Zen Mountain Monastery in the Catskill Mountains of New York and took an introductory weekend on Zen practice. To my surprise, I discovered that practice was *hard*, but there was something about it that kept bringing me back. Well, as they say: When the student is ready the teacher appears, and so it was for me. After moving from New York City to the farm country of New Jersey I had no reason to hope that I would stumble across, as I did, a sangha and a teacher and that my life would become so wonderfully alive because of it. But the world has a way of wanting you to wake up and if you open your mind you will see the lessons everywhere. The discovery of Buddhist practice is a blessing like none other.

The EVERYTHING® Series

Editorial

Publishing Director	Gary M. Krebs
Managing Editor	Kate McBride
Copy Chief	Laura MacLaughlin
Acquisitions Editor	Eric Hall
Development Editor	Michael Paydos
Production Editor	Khrysti Nazzaro

Production

Production Director	Susan Beale
Production Manager	Michelle Roy Kelly
Series Designers	Daria Perreault
	Colleen Cunningham
Cover Design	Paul Beatrice
	Frank Rivera
Layout and Graphics	Colleen Cunningham
	Rachael Eiben
	Michelle Roy Kelly
	Daria Perreault
	Erin Ring
Series Cover Artist	Barry Littmann
Interior Photographs:	©2001 Brand X Pictures
	and ©Corel—Spirit of Buddha

THE

EVERYTHING®

BUDDHISM
BOOK

Learn the ancient traditions and
apply them to modern life

Jacky Sach

▲

Adams Media Corporation
Avon, Massachusetts

An Everything® Series Book.
Everything® and everything.com® are registered trademarks of F+W Publications, Inc.

Published by Adams Media, an F+W Publications Company
57 Littlefield Street, Avon, MA 02322 U.S.A.
www.adamsmedia.com

ISBN: 1-58062-884-2
Printed in the United States of America.

J I H G F E D C B

Library of Congress Cataloging-in-Publication Data
Sach, Jacky.
The everything Buddhism book / Jacky Sach.
p.   cm.   (Everything series)
ISBN 1-58062-884-2
1. Buddhism. I. Title. II. Series.

BQ4012.S23 2003
294.3–dc21
2002154917

This publication is designed to provide accurate and authoritative information with regard to the subject matter covered. It is sold with the understanding that the publisher is not engaged in rendering legal, accounting, or other professional advice. If legal advice or other expert assistance is required, the services of a competent professional person should be sought.
—From a *Declaration of Principles* jointly adopted by a Committee of the American Bar Association and a Committee of Publishers and Associations

Many of the designations used by manufacturers and sellers to distinguish their products are claimed as trademarks. Where those designations appear in this book and Adams Media was aware of a trademark claim, the designations have been printed with initial capital letters.

This book is available at quantity discounts for bulk purchases.
For information, call 1-800-872-5627.

Contents

Acknowledgments / ix

Top Ten Pearls of Buddhist Wisdom Found In This Book / x

Introduction / xi

1 Under the Bodhi Tree: The Buddhist Way / 1

Budhism Today **2** • Religion or Philosophy? **2** • Practice, Practice, Practice **4** • Everything Is Nothing **4** • Refuge **6** • The Sinless World **6** • Buddha's Contemporaries **8**

2 The Buddha: History and Legend / 13

Siddhartha Gautama **14** • Youth of Luxury and Pleasure **15** • Finding the Path: The Renunciation **18** • The Five Ascetics **20** • The Middle Way **21** • Enlightenment **22**

3 The Buddha's Teachings: The Four Noble Truths / 27

The First Sermon: The Dharma Wheel Turns **28** • The First Noble Truth: All Life Is Suffering **31** • The Second Noble Truth: The Cause of Suffering Is Desire **36** • The Third Noble Truth: Suffering Can End! **37** • The Fourth Noble Truth: The Way **38**

4 The Buddha's Teachings: The Eightfold Path / 41

The Way **42** • Right Understanding **44** • Right Thought **45** • Right Speech **46** • Right Action **46** • Right Livelihood **47** • Right Effort **48** • Right Mindfulness **49** • Right Concentration **49** • The Parable of the Poison Arrow **50**

5 The Buddha's Ethics / 51

The Five Precepts **52** • Do Not Destroy Life **52** • Do Not Steal **53** • Do Not Commit Sexual Misconduct **55** • Do Not Lie **56** • Do Not Take Intoxicating Drinks **56** • The Five Hindrances **57** • More Precepts **59** • The Precepts Versus the Ten Commandments **60** • Ethical Dilemmas Today **61**

6 The Buddhist Community / 65

The Three Jewels **66** • The First Jewel: The Buddha **68** • The Second Jewel: The Dharma **70** • The Third Jewel: The Sangha **72** • Finding the Three Jewels Today **74**

7 Karma / 77

Popular Misconceptions of Karma **78** • Karma As the Moral Center **81** • Karma and Cycles of Birth **83** • Rebirth: Life As the Wheel of Samsara **84** • The Power of Karma **88**

8 The Buddhist Cosmos / 91

Past Lives **92** • The Three Realms **93** • The Realm of Desire **94** • The Realm of Form **99** • The Realm of No-Form **100** • Making Sense of the Cosmos **101**

9 Buddhism in India: Life after Buddha / 103

The Buddha's Life and Death **104** • The Followers **106** • The First Council: The Council at Rajagriha **107** • The Second Council: The Council at Vesali **108** • King Ashoka and the Third Council: The Council at Pataliputra **109** • The Fourth Council: The Council at Jalandhar **110** • The Eighteen Schools **111** • The Pali Canon and Mahayana Scriptures **112**

10 The Three Vehicles / 115

The Diversification of Buddhism **116** • Theravada **117** • Mahayana **119** • Theravada and Mahayana on Emptiness **121** • Differences Between the Two Main Schools **122** • Vajrayana **123**

11 The Spread of Buddhism / 129

Sri Lanka **130** • Burma **132** • Thailand **133** • Cambodia, Laos, and Indonesia **134** • Northward Bound **136** • China: Pure Land and Ch'an **136** • Japan **139** • Tibet **140** • Korea **141** • The East Today **142**

12 Tibetan Buddhism / 145

In the News **146** • Buddhist Origins **146** • The Six Traditions of Tibetan Spirituality **148** • Common Threads **153** • The Quest for the Dalai Lama **154** • Contemporary Tibet **156**

13 Zen Practice / 159

Beginner's Mind **160** • *Zazen* **161** • Group Practice **164** • Koan Practice **166** • Work Practice **168** • Zen Study and Liturgy **170**

14 Meditation Practice / 171

Why Meditate? **172** • What You Will Need: Supplies **173** • Posture **175** • The Breath **176** • Techniques **177** • Mindfulness **182**

15 Nirvana / 185

Extinguishing the Fires of Desire **186** • No Place **187** • Nirvana in This Life **190** • Nirvana after Death **193** • Nirvana versus Heaven **194** • What the Teachers Say about Nirvana **195**

16 Ceremony and Celebration / 199

Pilgrimages **200** • Giving It Away: Engaged Buddhism **203** • Tea Ceremonies **205** • Holidays **209** • Practical Matters: Know Thy Neighbor **212**

17 Life and Death and Other Practical Matters / 213

Children and Practice **214** • Rites of Passage **215** • Education **216** • Visiting Monasteries **217** • Marriage **218** • Buddhism and Sex **220** • Women in Buddhism **221** • Death **223**

18 **Buddhist Art / 225**
Art Practice **226** • Architecture **226** • Buddhist Statuary and Images **228** • Sand Paintings and Mandalas **230** • Thangkas **230** • Gardens **231** • Haiku **232** • Zen Art **233**

19 **Buddha and the West / 237**
Westward Bound **238** • Thich Nhat Hanh and Jesus **239** • Thomas Merton **241** • The Western Face of Buddhism **242** • Contemporary Buddhist Literature **244** • The Zen of Everything **245** • Buddhism and Psychotherapy **247** • A Bird's-Eye View: Three American Buddhist Teachers **248**

20 **Practicing Buddhism / 253**
No Words **254** • How to Start a Practice **255** • Giving Up the Ego **258** • Knowing No-Thing Is Everything **258** • Fullness in Emptiness **260** • Mortal Teachers **260** • Here and Now **261**

Appendix A • Glossary / **264**
Appendix B • Resources / **266**
Appendix C • Buddhist Monasteries and Practice Centers in the United States / **271**

Index / 283

Acknowledgments

To my dharma teacher, Kurt, and to my dharma friends Alex and Bob. With much gratitude to all of the teachers who illuminate the path with brilliant books, Web sites, and tapes. A list of valuable resources is available at the back of this book, though the teachings of the dharma far exceed any space allotted here.

With special thanks to Eric Hall, a wonderful and supportive editor.

Top Ten Pearls of Buddhist Wisdom
Found In This Book

1. Identifying ourselves with others, we can never slay or cause to slay.
—THE BUDDHA

2. Each of you should make himself his island, make himself and no one else his refuge, each of you must make the dharma his island, the dharma and nothing else his refuge. —THE BUDDHA

3. Whoever honors his own sect and condemns other sects . . . injures his own more gravely. —KING ASHOKA

4. Life is a series of spontaneous changes. Don't resist them—that only creates sorrow. Let reality be reality. Let things flow naturally forward in whatever way they like. —LAO TSE

5. Even loss and betrayal bring us awakening. —THE BUDDHA

6. To live fully is to let go and die with each passing moment, and to be reborn in each new one —JACK KORNFIELD

7. When you paint Spring, do not paint willows, plums, peaches, or apricots, but just paint Spring. To paint willows, plums, peaches, or apricots is to paint willows, plums, peaches, or apricots—it is not yet painting Spring. —DOGEN

8. Die before you die and you shall never die. —SUFI SAYING

9. All the happiness there is in the world comes from thinking about others, and all the suffering comes from preoccupation with yourself. —SHANTIDEVA

10. If on the path you don't meet your equal, it's best to travel alone. There's no fellowship with fools. —*THE DHAMMAPADA*

Introduction

▶BUDDHISM TRACES ITS ROOTS BACK TO THE BUDDHA, who lived more than 2,500 years ago in northern India. The Buddha discovered a way to live that has changed people's lives for centuries as his teachings were passed down from teacher to student all the way to us. The Buddha taught a practice of mindfulness that opened the mind to another way of experiencing the world. He taught kindness, compassion, morality, and ethics. Buddhism shares similarities with most of the other great religions of the world—in fact, it shares the Golden Rule with *all* of the world's great religions.

After the Buddha's death Buddhism took on a life of its own and different schools and traditions arose. The traditions all have at their core the same basic teachings but the path to awakening might vary in some degree. Buddhism is a practice—it is a hands-on experience and involves the marriage of mind and body through various practices and studies. There is a long-standing yogic tradition in Buddhism and the Buddha himself practiced yoga.

Buddhism in the West is on the rise and as the practices spread in the United States it appears a new form of Buddhism is arising that incorporates practices and thought from each of the traditions that arose after Buddha. It is not difficult to find a place to practice Buddhism in any state in the United States. Monasteries, sitting groups, schools, and discussion groups abound. Buddhism is alive and thriving in the United States, in the minds and bodies of all kinds of Americans, as Buddhism knows no gender, no race, no distinctions.

Buddhists are known as a peaceful group, and historically have gone to great lengths to practice peace and protest war. Who can forget the image of the Vietnamese Buddhist peace activists making extraordinary sacrifices—including self-immolation—to try to end the fighting during the Vietnam War? Today, Buddhism makes headlines as the struggle in Tibet awakens international interest and the unrest in Sri Lanka strains toward peace.

The Dalai Lama is all over the bestseller lists teaching us how to be happy, and the Buddhism section in the bookstore grows larger daily.

Buddhism is a colorful, exciting, dynamic study with the power to transform lives.

More and more Americans are turning to Buddhism in one form or another for answers to the questions that hound them. Americans are incorporating Buddhism into their own religions as well. Christians and Jews alike practice aspects of Buddhism while retaining their own traditions and marking their own holidays. From celebrities to the clerk at the video store, this vibrant religion is capturing the hearts and energies of many of us. Anyone who is compelled to learn more about the nature of their own suffering, the world's suffering, the heart of truth, and how to understand conflict, will be pulled toward Buddhism. The Buddha embarked on an adventure to discover his true nature and the true nature of the world. He relied on nothing but his own experiences and invited everyone else to do the same. And now you, too, are invited to have an encounter with the truth and see what Buddhism is all about. It just might surprise you. Ⓔ

Chapter 1

Under the Bodhi Tree: The Buddhist Way

Buddhism is indeed one of the world's great religions. Behind Christianity, Islam, and Hinduism, it is the fourth most populous religion in the world. It is a complex and multifaceted belief system that can be difficult for many to understand. Just calling Buddhism a religion can cause argument, as many believe Buddhism to be an entire way of life. But what is Buddhism and where did it come from? Is it a religion or a philosophy?

Buddhism Today

Buddhism has fascinated people for years but has recently become more interesting to many as we struggle through a time of darkness and violence in a suddenly frightening and confusing world. Buddhism is a religion of peace and serenity, of nonviolence and pacifism—qualities that can be very attractive when surrounded by incomprehensible violence and pain. Even Buddhist countries are beset by violence, however. The Tibetan government has been in exile from its homeland due to the invasion of Communist China in 1949, and Sri Lanka has been battling war for the past nineteen years. However, Buddhists take up the path of least resistance—the path to peace.

In today's world, it has become almost unbelievable to consider that peace is possible. Many people are turning to Buddhism to see if it has some answers to questions we never thought we'd address.

FACT

According to Russell Chandler, the author of *Racing Toward 2001*, there were an estimated 359 million Buddhists in the world in 2000, with a projected growth rate of 1.7 percent annually. Buddhist world population should top 359 million by 2001; and an increasing number will reside in the West.

Religion or Philosophy?

Buddhism started with the Buddha, a man born to a prominent and wealthy family in India 2,500 years ago. Buddhism differs from other religions such as Christianity in that Buddha is recognized to have been an ordinary man; Buddha is not a deity. He was a man who spent his life in search of the nature of reality and the truth at the heart of life itself. Buddha never claimed any inspiration or inside connection to a god or higher power. He believed that every person was a potential Buddha and humankind was supreme, above all other animals, in that humans had the ability—if they tried hard enough—to achieve enlightenment. No other power exists higher than humankind or influences human life. Man is in charge of his own destiny. In other words, man's emancipation from suffering was solely his own responsibility.

Unlike Other Religions

Though Buddhists can be said to follow the teachings of Buddha, Buddha does not lead his followers to God. The teachings of Buddha lead us to the practice of a truthful life. Buddhist principles teach the path to awakening, or truth. Practicing a truthful life and awakening to the reality of the world is open to everyone. Buddha just shows us the way.

Buddhists believe that we are distracted from seeing the truth or reality of the world—from seeing things as they really are—by our delusions, our thoughts, and our desires. By following the principles and practices the Buddha has set forth for us, we can slowly part the curtain of illusion and experience life and the world as they really are—the essence of truth.

Not Quite a Philosophy

Buddhism manifests itself through personal realization—through the practice of its principles. In this way, it is not a religion of the word, as our other well-known religions are. Because Buddhism does not set forth a belief in a higher power separate from oneself—a god who created us and is separate from us—it is often classified as a philosophy. But if one practices Buddhism as the Buddha suggests, then words and beliefs are meaningless and must be left behind.

It doesn't matter what Buddhism is, it only matters that you get to the truth. The argument becomes moot, and we come to realize that the question itself is not important. Buddhism is, most important of all, a belief in the power of practice.

Mindfulness is the substance of a Buddha. When you enter deeply into the present moment, you, too, become a living Buddha. You see the nature of reality, and this insight liberates you from suffering and confusion.

—Thich Nhat Hanh

Practice, Practice, Practice

What do we mean by practice? Practice what? Buddhists believe that in order to achieve an enlightened mind and reach Nirvana they must follow a set of guidelines to living as laid out by Buddha. Included in these principles of living are meditation, mindfulness, moral action, and moral thinking. These principles will be covered in much greater detail in a later chapter, but it is important to stress that Buddhism is an active belief system: Buddhists live their religion and practice it on a daily basis.

The realization of Buddhist principles in daily life is no easy task. Which is perhaps one reason we call their application practice. It takes much practice to try to remain in the moment and live life one second at a time. We must practice these skills each and every day, at every possible moment in order to achieve some measure of success.

QUESTION?

What is Nirvana?
Nirvana is the cessation of suffering. The cessation of suffering involves the elimination of desire. The elimination of desire can be achieved by going forth on Buddha's path. Nirvana is available to each and every person on earth who diligently practices the Buddha's way. Nirvana is not a place separate from us but lies in each of us and is the very still center at the core of our beings.

Everything Is Nothing

Buddhists believe that thoughts and desires are at the heart of suffering—they foster the creation of illusion and distract us from the truth of reality. Therefore, the eradication of thought and desire can lead to Nirvana—a heaven on earth. In this way, it can be said that the way to get everything is to practice nothingness. Everything and nothing are therefore the same.

What Is Nothingness?

By trying to find a place in life where there are no thoughts, no desires, no love, no hate, no pain, no hunger, no sameness, no differences, we can find a place where we exist truly in the moment. This is a complicated but very simple proposition. Buddhism, as we can see, appears to be a mass of contradictions. But truly that is not the case—it *also* is an illusion. At the heart of reality, everything is truly nothing and nothing is all there is.

We speak of *nothing* to describe the truth not because nothing exists at the heart of life, but because it is like nothing we know otherwise and cannot be described. *No-thing.* However, the notion of nothingness often strikes fear in the hearts of many and we recoil from the idea that at the center of ourselves, at the center of the universe, lies nothing at all. You can think of this as you can puzzle over the substance of an atom. Science has proved that at the center of matter, in the substance of an atom, there is mostly nothing at all but space.

FACT

At the dawn of the new millennium, there are approximately 800,000 Buddhists living in the United States.

Our egos state loudly that this is impossible. *I am* something. I am real. However, sit quietly with yourself for long enough and this idea of *I* quickly comes into question. What am I? Who am I? I am a construct of ideas about myself that I have created with the input of others. If you start to push these ideas about yourself away, you will start to tap into the essence of the universe and the truth of our reality. Herein lies the bedrock of Buddhist belief.

Buddha's First Encounter

Soon after the Buddha attained enlightenment, he walked by a man, a fellow traveler. The man was struck by the Buddha's unusual radiance and peaceful demeanor.

"My friend, what are you?" he asked the Buddha. "Are you a god?"

"No," answered the Buddha.

"Are you some kind of magician?"

"No," the Buddha answered again.

"Are you a man?"

"No."

"Well, my friend, then what are you?"
The Buddha replied, "I am awake."

Refuge

The search for Nirvana, for enlightenment, can be thought of as a search for refuge. Not that we want to hide from the world in our enlightened mind, but a refuge as a safe place that provides protection from distress.

Our minds can be our worst enemies. When we desire something our egos can come out in full force and feel threatened at the idea of not getting what we want. We can become irritable, selfish, and stressed. Whether our desire is for a new home, a new job, a larger piece of pie, or peace of mind, the threat of not achieving our desired objective can turn us into unruly and unpleasant individuals. Trying to turn over our desires, to find a place in life where we are content just to be, filled with compassion and love for our fellow humans and our surroundings, is absolutely heaven on earth.

We are what we think. All that we are arises with our thoughts. With our thoughts, we make our world.

—The Buddha

In fact, enlightened mind is very much a heaven on earth. Buddhists could be said to believe that we create our own heaven and hell right here in life. Given the choice of heaven or hell on earth, why not choose heaven? Buddha can show you the way.

The Sinless World

In the world of Buddhist practice, there is no such thing as sin in the Christian sense of the word. There is suffering and not suffering. By the sixth century, the doctrine of reincarnation had been widely accepted. It was thought that one would be reborn after death into a new life that was determined by your actions in the past life. This is the notion of *karma*. If the quality of your life and *intention* of action was negative or wrong, you would be reborn as a slave, a plant, or an animal. Therefore it was in your best interest to live life as honestly, nobly, and as well as you could so that you were reborn into a better life, perhaps as a king or even a god.

FACT

Buddhist terms commonly occur in two forms: either Pali or Sanskrit. For instance, the word *Nirvana* appears in Sanskrit as *Nirvana* but in Pali as *nibbana.* This book uses both the Pali and Sanskrit terms throughout.

It wasn't sinful to lead a negative life, but it went against your own best interests as your karma would catch up with you and you would suffer in the next life. Karma has much to do with intention and motivation rather than action. If your intent is negative, you have bad karma. Therefore, stealing something to feed your starving children might carry different karmic implication than stealing money from your boss to buy an expensive pair of shoes.

The Cycle of Rebirth

The act of being constantly reborn was seen as suffering and Buddha strove to escape the repeating pattern of life and death. The idea of continually growing old, getting sick, and losing your facilities was seen as a horrible and painful process by the people of Buddha's time. If you could rise above the cycle of rebirth you would be free. This was the concept of Nirvana, and it was an optimistic and liberating outlook.

It is sometimes a difficult concept for Westerners to grasp. We emphasize the blessings of a long life, and live in a time of great comfort. However, if one were to truly believe that you never escaped the cycle of life and death, perhaps your outlook would change.

All Things Are As One

If one has enlightened mind, then one has realized to the deepest core of one's being that all things are as one, that there is no difference between you and me, me and the table, the table and the dog. If there is no difference between me and anything else, then to harm something else is to harm myself. Therefore it could be said that committing a "sinful" act goes against the grain of Buddhism. Once a Buddhist has achieved enlightened mind, it becomes part of the nature of the Buddhist to be compassionate and practice loving-kindness to everyone and everything. To do otherwise would be to hurt oneself. Therefore, Buddhists practice the Golden Rule.

The Golden Rule is the ethic of reciprocity: Do to others as you would have others do to you. It is found in the tenets of nearly every religion worldwide. It is frequently regarded as the most concise and general principle of ethics.

This widespread unhappiness with the state of life was not limited to Buddha's small part of the world in India. It afflicted a great part of the civilized world, and a great deal of the world's population was coming to believe that the spiritual practices of those who came before were no longer working for them. Buddha would become one of the most important and wise sages of this time, but he was among some good company.

Buddha's Contemporaries

Before we look at the life of Buddha himself, let us take a look at the people of his time. This time in history is often referred to as the Axial Age, the period between 800 and 200 B.C.E. The concept of the Axial Age is a controversial one, as it posits a time of great parallel growth the world over, a time of unique spiritual, political, and philosophical development in history. Why such great change occurred at this time is unknown. This was the age of all of the following:

- The prophets in Israel.
- The great philosophers in Greece.
- The creation of the Upanishads, the classical Hindu texts.
- Lao-tzu and Taoism in China.
- Confucius and Confucianism, also in China.

This was a time of great suffering for humanity, as people become aware of their limitations and impotence in the greater world. The world was changing and the new philosophies and belief systems that emerged at this time continue to feed men and women to the present age. Technological innovations occurred during the Axial Age, such as the use of iron, which was plentiful. Literacy in the form of the alphabet was born as well as religion in the form of monotheism. It was a time of great thought in the Eastern world and men with great wisdom provided the populace with new ways to cope and survive with their misery, and wonderful new ways to transcend the pain and suffering of everyday life.

Israel: Isaiah and the Age of the Prophets (770–700 B.C.E.)

Isaiah is said to have predicted the coming of Jesus. The Book of Isaiah in the Old Testament is attributed to him. It is said he foretold the fall of Egypt and Ethiopia and the invasion of the Assyrians. Also among the Prophet of Prophets' predictions were John the Baptist and the story of Jesus' life and death. Isaiah had an absolute faith in the divine and was instrumental in guiding the people of Jerusalem to a more optimistic outlook on the future of their time.

Isaiah railed against social injustice and he is said to have been an instigator of great morality in Jerusalem in the eighth century. He foretold an end to suffering and a time of great peace, spiritual awareness, and harmony. Partly due to Isaiah's predictions, the people of Jerusalem were able to look to the future with promise and hope.

FACT

The first written evidence of the existence of Buddhism is found four hundred years after the life of Buddha. King Ashoka of the Mauryan state of Northern India made inscriptions containing references to Buddhism that date from about 269 to 232 B.C.E.

Greece: Socrates (469–399 B.C.E.), Plato (427–347 B.C.E.), and Aristotle (384–322 B.C.E.)

The political turmoil of the fifth century—with the Persian Wars and the ongoing tension between Athens and Sparta—was a catalyst for great change as a flood of new ideas hit Athens, Greece. Athens had become the intellectual and artistic epicenter of Greek culture. The great intellectuals of the time were rejecting the traditional explanations of the natural world and were focusing their energies on philosophical thought as they were increasingly dissatisfied with the mythical conceptions of the past. Among the great philosophers who followed were Socrates, Plato, and Aristotle.

Socrates, the teacher of Plato, begat the Socratic method of teaching by question and answer as opposed to lecture. His student, Plato, in turn became the teacher of Aristotle. Plato founded the school in Athens called the Academy and presented his theories that ideals, such as Truth, exist beyond the realm of the physical world. He is best known for his dialogues on ethics and politics. In turn, his student, Aristotle, differed from Plato in that he did not believe in absolute forms, but believed in absolute facts: he believed that knowledge came from experience, and he is the voice behind the philosophy of Empiricism.

Persia (Iran): Zoroaster (ca. 600 B.C.E.)

At the time of Buddha much was also happening in Persia. Zoroaster, founder of Zoroastrianism, was most likely a priest. The dates of his life are uncertain. However, he is believed to have been born in northwest Persia. Zoroaster is said to have received a vision from his god, who called himself Ahura Mazda, who directed him to spread the gospel of the truth and tell people to believe in him, the god of good, instead of the god of evil, whose name was Aura Mainyu. Zoroaster began preaching his message of the battle between the god of good and the god of evil, and the will of humans to choose between the two.

According to Zoroaster, the end of the world as we know it would come when good overcame evil. This promotion of the idea of two heavenly judgments—one after your human life and one after a resurrection of all humankind—was a new concept never before promoted. Zoroaster's ideas of good and evil and resurrection greatly influenced the religions of Christianity, Islam, and Judaism. Zoroastrianism's dualism was part of an evolution toward monotheism in religious history.

▲ Meditating Buddha

India: the Upanishad Texts (ca. 550 B.C.E.)

The Upanishads, the great Hindu texts, are said to have been created around 800–200 B.C.E. They are the philosophical section of the Veda, written not in hymnal form but in prose. They are designed to help light the way, casting aside ignorance as they provide both spiritual guidance and philosophical argument.

One of the main figures of the Upanishads is Yajnavalkyam, who taught that the way to discover the truth was to cease all thought about it. The Upanishads emphasize that the chief cause of suffering is ignorance, and value the Vedic doctrines of self-realization, meditation, karma, yoga, and reincarnation—obviously great influences on the life and lessons of the Buddha.

China: Confucius (551–479 B.C.E.) and Lao-tzu (605–530 B.C.E.)

Other contemporaries of the Buddha are Confucius and Lao-tzu. Many people today are familiar with some of the sayings of the wise philosopher Confucius regarding nature, the state of the world, and human behavior. Confucius was a great teacher who stressed the importance of education and learning. He is the founder of Confucianism, a system of ethics that greatly influenced the culture of China.

Lao-tzu is considered the first philosopher of Taoism—the Way—and the *Te Tao Ching* is attributed to him. In Taoism, there is no right and wrong, just the Way: the force behind everything. Lao-tzu and Confucius lived in a time of great upheaval in China and sought to find meaning in the world through their wisdom, and spiritual and ethical practices. Lao-tzu saw the stability of the natural world and believed the way of nature to be vastly superior to the way of civilization and politics. Humans could flourish only in a healthy balance with nature. Lao-tzu developed the idea of the Tao: the origin of all—unknowable, unfathomable, and unobservable, except in the way it manifested itself in life.

As we can see, the Axial Age was a time of great promise and evolution. Great minds introduced new ideas to the East that would greatly affect the world's most important civilizations to come. Nations were going through a metamorphosis of tremendous proportion. The people of the world at large, and the people of India in particular, were ready for change, and Buddha began looking for answers to the deepest questions of life.

Chapter 2

The Buddha: History and Legend

Documentation on Buddha's life is rather sketchy and the known facts about Buddha are few and far between. However, historians do agree that he did actually exist and lived a long and prosperous life—he died at eighty years old after teaching for forty-five years, traveling all over India to do so. Although the first written accounts of Buddhism were found hundreds of years after his death, they are considered credible and accurate.

Siddhartha Gautama

Siddhartha Gautama was born sometime around 566 B.C.E. to a royal family in the Himalayan foothills, on the border of northern India and southern Nepal. Siddhartha's mother was Queen Maya, his father King Suddhodhana, and he was a blessing to the childless couple as they would now have a prince and an heir to rule over their small but prosperous kingdom. They named their son Siddhartha, which means "every wish fulfilled." He was a dream come true for the royal family of the kingdom of Shakya.

The Birth of the Buddha

There are many mythologies and stories surrounding the birth of the Buddha, but it is generally agreed upon (with some variation) that when Siddhartha was but days old, his father, King Suddhodhana, invited a large group of Brahmins to a feast at the palace so that they could tell the future of the newborn baby. Eight of the Brahmins concurred on the prediction that Siddhartha would either become a great and powerful ruler of all the land, or a wise and sage religious figure and spiritual teacher.

FACT

Siddhartha was not the first Buddha to grace the earth. Depending on your source, there have been anywhere from seven to innumerable Buddhas who have lived at one time or another. These Buddhas are spread out in time and the Buddha who was Siddhartha is known as the Buddha of our time.

They warned that if Siddhartha left the palace in search of a spiritual life, he would endure many hardships but eventually become a Buddha. If he remained within the cloistered palace walls, he would become a great ruler of the world. One of these Brahmins, Kondanna, was convinced, however, that the young boy would become a Buddha and warned of four signs that would influence the young Siddhartha and spur him to leave his home and commence a spiritual journey. Kondanna was later to appear once again in Siddhartha's life.

The Raising of a King

Suddhodhana had no wish for his son to become a spiritual man and teacher, but dreamed of a son who ruled over the land, the most powerful man as far as the eye could see.

He decided to protect Siddhartha from the possibilities of a hard but spiritual path and vowed to keep him cloistered in the palace, lavishing riches and luxuries beyond imagination on the young boy.

QUESTION?

What is a Brahmin?
The Brahmins were the priests, the highest class in the hereditary caste system of India. According to the caste system of Hinduism and Ancient India, there were four classes of people: rulers and warriors (the Kshatriyas), business people and artisans (the Vaishyas), the Brahmins, and finally the unskilled laborers or untouchables (the Shudras).

Youth of Luxury and Pleasure

Young Siddhartha was surrounded by beautiful things and kept captive within the palace grounds so he would not be subjected to the sicknesses and poverty of the people of the kingdom. Guards were posted all around the palace grounds and Siddhartha was discouraged from leaving and protected from seeing anything distressing to his young life. He had everything he could ever want: great teachers, beautiful girls, companionship, wonderful food. He grew into a talented athlete, an intelligent and charming young man. His future as a leader of the people seemed secure.

One afternoon from the young prince's childhood would affect him much later in life.

He had been sitting under the shade of an apple tree watching the plowing of the fields as the town prepared for the next year's crops. He noticed that the plowing had destroyed the grass and that the insects that had been nesting in these young shoots were dead. The young boy felt a sadness come over him as if he were attached to the insects, as though he had experienced a personal loss. But yet the day was beautiful and the shade of the apple tree wonderfully cool. Joy rose up inside him and he experienced a moment of utter perfection. Siddhartha was alive in the moment, his self set aside. The compassion and love he felt for the insects took him outside himself and he was momentarily free. Legend has it that as the day wore on the shadows moved, all but the shadow of the apple tree, which continued to shield the young Siddhartha.

FACT

Queen Maya was Siddhartha Gautama's mother. She died shortly after childbirth and Siddhartha was subsequently raised by her sister, Prajapati. She is often called "the Mother of Buddhism" because she played a pivotal role in bringing women into the Buddha's circle. After being denied several times, Prajapati's consistent pleas paid off and Buddha allowed her to start an order of nuns, thus allowing women to enter in the realm of Buddhist practice.

Marriage and the Birth of a Son

When Siddhartha was sixteen he won the hand in marriage of a beautiful young girl named Yasodhara. Yasodhara was Siddhartha's cousin and considered the loveliest girl in the kingdom. Legend has it that he managed to win her hand in a contest by piercing seven trees with one arrow.

At age twenty-nine, Siddhartha's life was as much the life of luxury as it had been before, except his wife was pregnant with their first child, indisposed and unable to entertain him.

She beseeched her husband to find his own diversion, so Siddhartha wandered outside the gates of the kingdom after overhearing someone speak of the beauty of the spring in the forest just beyond.

The Four Signs

Siddhartha begged his father to allow him to go beyond the palace walls. Suddhodhana hated to deny his son anything so he quickly tried to ensure that life outside the palace gates was just as perfect as life inside.

When Siddhartha wandered outside, everywhere he went he saw happiness, health, and good cheer. Then suddenly an old decrepit man with white hair, withered skin, and a staff to lean on crossed his path. Leaning over to his companion and servant, Channa, Siddhartha asked, "What is this?"

Channa explained that before them was an old man and told Siddhartha that everyone would age similarly one day. Siddhartha was saddened and shocked by the sight of the old man and wondered how he could continue to enjoy such sights as his garden when such suffering was to come later.

A second trip outside the palace grounds brought the sight of a maimed man before the young prince. He was assured by Channa that a similar fate would not befall him as he was healthy and well cared for. At home, the king continued to rain luxury on the prince, hoping to distract him from these disturbing visions and his newfound knowledge. But a third visit outside his sanctuary found him confronting a funeral procession and a corpse. Channa explained death to Siddhartha and told him it was inevitable and not to worry.

Buddha is also sometimes referred to as *Shakyamuni,* which means "Sage of the Shakya Clan," as he hailed from Shakya.

Siddhartha was overwhelmed. Sickness, old age, and death—how had he missed all this suffering in life? Finally, on another excursion with Channa—his driver and charioteer—Siddhartha came upon a monk in yellow robes with shaven head and an empty bowl. Channa explained that this ascetic had renounced all worldly goods. He praised the man so highly that Siddhartha returned home pensive. That night the opulence of the palace disturbed him deeply. The four signs had left their mark and the veil of luxury and riches had been removed. The world now seemed a place of suffering and pain.

◀ Gold Buddha

Finding the Path: The Renunciation

Yasodhara had borne Siddhartha a son. The cycle of birth and death seemed endless and oppressive to Siddhartha—life after life and death after death (or *samsara:* the endless cycle of birth into illusion) as the cycle of reincarnation and karma continued. Despite his love for his family and the birth of his new baby boy (who he most interestingly named Rahula, or "chain"), he decided to "go forth" into the world and stole out of the palace.

His faithful companion Channa followed him out into the night but was soon sent back by Siddhartha to the castle ground. Siddhartha was now on his way, and once outside the palace grounds, he shaved his head and donned the yellow robes of the mendicant monk.

Enormous Sacrifice

This is a remarkable occurrence in the life of this prince. He had been surrounded by all that many would consider necessary for a happy life: he had money, fame, power, love, family, health, and endless entertainment and learning. He was safe, had a promising future, and a beautiful wife and son. Yet suffering had entered his awareness and dulled his enjoyment of life. His awareness of loss, of the pain that attachment could bring, caused him dissatisfaction and stress, and he vowed to live an unfettered existence. Family was not part of the life of a spiritual seeker; family had to be left behind.

Imagine the pain and suffering it must have caused a man such as Siddhartha Gautama to leave the home and family he loved so much. The thought of losing his family forever to old age and death must have been a very powerful catalyst for such dramatic change.

Siddhartha's Coming of Age

Siddhartha vowed to try to save all beings from such suffering and set forth in the world to change the endless repetition of the cycle of loss. Awareness of *duhkha* had entered the consciousness of the young nobleman and was to change his life forever.

Duhkha means "dissatisfaction, impermanence, imperfection, suffering, disease, anguish caused by attachment and desire." *Duhkha* is a very difficult concept to translate into Western terms. Many use the word *suffering* as a substitute for *duhkha,* but suffering does not encompass all the subtleties that *duhkha* should convey.

The forests surrounding Suddhodhana's castle were fertile and green, and housed many seekers of the holy life. To seek a holy life was a worthy cause. The yellow-robed monks were not seen as beggars and dropouts but as crusaders and adventurers. People were praying for an enlightened one to save them from the life of suffering and unease. Therefore, Siddhartha must have felt a great sense of adventure leaving his safe haven and entering the woods by his home.

The young prince set out to find himself a teacher, and wandered far and wide over the Ganges plain, learning from the truth seekers he ran across on his travels. He practiced self-denial, meditation, self-control, and yogic exercises, searching for liberation from the ties of the material world. Siddhartha believed that if he could transcend the self he could free himself of the endless cycles of samsara and become enlightened—finally free from rebirth.

The Five Ascetics

Siddhartha joined up with five ascetics and practiced the principles of asceticism in an effort to achieve enlightenment and discover liberation. Asceticism was believed to burn up negative karma and free one from samsara. It was the ascetics' belief that if they suffered enough in this life they could perhaps save themselves in the next.

Penance

Together with his five companions he wore little or no clothing, slept out in the open no matter the weather, starved himself beyond measure, and even ingested his own waste matter. He lay on the most uncomfortable surfaces possible and inflicted much suffering on himself, convinced that external suffering would banish the internal suffering forever. He became very ill, his ribs showing through, until finally his spine could be felt through his stomach. His hair fell out and his skin became blotched and shrunken. But still he was plagued with desires and cravings.

FACT

One of the Five Ascetics who Siddhartha spent so much time with was none other than Kondanna, the Brahmin who had predicted his future as a great spiritual teacher.

All the while he continued to practice his meditations, silencing the voices within so he could try to banish his small self from the world.

Finally he had to admit that the ascetic life did not seem to be working and his ego was still alive and kicking. He was still the same Siddhartha, although he was ill and nearly broken.

Alone Again

No one could have put himself through more suffering than Siddhartha, so he had to admit defeat on the ascetic path. Frustrated that he could easily have died without achieving enlightenment, he vowed anew to find the way that would lead him to the truth.

At this point in time a young girl passed by Siddhartha on her way from the village to offer the forest gods a package of food. She offered Siddhartha some rice milk and he drank his fill, casting the ascetic life behind him. When the Five Ascetics saw him partaking of nourishment they grew disgusted with their companion and hurriedly distanced themselves from him. They thought he was returning to the life he had lived before and was leaving the life of a holy seeker.

The Middle Way

Siddhartha wandered away from the ascetics and continued on his journey. He was consumed with thoughts of his afternoon under the apple tree as a young boy. He remembered his moment of sheer joy as his awareness of his self dissolved and he was absolutely free of himself as he entered fully into the compassionate moment. Siddhartha realized that the life of self-inflicted punishment was an extreme path and the way to the truth was neither a life of denial nor a life on indulgence. The way to enlightenment could only be found somewhere in the middle.

Siddhartha must have slowly nursed himself back to health—adding some pounds to his emaciated frame, cleaning himself up, and rebuilding his body and spirit. He became very conscious of his movements in the world and paid close attention to how he reacted to his environment, watching his thoughts as they passed through his mind. He became aware of the movements he made while he ate, slept, walked, and squatted. Siddhartha slowly became *mindful* of his every gesture and thought. Mindfulness made Siddhartha aware of every craving that passed through him and of how transitory these cravings were. Everything changed: everything came and everything passed. Whether or not he worried on loss, loss was inevitable as change was inevitable. With change came fear. And with fear came suffering (*duhkha).*

Moderate effort over a long time is important, no matter what you are trying to do. One brings failure on oneself by working extremely hard at the beginning, attempting to do too much, and then giving it all up after a short time.

—The Dalai Lama

Enlightenment

The young traveler found a nice spot to meditate under the shade of a bodhi tree and arranged himself in a meditative posture. He began to notice that all things were interrelated. The fruit was attached to the tree that was attached to the earth that received nutrients from the sky when it rained. The earth nourished the insects and animals, which ate the berries that came from the trees that came from the earth that were nourished by the sky. The animals died, the plants died, and so would Siddhartha. Life was filled with interconnectedness and change. And impermanence. Everything that existed would die. He would die, his thoughts would die, his desires would die. The moment would die. And another would arrive in its place.

Siddhartha is known by many names, including: Siddhartha Gautama: his birth and family name; Shakyamuni: as mentioned earlier, Sage of the Shakya Clan; Buddha: the Fully Awakened One; and Tathagata: the Thus-Perfected One; the One Who Has Found the Truth.

The Bodhi Tree—the tree under which Buddha sat—comes from the Asiatic fig tree, and is also known as "the Tree of Wisdom." Bodhi trees are thought by some to be immortal. One sacred bodhi tree in Sri Lanka is thought to be 2,200 years old! Today, a descendant of the original Bodhi Tree sits just where Buddha sat so long ago. Followers of Buddhism visit the tree and meditate, hoping to achieve enlightened mind just like Buddha.

As he sat under the Bodhi Tree, meditating and watching his thoughts come and go, his mind started to break free of the constraints of his ego. He entered each moment fully present as his thoughts dropped away.

QUESTION?

Is there any significance to the Bodhi Tree?
The Bodhi Tree (or bo-tree) is the tree under which the Buddha attained enlightened mind. Similar trees have been planted next to many Buddhist temples in India, Sri Lanka, and Nepal as a tribute to its part in the awakening of humankind.

The Arrival of Mara

Siddhartha's battles were not over yet, however. Demonic forces came to threaten the spiritual seeker. Mara, the evil one, arrived, determined to distract him from his path toward Nirvana. Mara sent his daughters to tempt Siddhartha with lustful dances, and when that didn't work, Mara taunted him with words to arouse his ego and pride. He sent monsters to arouse Siddhartha's fear, then hurled questions at him aimed to undermine his motives. Over and again Mara threw all his evil power and destruction toward Siddhartha, determined to unseat the immovable man.

Finally, in desperation and rage, Mara yelled out at Siddhartha: "Rise from your seat. It does not belong to you but to me!"

But Siddhartha did not move. Mara's warriors and demons rose up beside their lord and swore that they bore witness to *his* right to Siddhartha's seat. "Who bears witness to yours?" Mara roared at the still unshaken Siddhartha.

Siddhartha sat motionless and then slowly reached out for help. He put out his arm and placed his right hand on the earth. The earth instantly roared like thunder back at Mara: "*I* bear witness!"

And Mara crumbled in defeat, disappearing from Siddhartha's presence.

◀ Tibetan sculpture of a demon

Mara As Symbol

The evil god Mara can symbolize the internal battle Siddhartha fought with himself as he waded his way toward enlightenment. Mara, in fact, was part of Siddhartha—that part of Siddhartha that we all have inside us: our character defects and the stumbling blocks we face on our path to enlightenment. Lust, fear, pride, and doubt plagued Siddhartha as he tried to detach from his delusions and free himself of his smaller self. In an effort to rid himself of his ego, he reached out to the earth, symbolizing that he is connected to the world, a part of the realm of nature.

It is not the evildoers and perpetrators of violence who are connected to this world, but the compassionate seeker of enlightenment who is most in tune with nature and the fundamental truth of the universe. The true nature of the universe is love, and it is the seeker of this truth who is most connected to the very essence of existence.

Only when faced with the activity of enemies can you learn real inner strength. From this viewpoint, even enemies are teachers of inner strength, courage, and determination.

—The Dalai Lama

The Buddha

Siddhartha had achieved enlightened mind and now in his place sat the Buddha, the Fully Awakened One. He had awoken to the true nature of the world and everywhere was a newfound freedom and compassion that was like nothing he could have imagined.

But the Buddha could not just sit under the Bodhi Tree forever, enjoying his newfound freedom and basking in the lightness of Nirvana. He was tempted not to try to speak of his experience and pass on his newfound knowledge, as he thought it would be difficult for people to realize that he had found enlightenment and now knew the way to the Truth.

The world was full of unawakened people, suffering people, who could use the Buddha's teachings to awaken themselves. A Buddha is essentially a most compassionate person, a person filled with sympathy and empathy for others. And so the Buddha listened to his heart and to his nature, got up from his seat under the Bodhi Tree, and ventured forth to share his teachings with the people who so desperately needed his help.

The Mustard Seed

A story that illustrates well the nature of the Buddha's teaching is the story of the mustard seed. A young woman, grieving over the death of her young child, goes to the Buddha and begs him to help her bring her child to life once more. She is carrying the young child in her arms and the Buddha can see she is out of her mind with grief. The Buddha realizes that it will be difficult to say anything that will cut through the anguish the young woman is experiencing.

Buddha smiled kindly at the young mother and told her what she must do. "Go to the nearby village and bring me back some mustard seed. However, the mustard seed must come from a home that has not seen any death."

The young woman eagerly heads off to the village and knocks on each and every door until she has no more doors to knock upon. Eventually she arrives back in front of the Buddha a transformed woman. Each and every household she visited invited her in and listened to her request. They comforted her but told her they couldn't help. Then each and every person shared their own story of loss with her, how they had lost their children, their mothers, their fathers, their sons, and daughters. The young woman realized that she was not alone in her grief and that the nature of life was impermanent—everyone experiences the anguish of grief.

The Buddha did not tell this woman she could be happy, but showed her in a gentle and profound way the true nature. She then asked Buddha if she could be his student and follow the teachings he had experienced himself.

Buddha was a compassionate and empathetic teacher, and he had a wisdom born of enlightened mind. He knew that words would not help the young mother but experience of the truth itself would, so he gently pointed her in the right direction.

On the Road

Buddha left the Bodhi Tree and went in search of his earlier teachers and fellow seekers of the holy life. Remembering fondly the Five Ascetics he had spent so much time with and who for so long had been so supportive—regardless of the way they had parted—Buddha headed toward the Deer Park at Isipatana outside Varanasi where they were rumored to be living. He would spend the rest of his life—the next forty-five years—sharing the message of the lessons he had learned and passing on the wisdom and beauty of awakening.

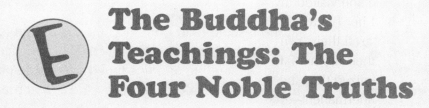

Chapter 3

The Buddha's Teachings: The Four Noble Truths

The Buddha's teachings were passed down orally until the first written record of the Buddha's lessons appeared hundreds of years after his life. It is believed that the teachings we have today are an accurate representation of what the Buddha taught 2,500 years ago. From the time he rose from his seat under the Bodhi Tree, to the time of his death four decades later, the Buddha taught all he came in contact with—starting to spread the dharma over the Indian subcontinent.

The First Sermon: The Dharma Wheel Turns

So there the Buddha was in the Deer Park of Isipatana, outside of Varanasi, preparing to give his first sermon to his disciples, the Five Ascetics. This is the moment that set the Dharma Wheel turning and was eventually to lead the five *bhikkus* (Buddhist monks) toward enlightenment.

But the Buddha had no texts to read from, no theories or theologies to offer his listeners. What he had was his own practical experience, the practice he had discovered, built upon, and fine-tuned over those past seven years. He had his experience and his hard work. He had practiced so diligently and ardently, so passionately, because he truly believed he would discover the path to Nirvana. And he *had* discovered the path to Nirvana. No one had come down from the heavens to light his way and give him words of advice. He had only himself, and upon himself he had relied, having a true faith that Nirvana and salvation were inside himself, that he himself was his only obstruction to an encounter with the Ultimate Reality.

FACT

Later Buddhist teachings would contend that a Buddha would only appear every 32,000 years, when knowledge of the Path—the dharma—had virtually vanished. A Buddha was defined as one who had not only achieved enlightened mind, but who had achieved it alone, with no teacher to show him the way. Although millions of people may have achieved enlightened mind in the past 2,500 years, perhaps none have achieved it without help.

Letting Go

So what the Buddha had to offer his *bhikkus* was his own life, his own practical experience. He believed they had to let go of everything they had learned to date in life. They must open their minds to a new way of life and a new way of practice. The best way to learn was to let go of all previous conceptions and be open. The Buddha believed that teaching was a means to an end, and once the lessons were learned the teaching itself should be discarded. He therefore did not offer the *bhikkus* lectures or theologies and ideas about enlightenment. There were no tablets, no bibles, no sacraments, no texts that could help the monks understand his ideology. He had no ideology. What he had was his practice.

Buddha told his audience about the man who needed to get across the river in order to reach the other side. He was desperate to continue his journey and had no way of crossing the raging waters. So he made a raft out of the materials at hand and slowly floated his way across the river until he reached safe haven on the other side. When he reached the other side, though, what was he to do with his raft? Should he tie it to his back and carry it across the land in case he needed it? Should he trudge around forever more, bound to the wood of the handmade raft? No, the raft had served its purpose of carrying him to where he needed to be. He did not need to be fettered with the vehicle any longer. So the traveler let go of the raft and continued his journey without it. To practice Buddhism effectively is to constantly let go of our notions and ideologies and to realize nonattachment in all things.

This was much the same with the teachings, Buddha tells us. The teachings are a way to get to Nirvana. Once you are there you no longer need them. To maintain that you do is to practice attachment. To practice attachment is to suffer. So let go of your notions, your ideas, and move ahead on your journey. Let go. The teachings are no longer needed once you reach the other side.

When we talk about the dharma, we talk about "the Path." *Dharma* means "what is, and what should be." Dharma is, most simply, the teachings of the Buddha. Dharma is everything: the Ultimate Truth, the teachings, all things and states conditioned and unconditioned, nature, morality, ethics, and that which helps one acquire virtue.

The Four Noble Truths

The Buddha's teachings were a pathway to letting go of suffering, freeing oneself from pain. The Buddha knew the only way was the

Middle Way. He knew that excessive pleasure—a life built on sensual delight—and excessive pain—such as the life of an ascetic—led to continual suffering and not to Nirvana. And so in the first sermon there at the Deer Park, the Buddha spoke of the Four Noble Truths and the pathway to Nirvana. He presented his truths as a program of action and not just the world of ideas.

FACT

The Buddha knew much more than he ever shared with his followers. He was a compassionate and wise teacher who gave each person what they needed to see the Truth and open themselves to the Path. He knew that to tell too much sometimes was a hindrance, and so he held back. We are left to wonder what he didn't tell us.

At the first sermon, where Buddha presented the Four Noble Truths, the light went on for one of his *bhikkus*, Kondanna, and Kondanna experienced the Truth directly as the Buddha spoke. He later said it was as if he knew all the time and couldn't understand why it suddenly was so apparent to him. Many people who experience a taste of enlightened mind say the same thing. When the moment of enlightenment occurs an overwhelming feeling of *I knew this* pervades your existence.

The Four Noble Truths are as follows:

1. The Truth of Duhkha (Suffering).
2. The Truth of the Cause of Suffering.
3. The Truth of the Cessation of Suffering.
4. The Truth of the Path That Leads to Nirvana (or the Cessation of Suffering).

You can think of the Four Noble Truth almost like a diagnosis and prescription from a doctor. The sickness is *duhkha*, the cause of the sickness is desire, the medicine for the sickness is the Eightfold Path. If we follow the Eightfold Path, we will recover and be well.

The First Noble Truth: All Life Is Suffering

The First Noble Truth is the Truth of *Duhkha*. As we learned earlier, the Buddha thought that life was filled with suffering. Does this mean that everyone is ill, poor, cranky, filled with bodily pain, ugly, deformed, in trouble, being tortured? No, suffering comes in many different forms. Even happiness can be a form of suffering, the Buddha tells us. But how can that be?

◀ Buddhist monk

You may think: When I am happy I am *certainly* not suffering. But right now, consider being happy. What are you happy about? Perhaps you are in love with a wonderful person and you are looking forward to going out to a nice dinner with your loved one tonight. Perhaps you are planning what you can talk about, what you will wear, what restaurant you will go to, and what you will eat. Perhaps the thought of a lobster and a big piece of pie is sitting just fine with you. Perhaps you are thinking of your loved one sharing your meal: what a wonderful person you are involved with! How much fun you are going to have together!

Suddenly the telephone rings and there is your beloved's voice. Ah, how wonderful to be connected this way! But now your plans seem to be threatened. Your loved one tells you that work is too much, that the boss is insisting the employees stay to finish the business at hand and therefore you are going to have to eat dinner alone. Much sorrow and many apologies are extended to you. How do you feel? Do you feel as good as you did ten minutes ago? Or do you feel anxious and disappointed, perhaps even angry? Perhaps you are even rude to your loved one when you receive this bad news. Now, you see, you suffer.

People have often thought when they hear that life is suffering that this is a pessimistic and nasty view of life. Life is good, they say! But this is indeed not a pessimistic view of life. It is realistic. Buddhism looks at what *is,* and tries not to judge what is. It is accepting of what is. Perhaps if we were to substitute a different word for *suffering* it would be easier to understand. You could say suffering is *impermanence* or *imperfection*.

Duhkha is, in fact, a very difficult word to translate and means much more than mere suffering. It implies a general dissatisfaction with even the wonders that life can bring—love, a good occupation, spiritual connection, warm friendship. Even a life lived well can leave one feeling that still *something* is missing. It is that nagging feeling of dissatisfaction.

The I Who Suffers

Who is this I who suffers? Who is the person who is disappointed by the cancellation of a nice night out on the town? Buddhism looks at the essence of that person *I* and comes up with nothing. In other words, there is no I. There is no me. Then who am I? We are constantly changing beings.

In order to understand the nature of the individual, I, the Buddha broke down the individual being into five groups, or five aggregates of attachment, in his second sermon at the Deer Park. By this time, each of the *bhikkus* was experiencing enlightened mind and was convinced that Buddha was onto something.

The five aggregates he named are as follows.

1. The aggregate of matter (eye, ear, nose, throat, hand, etc.).
2. The aggregate of feelings and sensations (sight, sound, smell, taste, thought, form).
3. The aggregate of perception.
4. The aggregate of volitions or mental formations.
5. The aggregate of consciousness (response).

So what does this all mean? Well, let's go back to the idea of change.

Change

Each aggregate previously listed is subject to change. Our body changes constantly. If you are over age thirty you know this more than most. Feelings and sensations change constantly as well. Our ideas change. For instance, maybe you used to believe in Santa Claus. Now you believe in credit cards and bank statements. Our volitions change as well—volitions can be thought of as our intentions, which we learned earlier are the basis of karma. Or volitions could be said to be the basis for our actions.

Volitional action changes as well. What we intend to do today will have an effect on what we do tomorrow. Or the intent with which we live our life today will affect our life tomorrow. And finally we have consciousness (or response), which also changes infinitely. You hear something with your ear and become conscious of the sound with your mind. You decide to act on the sound you hear. Your responses continually change.

Since you cannot act on that which you do not experience (you do not act on a sound you do not hear), we find that the fifth aggregate, consciousness, depends on all the other aggregates for its existence. The action or response you make based on the intention you had based on your perception of your senses from your body is *soley* dependent on each of the preceding phenomena.

Let's take a simple example: I pass by a pizzeria and my *nose* (body) twitches as I *smell* (sensation) the scent of fresh tomatoes and cheese. I *think* (perception), "Wow, a piece of pizza would sure taste good." My senses are aroused and I decide (*volition*) to go in to buy myself a slice.

I enter the pizzeria and put some money on the counter (*response*). Suddenly a dog enters the pizza store. I *see* (with my eyes, obviously) the dog and *think* how I should hurry home to walk my own poor dog, who has been alone since seven o'clock that morning. I *head out* the door toward home. We can see here that we move from sensory experience to perception to volition to response all day long. The aggregates of attachment are in motion again.

The person we call *I* is made up of these five aggregates and nothing more. These aggregates are constantly changing. Therefore the person we call I constantly changes as well. We find there is absolutely no fixed I! There is no permanent self, nothing to grab on to. The only way out of this endless cycle is to see that the perception of a fixed *I* is an illusion. It is an attachment. Letting go of attachment is to realize enlightenment.

Letting Go of Me

When I attended my first *sesshin* (a type of Buddhist "retreat" covered later in Chapter 13) I was told by my teacher that I would find through prolonged meditation and quiet my real self. I looked forward with great enthusiasm to discovering the REAL Jacky: the generous, funny, peaceful, kind, smart, wonderful me. I sat and I sat and I sat and I sat, meditating, and I waited for the real me to come out. And at the end of this *sesshin* I realized there was no me at all. There was nothing identifiable as Jacky. In fact, there were no borders at all to myself. I was borderless and unnamable. It was not a frightening experience at all: it was a very liberating experience.

The Squirrel and *Duhkha*

My husband and I were sitting outside one day watching the squirrels playing in the yard. "What is a squirrel," my husband asked me. "Are the little squirrel legs the squirrel? Are the little squirrel feet the squirrel? Is the gray fur the squirrel? Is it the little beating heart or the little squirrel kidneys? Are each of these things the squirrel or is it all of these things together that are the squirrel?" Fortunately he doesn't ask these questions every day. Is the squirrel an aggregate of all the squirrel qualities? Or do all the squirrel aggregates form the idea of a squirrel based on squirrel characteristics we agree upon? The characteristics that form the creature we call a squirrel are always changing. In Buddhism it would be said that the squirrel, in fact, is always *becoming* . . .

So, things arise and they pass. And they arise and they pass. And so on infinitely.

These five aggregates together (the aggregates that do not form an I and do not form a squirrel) comprise *duhkha,* or suffering. If you think of a river you will notice that the river is constantly changing. You cannot see one part of the river and stop to examine it and find it as fixed. We are much the same. We are not fixed. We are ever changing. The squirrel is not fixed. It is ever changing. If you understand this you will understand all of the Four Noble Truths. If you understand that all suffering arises from the constancy of our change as we try to fix ourselves in time—which also never stops changing—then you will understand what suffering is, where it comes from, why it must stop, and how you can stop it.

Anatman: **No Soul**

This no-self is the concept of *anatman,* also known as "no-soul." According to many religions, there is an everlasting identity that we all have and that identity is our soul. The soul outlives the body and the mind and continues on after our earthly life is over.

FACT

Anatman is the Sanskrit word referring to "no-soul." It also means nonself or no-self.

Buddhism is unique in that it denies the existence of a soul as it denies the existence of a self. Because, as we have seen, the self is an illusion born of the ego with no reality to base itself on, the self cannot have a soul. It is a very frightening proposition for many people to consider—that there is no soul and the ego that rules our life on earth is an illusion. Humankind created the idea of a soul so that we could find comfort in the afterlife and not have to deal wholly with the possibility of annihilation. In Buddhism the soul is an illusion, as the self is an illusion. Buddhism has no heavenly reward, but it does have Nirvana. Our dissatisfactions, our fear of impermanence, our sufferings, and our imperfections can all end. Buddhism has heaven on earth.

The Second Noble Truth: The Cause of Suffering Is Desire

The Second Noble Truth is the Truth of the Cause of Suffering. What is the cause of all this suffering? Of *duhkha?* The cause of suffering—or the origin of suffering—is desire, says the Buddha. Desire is not the only cause of suffering, but it is the root cause, the most important or immediate cause. Desire comes from somewhere, so it cannot be said to be the only cause of *duhkha.* However, it was the Buddha's belief that there was no beginning of anything (no origin theory); he believed that everything is causal, relational, and interdependent.

The Source of Desire

Desire comes from sensation and sensation is caused by contact with something that forces the sensation, and so on the circle of life and suffering and desire go infinitely. For instance, I feel unattractive (the sensation) and see a pair of glasses in a magazine (the contact that forces the sensation or in this case exaggerates the sensation) that I believe will change my life forever. My self-esteem, the glasses, the magazine, and my purchase are causal, relational, and interdependent (the purchase is based on the sight of the ad that I saw when I was feeling bad about myself).

This might be easier to understand if we use the simple example of a tree needing the rain that comes from the sky, which waters the ground, which feeds the soil, which houses the roots of the tree that provides the oxygen that creatures breathe . . . It is a cycle that never ends and has no beginning and no end, and nothing is separate from anything else. Today scientists call this *relational* theory.

But the *most* direct cause of suffering is wanting something—desire. This desire is not limited to material objects, though they can certainly cause us much suffering. Who doesn't want a beautiful body, a nice home, a new pair of shoes? But wanting, desiring, also extends to a serene disposition, a democrat in office, a healthy life, a well-behaved dog, attachment to ideals, ideas, and opinions. Desire refers to beliefs, wealth, power, concepts, and theories. When we want something we often deprive others to get it. If I want *this piece* of chocolate, you obviously cannot have it. In the process we also deprive ourselves of something. We deprive ourselves from experiencing life in the moment.

Clouding the Truth

This desire that we have for so many things keeps us from seeing the Truth. We are blinded by our desires and keep hungering after things that constantly change. Have you ever been in the grip of a desire so powerful that it hurt you? Addiction is a desire that can feel this destructive. But all desires are harmful, as they all lead us away from Nirvana and distract us from life in the moment. In his Fire Sermon, Buddha addresses this when he says, "*Bhikkus,* all is burning!" But awareness of this burning brings detachment from it. And detachment brings liberation.

The Third Noble Truth: Suffering Can End!

The Third Noble Truth is the Truth of Cessation of Suffering. Here's the good news! Liberation from suffering is a possibility. But in order to end suffering you have to end the cause of suffering. You have to end desire. If you end desire you can attain Nirvana, which is the cessation of suffering and the realization of no-self.

If we can end the suffering, we can see the Truth and enter the Ultimate Reality of enlightened mind. We can see things as they really are and not as we have been conditioned to see them. We can enter the moment and experience the world as it really is.

It's Never Enough

Most of us get to a point in our lives where we have attained some things. Perhaps we have a nice family, a good home, a solid job, a big car. But still we have that nagging feeling that something is missing. That there is *more*. This feeling is what often starts people out on the path to a spiritual life. Could you ever imagine that there could be an end to that feeling? That you could find what you are looking for and when found, you would say, "Yes, I *knew* this. I must have forgotten." Enlightened mind is like remembering something so basic and so instinctive, so beautiful and fundamental. Nirvana *is*. It just is. It is there; we just have to find it.

Arriving at Nirvana?

However, Nirvana is not a destination as Fiji is a destination. You cannot *arrive* in Nirvana. Nirvana is a practice, a path itself; it is the Truth. It is what is real. You know those funny pieces of art where you see a drawing and then stare at the drawing until your eyes relax and then, suddenly, another drawing appears and it's a 3-D drawing that's even wilder and more fantastic than the original?

Realizing Nirvana is like suddenly seeing what was obviously always there. Someone who has realized Nirvana is the happiest, most content, most free person in all the world. No neuroses, no obsessions, no worries. Pure enjoyment and peace. This person is free from the illusion of *I*. This person feels no separation whatsoever from the world anymore. This person is home.

The Fourth Noble Truth: The Way

The Fourth Noble Truth is the Truth of the Path That Leads to Nirvana. There *is* a path that leads to Nirvana. This is known as "the Middle Way." It does not promote excessive sensual pleasure or excessive self-denial. It is a moderate path that avoids extremes. The Buddha told us that the path to enlightenment is the Eightfold Path.

The Eightfold Path is a plan of action for realizing Nirvana. That path consists of the following actions, wisdoms, and disciplines:

1. Right understanding
2. Right thought
3. Right speech
4. Right action
5. Right livelihood
6. Right effort
7. Right mindfulness
8. Right concentration

We will cover the Eightfold Path in detail in the following chapter.

The Four Noble Truths are the basics of the Buddha's teachings. They teach us that life is full of suffering, that we suffer because of our desires, that there is an end to the suffering, and that end is to follow the Eightfold Path. The Buddha laid out a course of action for us to follow so we could live a happy and serene life.

> *The teaching of Buddha*
> *is like a great cloud*
> *which with a single kind of rain*
> *waters all human flowers*
> *so that each can bear its fruit.*
> —Lotus Sutra 5

QUESTION?

Do I need to sequester myself away from the world—like a monk would—in order to realize enlightenment?
The Buddha believed the Path was for everyone and no matter who you are you can realize Nirvana. Sometimes the most challenging practice takes place in the outside world as we are forced to work extra hard when confronted with so many distractions part in the awakening of humankind.

But that life is a life of practice. If some of the teachings seem like mental gymnastics to you, remember it is only words. The path is really quite simple—the path is the practice of ethics. Keeping things simple is at the heart of Buddhism, though human nature likes to complicate things. Even after one realizes enlightened mind, one cannot cease to practice. Even the Dalai Lama does the legwork necessary to realize equanimity and peacefulness. No one *arrives*. The path to Nirvana is a path of practice and action; it is about conduct and wisdom, and living a life well. But the Buddha had still more to teach and those teachings are laid out in the following pages. Ⓔ

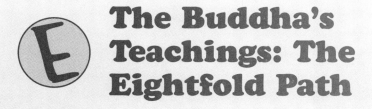

Chapter 4

The Buddha's Teachings: The Eightfold Path

The Middle Way, or the Eightfold Path, is our roadmap toward enlightened mind. It is here that the Buddha outlines our disciplines for practice. You might have noticed that the last of the Four Noble Truths is the first step toward the Eightfold Path. The teachings of the Buddha are interconnected and they build on one another as your practice grows.

The Way

Let's take another look at the Eightfold Path:

1. Right understanding
2. Right thought
3. Right speech
4. Right action
5. Right livelihood
6. Right effort
7. Right mindfulness
8. Right concentration

What is meant by the word *right*? The Buddha uses the word *right* in the way we would say something is proper, appropriate, or correct. So if you look at the list above, you will see that the Buddha meant for us to act properly, to concentrate correctly, to be mindful, and to put the appropriate amount of effort into everything we do. He meant for us to understand properly, to speak appropriately, to think the correct thoughts, and to have jobs that are proper, work that is respectful.

We in the West have been indoctrinated in dualistic thinking. So it is important to note here that the word *right* when applied to the steps on the Eightfold Path does not in any way imply that there is a wrong. This is dualistic thinking (this and that, you or me, right and wrong), and dualistic thinking is a Western creation, and is in no way, shape, or form part of the Buddhist way of life. In Buddhist thought there is no you and me, just *not me*. There is no right and wrong, only the Way. This is a very hard concept for Westerners to grasp as it goes against our entire way of thinking, and our dualistic thinking is an integral part of our culture.

The Three Divisions of the Path

The Eightfold Path can be divided into three different categories. The Sanskrit for each category appears in parentheses after the word to which it corresponds. They are as follows.

1. Wisdom (prajna)
2. Morality (shila)
3. Mental Discipline (samadhi)

All the steps on the Eightfold Path fall into one of these categories. Wisdom is comprised of numbers 1 and 2: right understanding and right thought. Morality includes numbers 3, 4, and 5: right speech, right action, and right livelihood. And finally, mental discipline is made up of the last three steps (6, 7, and 8): right effort, right mindfulness, and right concentration.

◀ Prayer wheels

Wisdom, Morality, and Mental Discipline

Wisdom is made of right understanding and right thought, and these two can be considered the hardest practices to master on the Eightfold

Path. Wisdom is gained through the practical experiences and insights that you have as a direct result of practice. It is not gained through book smarts, through text memorization, or the mastery of concepts.

Morality or ethical conduct is comprised of right speech, right action, and right livelihood. All three of these elements have as their core a spirit of loving-kindness and compassion.

Morality in Buddhist practice comes from a compassionate heart and mind and is expressed through the things we say, the things we do, and the occupations we choose. Finally, mental discipline consists of our meditations on right effort, mindfulness, and concentration.

Practicing

The eight steps are not meant to be done sequentially but are to be practiced all the time, simultaneously, each and every one. Every day is an opportunity to practice these steps. Unlike the Four Noble Truths, which are not actions you can take, the Middle Way is a program of action. You can picture these steps as spokes of a wheel. In order for this Dharma Wheel to turn, all the spokes must be in good working order and well oiled. Once you have understood what each step means, and have undertaken an attempt to practice the steps in your daily life, the Dharma Wheel starts rolling and you are headed down the path toward Nirvana.

Practicing the Eightfold Path is to do the footwork of Buddhism. It's the everyday sweat, and it is not an easy practice. We live in a world of great temptation. There's always a lazy way out of everything and choosing a life of diligent practice may not, perhaps, appeal. But as we've said before, Buddhism is a religion, a lifestyle, that relies on practical experience.

Right Understanding

What did the Buddha mean by right understanding? We all bring our own notions and preconceptions to every decision, thought, conversation, or exchange we experience. Right understanding means to see things as they are and not as we would see them through our own experience, with our own personal bias. One can master the discipline of right understanding—

a very difficult discipline—through the practice of the mental discipline of meditation.

When we meditate we try to stay in the first part of every moment. We experience the moment, but we don't form a judgment about the moment. We don't allow ourselves to proceed to the judgment part of the moment. For instance, we are meditating, breathing in and out, deeply concentrated on our breath. We hear a bird call out. But we just hear a bird. We don't proceed to the part of the moment where we hear a bird and it is a *beautiful* sound. We don't even proceed to the part of the moment when our mind says, "I hear a bird." *We just hear the bird.*

To see things as they really are, without naming them, without creating a dualistic situation of *this* and *that,* or of just *this is,* is right understanding. When we name something we rob it of its essence and we make it ours. Let go. Right understanding takes us back to the basics of the Four Noble Truths. If we understand the Four Noble Truths we are seeing the Ultimate Truth and we understand the nature of reality. We see things as they really are. Being in the moment is practicing right understanding.

Right Thought

Right thought involves our intentions (not the intentions again!). The spirit in which we approach everything—a spirit of kindness, compassion, and harmlessness to our fellow beings—is essential to right thought. Our process is to move away from the ego, to head toward a life where service is your lifestyle and your motivations are not ego-driven but entirely selfless.

It is very interesting and important to note here that thoughts of selfless detachment, love, and nonviolence are grouped on the side of wisdom. This clearly shows that true wisdom is endowed with these noble qualities, and that all thought of selfish desire, ill-will, hatred, and violence are the result of a lack of wisdom . . .

—Walpola Rahula

It is important to note that just like twelve-step programs, this program is one of progress and not perfection. Do not expect that you will automatically wake up one morning with a wonderful loving feeling toward everyone that you express through tireless works of selflessness. Egos are stubborn little things that are extremely persistent in their efforts to exert themselves. The Eightfold Path is a path of *slow* progress. Have faith in the power of your practice. If nothing else, you will be a very nice person.

Right Speech

Right speech is a little easier to grasp than right understanding or right thought. While you might not always be certain of the right thing to say, we are all pretty sure we know the *wrong* things to say. Here are some of the examples of speech you might want to avoid when practicing right speech:

- Lies
- Slander
- Cursing or abusive language
- Raising one's voice unnecessarily
- Harsh words
- Speaking too much (rattling on)
- Gossip
- Creating enmity

Think before you speak and try to restrain your tongue.

Right Action

Right action is similar to right speech. Your actions should be harmonious with your environment and should not produce enmity or ill-will, but peace. Do nothing that will cause harm to others. Obviously harmful acts include the following.

- Stealing
- Taking of life, human and otherwise
- Destruction of person or property or peacefulness
- Overindulging

Right action includes sexual responsibility—no adultery or prostitution. It also includes abstaining from alcohol and recreational drugs.

Not all Buddhists are vegetarians. If one intends to live a compassionate life it can be argued that eating meat does not promote kindness toward animals. At the time of the Buddha, however, monks were mendicants and relied on the generosity of the laypeople for their food. If they received meat, they would eat what was given to them. It is an individual choice.

Right Livelihood

What do you do for a living? Right livelihood forces us to look at our choices for work and decide if what we are doing to put food on the table is causing harm to anyone or anything else. Even more than not doing harm, right livelihood goes a step further and encourages us to do work that is helpful to others. It requires that we live an honorable life. Occupations a Buddhist might want to avoid include but are not limited to the following:

- Arms dealing
- Prostitution
- Drug dealing
- Working with intoxicants and poisons
- An abattoir worker
- Executioner

In today's world right livelihood can cause some confusion. You want to occupy yourself with activities that promote harmlessness and peace and cause no injury to others. Is being a bartender practicing right livelihood? That is up to you. As a practicing Buddhist, you are expending all of your energy toward a serene existence so you can realize enlightenment. Negative energy that you spend in the world will take away from your serenity and post unrest in the environment. Can you practice harmlessness and drill oil? Can you work with nuclear weapons and maintain serenity for yourself and others? Right livelihood asks that we examine our occupations and spend our work time practicing peacefulness and kindness in the world.

It should also be noted that no war was considered a just war by the Buddha. Therefore a profession in the military would not be considered right livelihood. Acts of violence were clearly against the Buddha's teaching and there were no exceptions.

FACT

Interestingly enough, Mitch Kapor, computer programmer and developer of the Lotus 1-2-3 program, is a practicing Buddhist. Where did you think the name Lotus came from?

Right Effort

The next three disciplines are all mental disciplines and directly relate to our meditation practices. All this practice takes quite a bit of effort, so now we need to make sure we are using right effort. Here we want to consider that we will use the appropriate amount of effort in living our lives fruitfully. We can overdo things as well as get lazy, so checking your level of effort is necessary.

Right effort also means getting rid of improper attitudes and thoughts. We need to expend our efforts to keep ourselves on the path. When unproductive or unsavory thoughts arise we must expend the necessary level of effort to dispel these thoughts and move toward harmoniousness.

Remember how the Buddha expended such effort to realize enlightenment. He sat through the arising of his ego, his pride, and the scorn of his companions. He left his wonderful family and summoned the appropriate effort to keep himself in the Middle Way.

Right Mindfulness

Right mindfulness has to do with living our lives in the moment and being mindful of everything we do. Entire books have been written on mindfulness. When you eat, eat. When you wash the dishes, wash the dishes. When you read, read. When you are driving the car, be present in the car and participate in your journey. Usually we are two weeks down the road living everywhere but where we are. We are planning our vacation, what we will say to our boss, what we will wear, what we will cook for dinner. We are reliving the past: thinking of our childhoods, about what happened at work that morning, about what our spouse said to us in anger, about our children's behavior.

The Buddha was practicing right mindfulness when he was observing his thoughts, his sensations, his bodily functions, and his mind. The key to mindfulness is not to judge. It is to observe and to exist in the moment as discussed earlier. Right mindfulness and right effort go hand in hand. Without right effort we would not have mindfulness, since mindfulness takes the appropriate degree of effort. Without mindfulness, effort would be wasted and futile.

When we are mindful of our thoughts, our actions, or sensations, and our mind, ethical conduct becomes possible in our everyday lives. It is hard to act unethically and immorally when we are constantly observing ourselves. Meditation practices help us to behave with compassion and loving-kindness as we strive to be mindful, aware, of what we are doing all the time.

Mindfulness is the miracle that can call back in a flash our dispersed mind and restore it to wholeness so that we can live each minute of life.

—Thich Nhat Hanh

Right Concentration

Right concentration could be considered the pathway to right mindfulness. It is by practicing the appropriate forms of concentration that we attain mindfulness. Concentration in the Buddhist sense is to focus all of your attention on awareness. One technique used in meditation for right concentration is concentration on the breath.

The meditator focuses on only the breath. He or she watches the in-breath; watches the out-breath. When thoughts arise, as soon as they are noticed, the meditator returns to the breath and lets the thought go. Thoughts, distractions, emotions—they all come and go, and the one who meditates goes back to the breath.

This type of meditation is called *one-pointed meditation.* We are focused on one point and one point only. By practicing right meditation we can come to mindfulness of the moment. Right concentration supports right mindfulness. Together with right effort they form the third element of the Eightfold Path, known as mental discipline.

The Parable of the Poison Arrow

Buddha's followers found that they had many questions to ask their teacher. You also might be bursting to ask the Buddha some things. Such questions might include:

- What about God? Do you believe in God?
- What about Heaven and the Hell?
- What happens to us after we die?
- Is there an afterlife?

What would the Buddha say if we were to ask him such questions? When the Buddha was posed with similar questions 2,500 years ago, he told the man who was searching for answers that he was like a man who had been shot by a poisoned arrow. Before he will allow his companions to remove the arrow he wants to know where the arrow came from, who shot the arrow, what kind of poison was used, why he was shot, etc. He would most likely die before his questions were ever answered. Ⓔ

Chapter 5

E The Buddha's Ethics

What makes a person a Buddhist? There are no ceremonies of initiation, no tests to take, no manuals to study. So when can you call yourself a Buddhist? If you whole-heartedly believe in the teachings of the Buddha and follow the Buddha's path, you could probably consider yourself a Buddhist. It is traditionally accepted, however, that one who has taken refuge in the Three Jewels and practices the Five Precepts is a Buddhist.

The Five Precepts

The Five Precepts are our ethical requirements for living a basically good life. These are the ethics that the Buddha set forth for a morally substantial existence. They are the *minimal* essential ethical values we live by and a counterbalance for the three poisons of craving, hatred, and ignorance (See Chapter 6). To take the precepts means to vow to honor them.

The Five Precepts are:

- Do not destroy life.
- Do not steal.
- Do not commit sexual misconduct.
- Do not lie.
- Do not take intoxicating drinks.

If one is to join a monastic order there are more precepts that one must follow, which we will take a look at later on. But for laypeople practicing Buddhism, the Five Precepts outlined above are a plan of action for ethical living. Let's now explore the precepts in depth.

FACT

According to Donald S. Lopez, Jr., in *The Story of Buddhism,* when a vow is taken, from the Buddhist perspective, it takes on a subtle physical form in the body itself and remains so until death or until the vow is broken. As long as the vow is in the body, the person accumulates merit for it.

Do Not Destroy Life

The obvious action implied here is not to commit murder. For most of us, that may be an easy pitfall to avoid. But there are many more subtle areas to consider that might fall under the heading of destroying life. Some will ask if killing bugs is against Buddhist teaching or if eating meat and fish is prohibited. Some will say yes, and some will say no. It is an individual choice. It would be impossible to go through life without harming another living thing, however hard we try.

Take reasonable precaution to avoid killing anything. Do not participate in the senseless killing of animals for sport, such as hunting turkeys or watching a bullfight. Our intention toward our action will go a long way to deciding if we are living up to a precept. Approach every living thing with kindness and compassion in your heart and you will most probably stay on the path. However, if you approach a living thing with hatred, anger, or greed in your heart, you are probably not living true to your ethical basics.

Perhaps you could ensure that you use products that have not had the destruction of life as part of their journey to your shelf. Did your shampoo get tested on a rabbit that died for your shiny hair? Did a cow die so you could have a beautiful couch? Where do you draw the line? Is wearing leather something you feel breaks your ethical code or is that something you can comfortably live with. Perhaps you eat only free-range meats, or vegetarian eggs.

Destroying life does not necessarily mean killing something, however. You can destroy life or disrupt life in many other ways. Respect others' need for quiet and privacy. Give people room for their own thoughts. Do not create any unnecessary disturbances, such as setting off firecrackers late at night, playing loud music, or raising your voice. Do not disturb others with incessant talking or forcing your unwanted lifestyle or view on another. Keep your belongings and your living space neat and clean and do not infringe on others' space and their right to a clean and orderly life.

Do Not Steal

The second precept discourages us from stealing from another. This does not just include stealing tangible objects, but intangibles as well, such as ideas or time. More accurately, this precept directs us to not take what is not freely given. Develop a sense of generosity toward others and respect others' property.

What to Do

Return borrowed items in a timely and gracious manner. Do not take up too much of someone's time unless it is freely given to you. This includes phone calls and idle conversations both at home and at work. It includes "borrowing" office supplies and limiting another adult's autonomy. Taking what is not freely given can cover a wide range of activities, so practice kindness and trustworthiness with others at all times.

We tend to demand more than our fair share of things, whether it be pie or financial security or love. Americans especially have much, much more of most everything than much of the world's population. We are an indulgent and spoiled population.

◀ Young monks

Reflect on Yourself

Are you taking more than your fair share? Since you cannot realistically pack up your lunch and send it over to a Third World country for consumption, you can practice generosity here in other ways. Limit your consumption. Eat less, live a simpler life. Do not use up all of our resources. Walk if you can and shut off your lights. But also keep in mind that you are trying to live a life in the middle.

FACT

The simple living movement is on the rise in the United States. More people each day join in against the overconsumption that is stressing our planet. Simple living proponents promote: frugality, stress management, avoiding unnecessary consumption, sometimes social and ecological justice, and, in general, trying to make do with less. Less is more!

The Buddha stressed that economic security was an important element to life in the middle. Life should be balanced. Remember, a life of asceticism is not a positive in Buddhism. As Westerners, we tend to have it ingrained in us that suffering is the road to salvation. Not according to the Buddha. Do not run out and give away all your possessions. You are striving for a moderate, fair existence; you don't want to be on the other side of the equation either!

Do Not Commit Sexual Misconduct

The third precept is sexual respect for yourself and others. Do not have sexual relations lightly with anyone you choose. The time of sexual promiscuity has come to an end in your life. Do not cheat on your partner or flirt outrageously with others. Do not act inappropriately or act out sexually. Do not participate in prostitution, incest, rape of any kind, or any other form of sexual misconduct. Do not harass people sexually at the office, at the supermarket, or anywhere at all. Do not catcall or make inappropriate sexual comments.

If you turn on the television or look at a magazine you will see that we are a culture obsessed with sex. Sex sells everything from toothpaste to violence, houses to hair gel, clothing to furniture to perfume. Through our sexual selling we have created a culture of shame and self-hatred.

We live in a time when we have to worry about our children in our religious institutions. Be a proponent and a catalyst for sexual healing in your own environment. Act with respect and behave with sexual responsibility. Foster intimacy in your personal relationship and create a bond of love, harmony, safety, and enjoyment with your partner. Do not take sexual behavior outside your partnership, whether it be verbal or physical, an overt look or a lingering touch. Sex on the Internet is included in this category. Be respectful of yourself and all others and promote sexual healing in our world.

Do Not Lie

This precept is much like the right speech of the Eightfold Path. Do not lie, slander, be dishonest in any way, speak with insincerity, promote falsehood, misrepresent information, or gossip maliciously. Do not be indifferent to the truth in any situation with any event that arises.

Lying doesn't necessary mean speaking, however. Your behavior can be just as dishonest as your words. Be truthful in everything you do and bring love and kindness into being in your environment.

Do Not Take Intoxicating Drinks

As we noted earlier, Buddhists do not drink alcohol. The category of intoxicants would also include recreational or unnecessary drugs. Some include caffeine and tobacco as well. This precept allows us to develop inner clarity, keeping our minds free from unnecessary confusion.

The precept prohibiting intoxicants can also be read as prohibiting toxins. Do not pollute your body, as a mindful practice requires little distraction. Caffeine, tobacco, alcohol, and drugs have the propensity to become addictive substances—therefore, although prohibiting the consumption of alcohol may seem like an extreme path and not a path of moderation, the fact that the possibility exists of abuse certainly may influence the argument against any use whatsoever. Remember, even a small amount of an intoxicating substance can disrupt consciousness. You cannot be present in the moment when you are falling down drunk or even marginally impaired. Mindfulness, concentration, and effort are the vehicles that will drive you toward enlightened mind. Polluting your mind with intoxicants is a strike against your right-minded efforts.

QUESTION?

Why are the Five Precepts pretty much negatively worded?
The Five Precepts start out telling us what we shouldn't do. It is easier for us to understand what we *cannot* do than to understand what we *can* do. As we practice not doing these things we start to understand how we *should* act, and we start living on the positive side of the Five Precepts.

The Five Precepts help us recognize the bad behavior we have been partaking in, and help us to cease and desist. For instance, if you stop lying you become a more reliable and trustworthy person. You recognize the benefits of telling the truth and being honest in all of your dealings and others rely on you, as they trust you more. You are a better friend and worker. You notice the effect your behavior is having on others as you become a person who promotes peace instead of negativity. Living the Five Precepts can turn your attitude around as you start to become a positive influence in the world.

The Five Hindrances

The Buddha believed that he could find release from samsara by walking the Eightfold Path. He would not be reborn into the world of *duhkha* if he realized Nirvana in his lifetime. As he related his experiences with the Four Noble Truths and the Eightfold Path, he also told of the Five Hindrances to spiritual progress.

The Five Hindrances are:

1. Doubt
2. Lust
3. Hatred
4. Worry
5. Languor

These are the hindrances to any kind of clear understanding of the truth. As you practice mindfulness and meditation you will become aware of each of the Five Hindrances arising in your mind. You will doubt that what you are doing is meaningful and worthwhile. Don't you have a million other better things to do? What is so important about just sitting there? Images of lustfulness will come up. You will deal with anger and hatred, restlessness and worry, languor and fatigue.

Overcoming Them

Each of these hindrances is something to work through. They can actually be looked at as gifts that further our progress. We must practice that much harder so we can move through our encounters with the hindrances, just as the Buddha sat through Mara's assaults under the Bodhi Tree.

FACT

Ayya Khema, a noted Buddhist author of twenty-five books, become ordained as a Buddhist nun in Sri Lanka in 1979, when she was given the name of *Khema,* which means "safety." In 1987, she coordinated the first international conference of Buddhist nuns in the history of Buddhism, which resulted in the creation of the worldwide Buddhist women's organization, Sakyadhita. In New York in 1987, she became the first Buddhist to ever address the United Nations.

It is important not to attach to any of the hindrances. Do not attach to your worry or your restlessness. Merely observe your feelings and watch them arise and watch them pass. As Ayya Khema said in *When the Iron Eagle Flies,* "Cessation of suffering is not due to the fact that suffering stops. It is due to the fact that the one who suffers ceases to exist." It follows that the doubter, the luster, the angry one, the tired one, the worrier . . . these cease to exist as well.

More Precepts

The Five Precepts previously outlined apply to laypeople practicing Buddhism. However, there are other precepts, and these precepts apply to only monks, or *bhikkus*. A more rigorous set of ethics applies to those practicing a monastic life, and the number of precepts a monastic might vow to undertake varies from one Buddhist tradition to another. Here, however, are five additional precepts that are traditionally taken by monks entering monastic life:

1. Do not take food from noon to the next morning.
2. Do not adorn the body with anything other than the monk's robe.
3. Do not participate in or watch public entertainments.
4. Do not use comfortable beds.
5. Do not use money.

These additional precepts are designed to separate monks from life outside the monastery. Feasting, comfort, financial freedom, personal style, and entertainment are all restricted. These restrictions serve to focus the attention of each monk on the task at hand: the search for enlightenment through practice. There are few distractions from practice for monks.

Each of these additional precepts serves to widen the gap between the monk's life and the life of the laypeople in his community. Though monks are encouraged to live among the population in order to better serve them, their focus is on meditation, mindfulness, the acquisition of wisdom, and the practice of the precepts. A monk's life is dedicated to selflessness and getting rid of ego. Each of the additional precepts a monk might undertake emphasizes the abandonment of ego and the practice of selflessness.

In addition to the men and women who took monastic vows, there were also the bodhisattvas. A bodhisattva is one who puts off his or her entrance into Nirvana and works for the ultimate enlightenment of all humanity and all beings everywhere. The bodhisattvas remain in the samsaric realm in order to help others along the Eightfold Path.

The Precepts Versus the Ten Commandments

What are the differences between the precepts and the Ten Commandments? The Ten Commandments are:

1. Do not have any other gods before me.
2. Do not make unto thee any graven image.
3. Do not take the name of God in vain.
4. Remember to keep the Sabbath day holy.
5. Honor your father and mother.
6. Do not kill.
7. Do not commit adultery.
8. Do not steal.
9. Do not bear false witness against a neighbor.
10. Do not covet anything belonging to your neighbor.

We can see there are similarities between the precepts and the commandments.

The precepts are our instructions for ethical living as are the commandments. Commandments five through ten certainly share the Buddhist practice of being compassionate to all living creatures. Honoring our parents, being kind to our neighbors, refraining from untruthful thought and behavior, stealing—we can see that the commandments and the precepts are in line with each other here.

FACT

Avalokiteshvara is the embodiment of all the Buddha's compassion and symbolizes infinite compassion in Buddhism. Avalokiteshvara is the bodhisattva of compassion.

However, commandments one through four have no common ground with Buddhist thought. There is no higher power in Buddhist tradition, and each of these commandments focuses on the treatment of the Christian god: Do not take another god, do not take God's name in vain, do not hold any images of God, and honor God on a holy day of the week. The commandments are edicts from God; the precepts are suggestions for ethical living. If you break one of the commandments, you risk the wrath of God; if you break one of the precepts, you risk no higher wrath, but you do try over and over again to live within the precepts without breaking them so that you can break the cycle of samsara. Our suffering, therefore, in Buddhist thought, is self-inflicted.

If we were to compare the Ten Precepts here with the Ten Commandments, we'd see the additional precepts that monks take are designed to humble the monk and promote selflessness, and have no mention of a higher power. So we can see that there are similarities in the ethical principles of Christianity and Buddhism; however, they diverge on the subject of God.

Ethical Dilemmas Today

Today we are faced with different ethical issues than perhaps the Buddha and his contemporaries faced. We live in an era where such topics as assisted dying, abortion, suicide, and capital punishment come up in dinner conversation. A Buddhist could look at any ethical issue at hand and try to apply the Buddhist principles of compassion to all living creatures, karma, and mindfulness to the problem at hand. To act with compassion and good intention is to act as a Buddhist.

A Christian friend always says to me, "God will keep giving you the problem until you figure out the answer." This is not so far from the idea of karma. The intention you have going into an action affects the result and impacts your karma. Therefore, if you approach something with hatred or anger in your heart, instead of love and compassion, you will be reborn into a life of suffering once again. In this sense, "God will keep giving you the problem" until you learn how to do it the right way—the way of loving-kindness. As we have seen, the task of making difficult decisions falls to the individual.

Assisted Dying and Abortion

Here are two topics many people raise when contemplating the first precept, do not destroy life. Is abortion destroying life? Perhaps you could side with both the fetus and the mother on this issue. Perhaps the mother's life is at risk or the baby will be born into circumstances of terrible suffering.

Though abortion would seem to override the principles of the first precept, one could see there would be circumstances where compassion necessitates such an act. The same could be said for assisted dying. These are difficult decisions for any individual to make and should be made with the precepts in mind and an attitude of compassion for all living things.

Suicide

In Buddhist thought, suicide is not a sin as it is in Christian belief systems. Remember, in Buddhism morality and ethics have to do with how we treat others and what our intent is as we approach a decision to act. However, suicide is not an act of compassion toward oneself, but is an act of self-annihilation.

The Buddha taught that all sentient beings possess buddha-nature and are considered fundamentally good. Buddha-nature is our potential to awaken and achieve enlightened mind. Buddha believed that everyone has buddha-nature, no matter what they have done or how they look on the outside.

Suicide is subject to the laws of karma. If one commits suicide, one will most likely be born into suffering once again.

The Death Penalty

In some Buddhist countries, such as Japan, Thailand, and Bhutan, capital punishment does exist in certain circumstances. However, these countries—which have large Buddhist populations—are run by secular governments. The Buddha was clear that life is precious and we should not under any circumstances take the life of another living creature. Capital punishment would clearly seem to be against Buddhist thought.

The Buddha further felt that every person had the potential to be a Buddha and start to walk the Eightfold Path at any time. It would seem therefore that the opportunity to turn oneself around at any time, no matter what the crime, should be provided. Appropriate punishment, doled out with a compassionate heart, would seem more in line with the Buddha's intentions.

Treasuring the lives of those who, in many cases, have not valued the lives of others is an act of spiritual courage.

—Damien P. Horigan

The precepts are suggestions for a moral and ethical life. If we follow the precepts—if we do not take life, refrain from stealing in any form, stay away from intoxicants, be truthful in all our affairs, and act sexually responsible—we will have the opportunity to awaken and experience heaven on earth. We will relieve our own suffering, here and forever after, and the suffering of those around us. We will make the world a nicer place to live. Practicing compassion in the world is a wonderful way to live. The precepts show us how. Ⓔ

Chapter 6

The Buddhist Community

Community is an important part of Buddhist practice. As in other great religious traditions, community plays an essential role in keeping the practitioner on the right path, supported by others who share similar beliefs and interests. In Buddhism, each member of the community helps other members to continue on the Eightfold Path.

The Three Jewels

As we have seen, you might call yourself a Buddhist if you practice the Five Precepts as laid out for us by the Buddha, and if you take refuge in the Three Jewels. But what is meant by the Three Jewels of Buddhism? The Three Jewels are more elemental than the Five Precepts and the Four Noble Truths. The Three Jewels are the basic components of Buddhist belief. The Three Jewels of Buddhism are:

- The Buddha
- The Dharma
- The Sangha

We already know what the Buddha is. Buddha means the Fully Awakened One. The Enlightened One. This means we take the Buddha as our refuge. Dharma is the Buddha's teaching, the Path. And the sangha is the Buddhist community. Sangha can generally mean the community in which you practice or it can refer to a specific monastic setting. For instance, if you have a group of people with whom you meet to meditate together on a regular basis, this would be your sangha. Or if you go to a monastery to meditate there, that group would be your sangha. The Three Jewels are often contrasted with the Three Poisons.

The Three Poisons

The Three Poisons are as follows:

- Craving (greed)
- Hatred
- Ignorance

These poisons are not helpful influences in life and can detract us from the dharma. We all experience various forms of these emotions at one time or another. Who hasn't been overcome with desire for some new, shiny possession such as a brand-new car, an addition for your house, an awesome new coat, or even a chocolate double-dipped ice cream cone? Daily life is filled with cravings, and cravings certainly make us suffer. Hatred overtakes us as well. Did someone cut you off in traffic today on the way to work Did you yell out a word perhaps you'd rather your mother didn't hear? What about the person who got your promotion at work? Or the terrorists who caused the destruction of the World Trade Centers? Do the leaders of Enron perhaps inspire feelings you'd rather not have? The stock market?

FACT

When a person decides to live the Buddhist way of life he or she can recite the following as a tangible way of admitting this belief: I take refuge in the Buddha; I take refuge in the dharma; I take refuge in the sangha.

We all experience ignorance as well. Our ignorance of the root cause of suffering is certainly one example of how we don't see clearly. If we knew all along that desire was the root of all suffering, perhaps we wouldn't spend so much time chasing our own tails.

Refuge

Taking refuge in the Buddha does not mean we are hidden and protected by a great and powerful force. It means we align ourselves with the Buddha and strive to become a Buddha ourselves. Similarly, we take refuge with the dharma—we align ourselves with the teachings—and the sangha. We do not hide in the sangha and ask the sangha to protect us from the evils of the world. We find strength in our practice with the sangha. It is much easier to practice with many than it is to practice alone. Sometimes, the only thing getting you in line with the other two jewels is the sangha itself. The sangha can be a very powerful motivator.

Taking refuge in the Three Jewels is like feeling very sick and checking yourself into the hospital. You take refuge in your doctor's care and feel certain she will cure you and get you back on your feet once again. If you recognize your suffering in life, you can similarly take refuge in the Buddha, the dharma, and the sangha, and feel certain that by doing so you will be well on your way to healing yourself from what hurts you.

The Buddha sat under the Bodhi Tree and experienced Nirvana. Once he realized that he had found the answers he had been seeking to the questions that plagued him, he set out to share his newfound knowledge with the people of the Ganges basin. He went to his original fellow spirit seekers, the Five Ascetics, and told them of his experiences. They became his first sangha. His teachings were the dharma. And so the Three Jewels were identified.

When we say, "I take refuge in the Buddha," we should also understand that "The Buddha takes refuge in me," because without the second part the first part is not complete. The Buddha needs us for awakening, understanding, and love to be real things and not just concepts. They must be real things that have real effects on life. Whenever I say, "I take refuge in the Buddha," I hear "Buddha takes refuge in me."

—Thich Nhat Hanh, *Being Peace*

The First Jewel: The Buddha

The Buddha was a man who walked the earth in search of relief from the suffering he experienced. He saw that people age, people get sick, people go hungry, people die, and life was filled with suffering. He saw that the nature of the world was transitory, things come and things go. He identified his cause of suffering as desire: desire for animate things, desire for inanimate things.

He was prince of his kingdom and he was also a beggar on the streets. He was a husband, a father, and a monk. He was a son and a friend, a spiritual seeker, and a man like any other. He was a yogi, and was familiar with excess and with deprivation. He became the living spirit of compassion and a living embodiment of all that is kind and fair.

Respect

We take refuge in the Buddha for all of these reasons and more. We respect the man that the Buddha once was. We respect the sacrifices he made so that we, too, could experience the reality of awakening and live a heaven here on earth and be released from the cycles of samsara. When the Buddha realized his awakening, he didn't sit in his little piece of heaven, alone, for the rest of his life. He took to the challenge of spreading his knowledge so that we, too, could have the opportunity to awaken. Everything on earth, everything in the world, is willing us to wake up to the true nature of life. And the Buddha set forth the path for all of us to see. For this we take refuge in the Buddha.

We can relate to the Buddha: He was a man who traveled his path for six years looking for the answers. He sat and meditated in pain, just as we all sit and meditate in pain. He experienced the same distractions, the same physical pains, the same temptations, as illustrated by the visits from Mara. He was not a man separate from each of us, but one exactly like each of us. We can all have the same experience, and the Buddha assures us that each and every one of us, with diligent practice and utter mindfulness, can also wake up to the Truth.

The Buddha does not tell us to believe in him, to pray to him, and he will bestow great peace of mind on us. The Buddha tells us to do it ourselves, the way he did it. He shows us a path that we are free to take all on our own. Each and every one of us can find out for ourselves if the path works, if the path is what we are looking for. There is no blind allegiance; there is only practice. It's as if all Buddhists are from the state of Missouri with its state proclamation: "Show me!"

See for yourself: You, too, can take refuge in the Buddha.

Living Buddha

Taking refuge in the Buddha can also mean finding an appropriate teacher today. You might know of a Buddhist who is qualified to teach you the dharma. If so, you can take refuge in a qualified teacher of the dharma as well. Find yourself a teacher who embodies the teachings of the Buddha. When you find a living Buddha—when you witness the compassion and loving-kindness that is possible in our everyday world— you can wholly take refuge in the Buddha with an open heart and exquisite anticipation of the possibilities that really do exist. To take refuge in the Buddha is to take refuge in any Buddha at all.

◀ Buddhist statue in front of a temple

The Second Jewel: The Dharma

The second of the Three Jewels is the dharma. The dharma is the entire collection of Buddhist scripture and thought, including all modern Buddhist teachings, as well as the traditional, original teachings, such as the Dhammapada, the Tibetan Book of the Dead, and the sutras. The dharma is all the written text and spoken word passed down through the generations, and all language, concepts, and material on Buddhism.

Today we have many sources for the dharma. We have books, video, CDs, tapes, teachers, classes, and the Internet. There are two types of dharma: that which can be read or heard—transmitted from person to person—and that which is realized. *Realized* dharma is dharma experienced through the practice of the Eightfold Path—the realization of the Truth, or awakening.

The dharma surrounds us. Anything that helps you awaken is the dharma. Have you ever found yourself sitting outside, perhaps by a stream, enjoying the wonders of a beautiful day? Suddenly you hear a bird call out and its call is pure and sweet and fills you. You lose yourself completely in that moment, just listening to the sounds of the bird. The bird is the dharma; the bird teaches you something about awakening. In that moment your small self disappears and you awaken to understanding and the truth. Then the moment disappears. Anything can be the dharma: water, a bird, a work of art, a cup of coffee, a dog barking, the rain . . . anything at all that helps us to awaken for just a moment. Everything that exists is constantly trying to teach us the Truth.

Roshi is a title given to a Zen master, under whom a student must study if he or she hopes to reach enlightened mind. In Japanese it means "venerable master."

Earlier we read about the man who wanted to cross the river on his raft. Once he crossed the raging waters, he wondered what to do with his vehicle. Should he take the raft with him on his journey? No, and you shouldn't carry the dharma with you as you cross into enlightened mind, either. The Buddha taught us to leave behind that which we no longer need. Do not take the dharma as an absolute, definable, and fixed reality. It changes just as everything changes. Do not burden yourself with that which you believed to be fixed. It is an illusion. As you journey on the path toward enlightened mind, let go of what you learn on the way and keep your mind fresh and clean. Zen Master Suzuki Roshi tells us that it is difficult to keep our mind pure. In Japan, there is a phrase, *shoshin*, which means "beginner's mind." In Buddhism, the aspiration is always to keep this beginner's mind, this openness and readiness. Suzuki tells us, "In the beginner's mind there are many possibilities; in the expert's mind there are few."

FACT

Shunryu Suzuki, a Zen priest of the Soto lineage, was one of the most influential Zen teachers of his time. In 1959, he left Japan and went to San Francisco, where he was impressed by the "beginner's mind" quality he found among Americans practicing Zen. He settled in San Francisco and brought the way of Zen into the daily lives of an appreciative American population. He died in 1971.

The Third Jewel: The Sangha

The last part of the Three Jewels is the sangha. The sangha traditionally referred to the monastic group studying with the Buddha. As the Buddha traveled around the Ganges River area spreading knowledge of the lesson he had learned, thousands of people gave up family lives to join his sangha and take the vows of the *bhikku*. The sangha therefore was originally a monastic community.

However, especially in the West, the sangha has come to mean any community of Buddhist practitioners, monastics, or layfollowers. There is some controversy over what some see as a dilution of the integrity of the sangha. By everyday folk calling their community a sangha, some traditionalist feel it weakens the strength of Buddhism and corrupts the strength of the sangha itself. Others disagree.

Vacchagotta approached the Buddha and asked him if there were layfollowers practicing the Buddha's principles who achieved "high spiritual states." The Buddha told Vacchagotta that yes, there were "not one or two, not a hundred or two hundred or five hundred but many more" who did.

The monastic setting certainly provides a place for individuals willing to devote their entire life to their spiritual development and to the service of all. However, it is not realistically possible for most of us to do so. Should those who cannot devote their entire lives to service of this kind be pro-hibited from a community in which to practice the principles the Buddha put forth? What would the Buddha say? It is up to the individual to decide.

As we know, there is power in numbers. What you find difficult alone, you might find much easier with the strength of numbers behind you. It can be very difficult to practice a spiritual program on one's own. The world around you is often not quite on the same spiritual page as you are. And it often feels as if it is working directly against you. If you are trying to be mindful, to be courteous, to practice the Five Precepts in all your affairs, it can be difficult when you are up against a greedy coworker, an incessant talker, a liar, or number of other distractions. Sometimes you can feel overwhelmed by the noncompliance of others. Having a group that supports your belief system, that encourages you to proceed against the odds, can make all the difference in the world.

As you sit to do your meditation, perhaps you start wondering *why* you are sitting on a cushion when you could be watching *Law and Order* or playing a round of golf. Perhaps work beckons or the house needs cleaning. Without a sangha to keep you on track, over time the voices in your head that discourage you from your practice will get louder and louder until they crowd out that little voice inside yourself that urges you onward to discovery.

Remember, if your mouth is moving you aren't learning anything new. We can come to believe that we know the answers and that the answers lie with our favorite pillow on the couch or at the seventeeth hole on the green. The sangha can help bring you back to the path and hold you there. There has been many an early morning when the only thing that got me sitting on a cushion in the middle of my community group was the idea that if I didn't show up, maybe—just someday—nobody would, and then what would I do? Sometimes the sangha is the only thing pushing us forward. The sangha can be a powerful force of encouragement.

Sangha can be expanded to mean the entire world. The universe around us can be our community. We can treat all of our surroundings as our sangha, and feel a part of the world itself as we do feel a part of our sangha.

We take refuge in the Buddha because Buddha is our great teacher . . . We take refuge in the law, in the Dharma, because it is good medicine . . . We take refuge in the Buddha's community, or sangha, because it is composed of excellent friends. . . .

—Dainin Katagiri

Finding the Three Jewels Today

How can you find refuge in the Three Jewels today? If you are just setting out on the Eightfold Path and your journey toward enlightenment, where can you find a living Buddha, the teachings you will need, and a group to support you? There are many Buddhist communities all over the world today.

Buddhism Is Your Neighborhood

Buddhism is found the world over. In the United States, there are approximately 3 to 4 million proclaimed Buddhists, out of a total population of approximately 261 million people. There are somewhere between 500 and 800 Buddhist centers in the United States. See Appendix C at the back of the book for a list of Buddhist centers near you and check one out to see if you think it's right for you and your practice. Visit a few centers if you can and sit with a few different groups. Buddhists live in Australia, South Africa, Hungary, Poland, Russia, Italy, the Netherlands . . . they're everywhere!

If there is no Buddhist monastery anywhere in your vicinity, you can always look online for sitting groups within a reasonable distance of your home. I live in a rural area of northwestern New Jersey and would have thought the likelihood of finding a local sitting sangha was slim. However, I was very surprised to find a number of groups within a reasonable drive and have been a very happy member of the same group for several years now. For example, I did a search on Google for "Buddhist Sitting Groups New Jersey" and got more hits than you'd imagine.

Your phone book is also a good source of support. Look under Religious Organizations or Churches. I also noticed in my local paper that a monastery close to my home was offering lessons on the weekends. Sometimes your community bulletin boards are wonderful sources of information. You could also get some like-minded friends together and start your own sitting group.

You can find a teacher at a monastery or through members of your sitting group. If you find an established sangha in your area, you will most likely find a teacher comes along with the sangha. I was lucky to find my teacher through a friend. We started speaking and it quickly became evident that we shared some very similar belief systems. My friend mentioned his teacher, and before long I found I had someone to lead me through my own practice.

The Teacher Appears!

When the student is ready, the teacher appears! I do believe it is important to find a teacher who embodies living compassion. If you want what your teacher has, and you are willing to go to any lengths to have such compassion, humility, sanity, and love, you will find yourself very committed to the path. It's amazing to meet a real, live, living Buddha. Buddhism is a show-me belief system and finding living proof of the reality of enlightenment is very encouraging and inspiring. It can change the way you view the world entirely.

QUESTION?

Where can I find a list of reliable sources on Buddhism?
A comprehensive list of resources appears in Appendix B at the back of this book. But also try your library, bookstores, and the Internet. There's a vast array of information out there on Buddhism in all its forms.

Your teacher can show you the dharma, but the world is open to present the dharma to you. You can find information on Buddhism everywhere. My tiny local library had quite a selection of Buddhist texts, as well as the ability to order books from other libraries.

Bookstores, the Internet, other Buddhists, audiotapes, CDs . . . it's all out there. The world is your classroom and the dharma is everywhere; just open your eyes and your ears and you will be amazed at what you will learn.

Your journey down the Eightfold Path can begin today. If you embrace the Three Jewels of Buddha, dharma, and sangha, along with the Five Precepts as outlined in Chapter 5, you will have started your Buddhist practice. If you have decided you would like to adopt a Buddhist's way of life, and would like a more formalized initiation ceremony, you can always recite "I take refuge in the Buddha; I take refuge in the dharma; I take refuge in the sangha," alone or with friends. What a beautiful way to begin . . . Ⓔ

Chapter 7

Karma

Karma is one of the fundamentals of Buddhism. Without a good grasp of the meaning and implications of karma in our lives, we cannot truly understand the Buddhist belief system. This chapter will take a look at common misconceptions about karma, how karma serves as the moral core of Buddhist belief, the cycles of birth, and finally rebirth, preparing us for the insights that follow in Chapter 8.

Popular Misconceptions of Karma

Let's take a look at some of the most common incorrect assumptions about karma, that karma is retaliatory, personal, and passed down.

Misconception: *Karma is retaliation from a force outside ourselves*

How many times have we heard someone say, "She has bad karma," referring to someone who has had a run of bad luck. In the West, karma has often been interpreted as equal to the principle of "an eye for an eye"—the retaliatory principle that we are punished with the same punishment we inflict on another. However, this is a misconception and misunderstanding of the meaning of karma. Karma means *action*. We are not made to pay for past mistakes, nor are we rewarded for our past good deeds—but we *are*, in fact, what we *do* or intend to do. More to the point, karma is the process by which our thoughts shape our lives.

If we commit an act of insult or a crime, such as murder or adultery, we will not be punished by being reborn as a pig. Anyone who has spent time with a pig might notice that the pig seems quite happy to be a pig. Pigs like to roll in the mud, eat their food, and play. So therefore, a human who is born as a pig is not a human stuck in a pig's body, but a pig in a pig's body, having a pig's day and a pig's life experience.

QUESTION?

Is karma a punishment or reward from God?
No, karma has nothing to do with a higher power or an objective judge. In the words of Shantideva (an eighth-century Buddhist teacher), "Suffering is a consequence of one's own action, not a retribution inflicted by an external power . . . We are the authors of our own destiny; and being the authors, we are ultimately . . . free . . . "

Karma is not something inexplicable. It is not an immutable force from the past for which we hold some ephemeral responsibility and are powerless to change. We do not resign ourselves to our bad karma and throw our hands up in despair because we have been "cursed" with bad karma. Karma is a natural law in the world, like the laws that govern gravity. Karma *is*. Our rebirths are the natural result of our actions, not a punishment for a force outside ourselves.

Misconception: *Karma is not personal*

Karma is not something that is carried by an individual from life to life. There is no individual in the sense of the Christian soul—you are not the same person after life as you are in life. Indeed, the human you may be in this life is a direct result of the actions you took in the last life. In other words, bodies and manifestations are the *result* of karma, not the other way around. (You are who are you now because of what you have already done; you are not the same *you* with a more painful life, you are an entirely *new* you *due* to your past life.) Karma is not something, like a curse, that is carried by someone, but karma is in its entirety, the person him- or herself. Karma is not the individual person or manifestation, but it is re-created with every new action or choice we make.

FACT

Karma means "action" in Sanskrit. However, we do not substitute the word *action* for *karma* as karma carries much more weight than the simple understanding we have of the word *action*.

Just as you are not the same person you are now as you were when you were a baby, you will not be the same being in the next life as you are now. We are all constantly changing. Although we seem to like to view ourselves as fixed individuals, as we have seen in earlier chapters, we are not fixed, but fluid, constantly flowing and changing like a river.

Misconception: *We inherit other people's karma*

For an example of this misconception we can take a look at the Kennedy family. President John F. Kennedy was killed by an assassin in November 1963. Five years later, in 1968, Robert Kennedy, John's brother, was also killed by an assassin. When John, Jr., died in a plane crash at thirty-eight years old with his wife, Carolyn Bessette, and her sister, there was much talk about the Kennedy curse. However, in Buddhist belief there is no such thing as a curse and you cannot inherit your relatives' karma. President Kennedy, therefore, did not inherit the curse of his father, and neither did Robert Kennedy, nor John Kennedy, Jr. In fact, if each Kennedy had bad karma, it would most likely have been due to actions in a past life and not this one.

Our karma is ours individually and cannot be passed on or shared—which still does not mean that karma is personal. It would be safe to assume that the karma of those who assassinated the Kennedy brothers was not positive karma in that particular lifetime and could and would affect how the assassin would be reborn in the next lifetime. The Kennedy deaths are tragic, and very sad losses for a family as well as an entire nation. However, once an action is committed, the consequences for committing that action fall to the individual or manifestation that committed the action to begin with, and never to anyone else.

In fact, where you come from and who you come from has little bearing on your karma at all. However, what you do with your life *now* is everything . . .

Misconception: *Karma involves all actions*

Karma only involves intentional actions. Therefore, if you were to step on a spider on your way to the curb with the week's recycling matter, you would not incur bad karma.

You unintentionally stepped on the spider. There was no intent to hurt the spider at all.

However, if you decide beforehand that you are going to kill the damn spider that is living in the garage and stomp on him with malice aforethought, you do incur bad karma as a result of your negative action. You do not always have to act with malice, however.

Sometimes you intentionally set out to cause harm with no malice in your heart whatsoever. You might decide to whack your dog over the head with a big stick because he won't sit when you tell him to. You may even believe you are doing the dog some good, as he will have better manners and be better behaved. However, you are intentionally harming another creature, and this cannot be construed as a positive action.

Thinking about bad actions involves negative karma, but acting on them makes it that much worse. Thinking on good actions involves positive karma, and acting on them increases the good karma. Regretting bad actions can also increase good karma, or better said, lessen the bad karma. In this way, you can create your own destiny.

If you are a negatively thinking person who constantly harbors bad or negative thoughts, this could be a result of some previous bad karma. However, if you try to change your thought patterns and become a more positive-thinking person, you can lessen the bad karma and increase the good karma. One should always strive to improve in the present.

It is mental volition, O monks, that I call karma. Having willed, one acts through body, speech or mind.

—The Buddha

Karma As the Moral Center

As you can see, in Buddhism our actions matter very, very much. And therefore karma serves as a moral compass for our lives today.

Karma is not a complicated concept. It is as simple as this: What you do, what you say, will have an effect. For instance, I'm sure you have run into someone in the course of your day who has gotten up on the wrong side of the bed. Perhaps you are at work and your boss is in a difficult mood. She has made a judgment in error herself and decides to take the mistake out on you. She calls you into her office and criticizes you on work that you are quite proud of and for which you have put in a lot of hard work. You are deflated and in turn you are angry yourself. Your wife calls you and you take your anger out on her. As we can see, actions have effect. Similarly, we are walking down the street and a stranger gives us a big smile, a compliment, and remarks what a wonderful life it is we are living. You walk away yourself feeing a lift you hadn't felt a moment before. His actions had an effect on you. This is a very simple example of karma.

The man who has had a positive effect on others with his smile and kind words will be happy. That is the karmic result of his kindness. The boss who takes out her anger on her subordinates is left remorseful. And that remorse is the karmic result of her negative action.

Effects of our Actions

But our actions have much greater effect than one day's span. Karmic actions include thoughts, words, deeds, in fact, all of our intentions. Karma is vast. We as a nation are part of a common karma. Our actions as a nation, although you might personally disagree with them, are part of your karma. Karma can also change. If you do good acts now you can change your later karma. Karma overcomes death and is passed on from one life to another. Believing in karma will change the way you live your life. For Buddhists, the belief in karma is as guiding a moral compass as the Ten Commandments are for some believers. However, do not worry or obsess on past actions. Take care of your life today. Live in the moment and change the present. Thereby you might change the future as well.

FACT

Shantideva was an Indian Mahayana monk and scholar who studied at the renowned Buddhist University Nalanda. He was born during the last half of the seventh century and was known for teaching the Bodhisattva's Way of Life.

Wholesome Versus Unwholesome

In Buddhism, good action is referred to as "wholesome" action, while bad action is referred to as "unwholesome." Unwholesome actions incur harm in others or oneself. The harm can be spiritual, mental, or physical; it is not limited to physical harm.

Wholesome action is action that does no harm to others or to oneself, but also promotes some kind of wholesome growth. For instance, greed, hatred, and delusion will promote unwholesome action. Sincerity, compassion, generosity, clarity, and loving-kindness will promote wholesome action. If someone speaks to you unfairly and negatively and you respond with forbearance and loving-kindness, you will be promoting wholesome action.

Karma and Cycles of Birth

In Chapter 8 we will take a look at how the Buddhists view the world—the heavens and hells of birth and rebirth. Moving between lives and rebirths is not a random act, but is determined by your actions in your current life. In this manner, we are heir to our actions. As Peter Harvey tells us in *An Introduction to Buddhism,* if we commit acts of hatred—violent acts, such as murder, rape, incest, or bodily harm—we will be reborn into a life in hell.

A Lower Rebirth

If we commit acts of ignorance and delusion, we will be reborn as animals. And if we commit acts of greed, we will end up as a hungry ghost (see Chapter 8 for more on this subject). Our acts in this life tend to dictate our life form in the next life. We will not necessarily be born again as a human. We might end up as an inhabitant of hell, a spirit, an animal, or even a god. We are not in the circumstances we are in during this lifetime due to our actions in this lifetime, but because of actions we have perpetrated in another lifetime and another life form.

The Tibetan Book of the Dead is a classic of Buddhist wisdom on the process of dying. It is a wonderful source of information on the Buddhist cosmos, life and death, and life and rebirth. It has become an influential text in the Western world for helping us cope with death and dying.

Taking a Step Up

In this same way, we might be reborn into higher life forms if we commit good acts in this lifetime—if we are generous, spiritually fit, kind, loving, and sincere. If we practice the Five Precepts and the ways of the

Eightfold Path, we will have a much greater chance of being reborn into a life in a higher form, such as a human or god.

Picture a woman in a church. She is going to light a candle to honor the soul of the dead and pray for the lost ones. She takes an unlit candle from the altar and holds it up to a lit candle so that the flame may be shared. When the flame lights up on the new candle, is it the same flame that was on the old candle? It is not exactly the same; however, it is not exactly different either. Much is the same with a life and rebirth. It is not the same life. However, it is not an entirely different life either.

It wasn't until I moved to the country from the city that I noticed the seasons were constantly changing. Buds appear in early February during the snow; spring doesn't suddenly announce itself one day with a mass budding and flowering profusion. Similarly, leaves start dropping at the height of summer. Fall isn't limited to September, October, and November. Again, nothing is fixed. We are constantly changing as well. Nothing is the same from one second to the next.

FACT

The changing of everything in the world from one form to another, the truth that nothing lasts, is called *impermanence*. Our inability to understand impermanence leads to our suffering.

Chögyam Trungpa Rinpoche, one of the most dynamic teachers of Buddhism ever to grace the West, tells us that impermanence is indestructible. Are we to take comfort in these words? Yes, for if we didn't have impermanence, then winter would never give way to spring, a seed would never give way to a tree, a match would never give way to a fire. We would never change and grow. Everything would be frozen in time, immutable, and dead to the life force that changes us all.

Rebirth: Life As the Wheel of Samsara

The cycle of samsara is often depicted as The Wheel of Life. The Wheel of Life illustrates for us the cause of all suffering and evil. The wheel itself is held by a monster, who snarls at us and shows us that to be caught up in the cycles of life is suffering itself. The different parts of the wheel symbolize different parts of the cycle of life and suffering.

The Inner Hub

In the very center of the wheel, at the hub of the wheel, are three animals:

- The cock
- The snake
- The pig

These three animals represent the Three Poisons. As we saw in Chapter 6, the Three Poisons are greed, hatred, and ignorance. The cock represents greed, the snake represents hatred, and the pig represents ignorance.

Circling the center of the wheel is a narrow path that is cut in two. The right side of the path represents the Dark Path. If you take the Dark Path you have chosen to live with the Three Poisons of greed, hatred, and ignorance. The left side of the path is the White Path.

If you choose the White Path, the path will lead you to rebirth and eventual liberation.

The Heart of the Wheel

At the main body of the wheel, just outside of the Dark Path and White Path, are the Six Symbolic Worlds. To understand the meanings of the Six Symbolic Worlds, read about the Buddhist cosmos in Chapter 8. The main body of the wheel is broken up into six slices of pie. At the top of the wheel is the slice that represents the world of the gods. The gods symbolize vanity. The Buddha appears to the gods playing a lute, which symbolizes the nature of impermanence. The gods become comfortable in their god realm and forget that they are subject to rebirth. Buddha gently reminds them.

To the right of the gods you will find the world of humankind. Humans symbolize egoism and ignorance. The Buddha appears to the humans as a monk, showing us that we can be saved through practice.

Next to the right is the realm of the animals. The animals stand for oppression, as they are oppressed by other beings. The Buddha appears to the animals with a book, symbolizing, perhaps, that they too can be saved.

At the bottom of the wheel are the hells of the Buddhist cosmos. The Buddha brings to hell a flame, showing that he will light the way out of their suffering.

The Dhammapada, or the Sayings of the Buddha, is the Pali version of one of the most popular texts of the Buddhist canon, and ranks among the greatest of the world's religious literature. It belongs to the Theravada school of Buddhist tradition.

To the left of the hell realm is the realm of the ghosts. The ghosts symbolize greed, and the Buddha brings them nectar, to try to appease their incessant craving. To the left of the ghost, between the ghosts and the gods, can be found the titans. The titans symbolize war, and the Buddha brings to them a flaming sword, to symbolize the end of their raging.

The Outer Rim

The outer rim of the Wheel of Life contains the twelve interdependent causes and effects. This section of the wheel is divided into twelve pictures. Each picture represents the dependent, conditioned, and relative phenomena that make up life. These pictures symbolize that a life cycle is made up of twelve conditioned phenomena that form a circle of repeating, dependent causes and effects:

1. Ignorance: symbolized by a blind man.
2. Actions (how we shape our own karma): symbolized by the potter.
3. Consciousness (how we flit from thought to thought, object to object): symbolized by the monkey jumping from tree to tree.
4. Name and form (our physical and spiritual energy): symbolized by a boat with two passengers.

5. Five senses and thought: symbolized by a house with five windows and a door.
6. Contact: symbolized by lovers embracing.
7. Emotions: symbolized by an arrow through a man's eye (ouch).
8. Desire: symbolized by a woman offering a drink to a man, or by a man drinking.
9. Attachment or sensual entanglement: symbolized by a woman plucking fruit from a tree (the desire to take something and keep it).
10. Procreation or becoming: symbolized by a bride or a pregnant woman.
11. Consequence: symbolized by a woman giving birth.
12. Old age and death: symbolized by a corpse or an old man.

What do we mean by dependent and relational causes and effects? Well, we can see that ignorance leads to our actions. Actions give rise to our consciousness, which in turn gives rise to name and form. (We do, we think, we name.) Name and form leads to the five senses and thought, which in turn give rise to our impressions (our contact). Our contact leads to our emotions, which leads to craving and desire. Desire leads to attachment (I want to keep what I have), and attachment leads to becoming. Becoming leads to birth, and birth leads to death, which leads to rebirth and ignorance. This is the pictorial presentation of samsara. We are trapped in samara until we can reach enlightened mind and freedom.

FACT

Chögyam Trungpa Rinpoche was one of the twentieth century's greatest teachers of Buddhism. He brought Tibetan Buddhist teachings to the West and introduced many important Buddhist concepts here. In 1974 he founded the Naropa Institute, the only accredited Buddhist-inspired university in North America. Rinpoche died in 1987 at the age of forty-seven.

◀ Buddhist statues

At the top of the Wheel of Life, to the left, above the monster, is the Bodhisattva Avalokiteshvara. Avalokiteshvara is the bodhisattva of compassion. He represents the link between the beings trapped in samsara—the mundane—and the transcendental.

On the top of the Wheel of Life, to the right, above the monster, is the Buddha. The Buddha represents the transcendental, Nirvana, and the path to freedom.

The Power of Karma

An ethical, moral life is not necessarily followed by a desirable rebirth. Sometimes our past karma is powerful enough to inhibit our present and future good karma. If there is a strong evil action in your past, perhaps it will take some time to work out the bad karma and exhaust it. Similarly, if you had a shining example of good behavior in a faraway past life—if you perpetrated good and were a positive influence on the world—but you were most recently living a life full of negativity, then you will not necessarily have a bad rebirth either. Your past good karma could carry you through a negative life form.

While karma is a very important concept and fundamental to many Buddhist's belief system, it is not critical. The most important teachings are the Four Noble Truths and the Eightfold Path. The belief in karma can make it easier to stick to the teachings of the Eightfold Path, as the consequences of an unethical and moral life can be extreme and unpleasant. We will investigate the possibilities of rebirth in the next chapter.

Chapter 8

The Buddhist Cosmos

Buddhist cosmology came from a mixture of pre-Buddhist Hindu thought and later additions by early Buddhists. The view of the cosmos held by some Buddhists is a far cry from traditional Western worldviews. The concept of karma plays a major role in Buddhist cosmology, as does the belief in the cycles of samsara, both borrowed from the Hindu belief system, prevalent during the life of Siddhartha Gautama.

Past Lives

On the night of the Buddha's enlightenment he is said to have remembered 100,000 past lives. Can you imagine? This belief in the endless cycle of birth and rebirth is fundamental to Buddhist belief, and once this foundation is understood it is easier to comprehend the compulsion Buddhists felt for finding a way out of the infinite repetitions of suffering. We in the West, with our emphasis on the material, might find it a hard concept to grasp. Doesn't everyone want to live forever? The answer for Buddhists was most certainly *no*. The Buddha believed there was no beginning of life, just an endless circle of samsara. Just imagine never resting, finding an end, knowing that you were endlessly destined to repeat the pattern of life. Knowledge of such repetition would most likely feel exhausting.

Within the system of birth and rebirth, there were considered to be many worlds and many ways in which one could be reborn—*endless* worlds and *endless* ways to be reborn. The Buddha is said to have remembered ninety-one *kalpas* of time. A *kalpa* is an enormous amount of time, more than we can easily comprehend. (Although there is much discrepancy in sources over the number of *kalpas* Buddha remembered, it can be understood to mean that the Buddha saw a large amount of worlds.) For example, if there was a mountain that reached many miles into the sky, and that mountain was made of pure granite, and once every 100 years that mountain was stroked with a cloth such as silk, then a *kalpa* would be the time it took to wear the mountain away to nothing. Such is the context in which one can understand the meaning of samsara.

These cycles involved not only human births. A person was not necessarily born as a human in every lifetime. There are also animals, spirits, gods, titans, and the inhabitants of hell. The early Buddhists rejected the Hindu caste system, so in rebirth it was possible to move from a god to a human, an animal to a god. There was no safety in reaching a higher life form. Every life form was subject to death and therefore rebirth. Most Buddhists in the Western world would take these realms and forms as being metaphorical or mythical, but as they do show up in even the most advanced Buddhists texts the student of Buddhist life should be familiar with them.

The Three Realms

According to Buddhist cosmology, there are three realms—or types—of existence in each of the innumerable worlds: the Realm of Desire, the Realm of Form, and the Realm of No-Form.

◀ Meditating Buddha

These realms can simplistically be considered to be like hell or like heaven. They can also be understood symbolically as spiritual, psychological, or emotional states.

In Buddhist thought, [karma] has nothing to do with fate—it is an impersonal natural process of cause and effect. Our karma at a given moment is the overall pattern of causal impulses resulting from former actions connected with our life-continuum.
—Tibetan Book of the Dead

The Realm of Desire

Within the Realm of Desire there are six categories into which you can be born. The six categories are:

- Gods
- Humans
- Titans
- Animals
- Hungry ghost
- Denizens of hell

Whether or not you end up as a god or a hungry ghost largely depends on your karma and your intentions and actions in your last life. If you had good karma, you could advance upward. If you had bad karma, you would go downward. One can start to see why enlightenment is such an appealing solution. Enlightenment is the only way to stop the cycles of rebirth. There are endless possibilities for suffering in the different worlds, so there is a powerful incentive to find a way out—to end the suffering by ending the cycle of rebirth. Of these six forms, three are considered desirable form (gods, titans, and humans) in which to be reborn and three are considered undesirable (animals, hungry ghosts, and denizens of hell).

FACT

According to John Snelling, in *The Buddhist Handbook,* the most fortunate age to be born in is termed a *Bhadra Kalpa.* During a Bhadra Kalpa, at least 1,000 Buddhas will be born (over the course of 320,000,000 years). Each Buddha will discover the dharma, and teach it for anywhere from 500 to 1,500 years, until a dark age sets in and the teaching is lost. We live in a Bhadra Kalpa now.

The Realm of Desire is named so because it is the only realm in which beings perceive objects through their senses and experience desirability or undesirability. Desire is the root of suffering, and there is much suffering in the Realm of Desire. The Realms of Form and No-Form are not subject to the same experiences.

Picture the endless mountain once again. The Buddhists call this mountain Mount Meru. If all of these inhabitants were living on the mountain, then the gods would live on the upper slopes. The titans would live on the lower slopes. The humans and animals would live at the bottom of the mountain in the planes and meadows, and the ghosts and the denizens of hell would live below ground.

It takes many *kalpas* for a being to change enough to advance into another type of being. Infinitesimal changes, over great periods of time, must occur in order for a being to be free from a particular life form. Once stuck in a lower life form, the chances of making it into a human life form are unimaginably small.

Gods

Gods live on the upper slopes of the Mount Meru. They keep an eye out on the goings-on of the realms below. There are different levels of gods on the upper slopes, some more superior than others. The gods who live on the uppermost levels have lives of incredible luxury and opulence. They live a life controlled by the mind and have more freedom than do humans. They are surrounded by the finest of everything and are rich beyond belief.

These gods live very long lives, much longer than human lives. However, they, too, eventually die and must be reborn as all others are reborn. They can easily fall into the lower realms, as their pride can overwhelm the force that has pushed them into the realm of the gods. At some time their good karma will wear out and they might find themselves born into a life as one of the lower life forms, such as animals or hungry ghosts.

Titans

What are titans? Titans might bring up visions of Harry Hamlin in *Clash of the Titans,* but in the Buddhist world, titans were typically depicted as warrior demons. They have taken their human traits and used them in the pursuit of power. The titans are angry, hot-tempered creatures who are prone to jealousy, rage, and war. They often leave their habitat to do battle with some of the other inhabitants of their world and are motivated by the desire to fight. They want to take the realm of the gods away from them. Because of their tendency toward war and jealousy, they often end up falling down to the lowest of the realms, into life forms of intense suffering and pain.

FACT

The warrior demons, the titans, were also known as *asuras*. Although the words *warrior, demon,* and even *titans* might conjure up negative, evil images, these powerful beings did not always perform negative acts.

The titans are generally understood to be a nasty sort and not as desirable a form in which to be reborn as the gods. There are always in foul temper, always causing trouble for someone or other, and do not symbolize rest or peace.

Humans and Animals

Humans and animals live at the bottom of Mount Meru. Living a life as an animal is considered one of the not so fortunate forms to take. The animal realm is considered a lower birth, and animals are considered to suffer more than human beings do. Animals are trapped in ignorance, and have no way of getting out of their instinct-driven behaviors. Their potential for freedom is almost nil, and it takes a long time and a lot of care for them to evolve into a higher form.

The human form, on the other hand, is a very desirable form to inhabit. It could be said to be the center of everything in the Buddhist cosmos. It is within the human form that you have your only chance for enlightenment and escape from samsara.

Depending upon your actions and intentions as a human, you can fall back down to the hell realm, become an animal or god or other, or escape entirely into Nirvana and end the cycle of rebirth. The possibility of achieving a human birth after you have fallen into one of the lower realms is extremely slim, however. But tiny positive moves on the part of the three lower realm forms can have a cumulative effect of pushing a being into one of the higher realms and human form.

QUESTION?

Will I remember my past lives?
No. Your past lives are all a part of who you are now. Everything that has come to be is part of who you are at this moment. The past is not separate from you; it is part of you. You are not the same individual that existed in the past life. To remember your own past life would be like trying to remember your cat's past life.

Although humans still have some very negative traits, they are free from the extreme negativities of life as a hungry ghost, animal, or hell-being. Over billions of lifetimes these traits have been made marginally smaller, and humans have gained some positive traits as well. Humans have the capacity to do right and wrong; it is therefore at the human life form level that positive or negative actions are performed. Gods do not have much capacity for action. Being one of the lower forms, such as animals, hungry ghosts, and hell-beings, means you have little intentional ability to affect your rebirth. However, your karma will eventually play itself out and when the bad karma from a previous life has exhausted itself, you might move into a more positive rebirth. It is only at the human level that you can directly affect your rebirth.

Hungry Ghosts

Hungry ghosts are pretty much exactly the tortured specters you imagine. They are often portrayed as having a huge stomach, a long, skinny neck, and a very small mouth. This image symbolizes the intense hunger these beings suffer; their small mouths and narrow necks an indication that their suffering is never eased, as they can never feed enough to appease their desire. Adequate amounts of food can never pass through the small mouths and the narrow necks, and when it does, immense pain is experienced by the hungry ghosts as the food tries to force its way through spaces too small to accommodate it. These hungry ghosts are disembodied spirits, floating around the human and animal forms, never finding rest.

Hungry ghosts have been the subject of many interpretations and can be seen as the embodiment of unsatisfied desire and attachment. An addiction could be viewed as a hungry ghost: never finding satisfaction but constantly craving the substance that hurts, an endless cycle of pain and dissatisfaction. Being reborn as a hungry ghost would certainly not be on the forefront of your list of choices for a new life. Hungry ghosts can be seen to symbolize greed.

Denizens of Hell

The worst place to find yourself in a rebirth situation is as a denizen of hell. As a member of this poor group, you can expect any of a number of tortuous lives. Early Buddhists, just like everyone else, had vivid imaginations when it came to suffering and torture. You could be endlessly cut up, burned, frozen, eaten, beaten, or tortured in any number of ways, only to die and wake up and do it all over again. Some areas of hell are all about abominable nightmares, untenable sensory experiences, and horrible visions. The denizens of hell symbolize hatred. There are as many as ten hells in the Realm of Desire and the inhabitants must make their way through all in order to escape the anguish and suffering.

FACT

In Hinduism, Brahma is the creator of what we would think of as our solar system. (There are many different versions of the creation or re-creation of the universe in Hinduism and this is just one.)

The only way out of hell is to be reborn into another form. In order to do so you must change your karma. You ended up in hell due to some action or intention you took in another life, so until your bad karma runs out you will be constantly reborn into another form of hell. While life in hell won't last forever, it certainly might feel like it does. This vision of hell is not so far from the Western visions of hell we know more familiarly—the hot, wicked place of endless torture depicted in numerous book and movies.

All of these realms together form the Realm of Desire. Lifetimes in the Realm of Desire last many, many *kalpas* and together with all the lifetimes in all the realms make up a vast and unimaginable passage of time.

The Realm of Form

The Realm of Form rises above the Realm of Desire. It also is separated into hierarchical levels. The beings that live here live in many different heavens and are a higher type of god than those in the Realm of Desire. There gods are called *Brahmas*.

The Brahmas are more peaceful than the gods found in the Realm of Desire and have no sensory perceptions: they do not see, smell, taste, or touch or desire. They have found freedom from desire and experience life in a pure, simple, and unspoiled form. However, because of their blissful life, they tend to forget their origins.

◀ Buddhist temple

It is interesting to note that in Buddhism the Brahmas were gods in the Realm of Form. Obviously, the Buddhist thought and beliefs were heavily influenced by Hindu beliefs.

The lifespan of the beings in the Realm of Form is very long—almost beyond comprehension. They can live many, many *kalpas*, far outliving the beings in the Realm of Desire. The beings who attain this realm are the ones who have achieved great skills in meditation but are not yet enlightened. They are beings who have practiced well in their last lifetime and can continue to practice in the Realm of Form.

FACT

On the highest levels of Mount Meru live the Four Great Kings. They each watch over one of the four directions. The Four Kings rank as gods and watch over the lower realms, reporting back to the higher gods above.

The Realm of No-Form

The Realm of No-Form is a place beyond shape and form. It is the highest level of life and beings live the longest in this realm. Existence is purely on a spiritual, mental level with no physical presence at all. There are four forms of rebirth at this level. One form is the form of infinite space. In infinite space no boundaries, no beginnings, and no ends can be perceived. The second form is the form of infinite consciousness. Infinite consciousness provides the being the ability to recognize and comprehend infinite space.

The third form in the Realm of No-Form is "nothingness." The beings can perceive that there is nothing—no-thing—in their existence. They perceive that everything is the same and at the heart of all is nothing. The last form is beyond consciousness and unconsciousness. This means that their consciousness is so ephemeral that it is neither recognized nor not recognized. This is highest form in the universe and lasts longer than we could comprehend. There are numberless gods here who are each driven toward the absolute and have left the worlds of form far behind. However, each of these lifetimes is also subject to rebirth and therefore each of these lifetimes eventually ends.

It is tempting to believe, based on this hierarchy, that the god realm is the most coveted life to inhabit. However the gods are up against their own pitfalls. They can easily believe that they are in the highest of meditative states and stay stuck there for eons. It is only in the human form that we can reach enlightened mind and freedom from rebirth.

Making Sense of the Cosmos

Teachers in recent times have said that the six states are symbolic, metaphorical states and not to be taken literally. With the increasing number of Western Buddhist practitioners one can see that without this stipulation many would turn away from such a frightening and foreign spiritual world. We are increasingly a world of show me, of people needing proof, and we strive to make sense of metaphor and symbols. Each of the six states can be seen as mindsets, and, indeed, the world is experienced through our thoughts and perceptions.

For example, we can see that the hell-beings are our inclinations toward hatred and anger. How many lifetimes does it seem that we spend in hatred? Hatred once felt, can seem to last an eternity. Our spiritual progress can be seen as a passage through anger and hatred to a higher spiritual plane. Similarly, the hungry ghosts symbolize our greed and the destruction we do to ourselves and others through our cravings for more. Animals are our ignorance, our inability to see the way out of our own pain.

As with other spiritual beliefs, such as the idea of a Christian hell of fire and brimstone, there are benefits to believing in such a system. With the idea that bad karma can lead us straight into the habitat of the denizens of hell, we perhaps will forgo our negative inclinations for more positive ones. We might strive for a better, kinder, more gentle life here on Earth.

The world in the Buddhist cosmos is vast and infinite, with no beginning and no end. There is terrible, awe-inspiring suffering and untold spiritual growth. Everything is constantly changing and nothing remains the same. It is possible to reach for the heavens from hell, and to fall to the depths from the highest spire. And there is no escape, but for one: to be born into the human realm and to strive to reach enlightenment.

Much as the belief in a Christian hell has kept Christians of all kinds on the straight and narrow, so can embracing the Buddhist cosmos prevent one from perpetrating unhealthy and unwholesome actions. Our fear of being reborn into a hell of unbelievable pain, or our desire to prohibit a birth as a donkey, can compel us into wholesome action and good karma. Our sincere hope it that as Buddhists we can meet with the teachings of a Buddha who can show us the Path. Only this way can we escape the endless cycles of rebirth and find true freedom.

Never forget how swiftly this life will be over, like a flash of summer lightning or the wave of a hand. Now that you have the opportunity to practice dharma, do not waste a single moment on anything else.

—Dilgo Khyentse Rinpoche

Chapter 9

Buddhism in India: Life after Buddha

The Buddha traveled all around India spreading the teachings and showing his followers how he reached enlightenment. His sangha grew until thousands were practicing the principles of the Four Noble Truths. This chapter looks at the end of Buddha's life, and how Buddhism spread through India and beyond, starting well on its way to becoming a major player in the world of religious practices.

The Buddha's Life and Death

The Buddha lived to be eighty years old. It was a time of unrest in India and the king at the time, Ajatasattu, had planned an offensive against the republics to the east of his kingdom, determined to wipe them out. Buddha had decided to avoid the carnage and headed north to the margins of the Ganges basin. As death approached and the Buddha prepared to leave this world, he lived a life of increasing solitude, searching out places of quiet and peace. He was ill and was intent on making sure the sangha knew everything they needed to know before he departed this world.

A Simple Life

It is easy for us to imagine the Buddha surrounded by riches and adored by many, much as we picture our great religious leaders today. However, the Buddha remained a mendicant monk for this entire lifetime, and he frequently lived outside, among the mango groves, begging for food for his meals. He practiced the principles of the dharma into his eighth decade, never wavering from his dedication to the Way.

His illness was particularly upsetting to his long-time companion Ananda. Ananda wanted to know who would take over for the Buddha, who would be the next in line to continue the teachings. But the Buddha knew that no one needed to take over. Each person himself had all that he needed inside himself. By practicing the principles the Buddha had set forth, each could become self-reliant and strive toward enlightenment. No authority figure was needed in the sangha. The Buddha had taught them all they needed to know.

Each of you should make himself his island, make himself and no one else his refuge, each of you must make the dharma his island, the dharma and nothing else his refuge.

—The Buddha

Final Days

The Buddha abandoned the will to live on and consciously decided to die, to head toward his final reward of Nirvana. He reminded the sangha that he had only taught them things he himself had experienced and had taken nothing on the word of another. He told them to do the same. They should practice the disciplines he had taught them and should always, most important of all, live for others with loving-kindness and compassion for the entire world.

QUESTION?

What is the difference between Nirvana and *paranirvana*? Paranirvana is attaining Nirvana plus the total extinction of the physical. So when the Buddha died he attained paranirvana. In other words, if you reach Nirvana in life, you can attain paranirvana in death.

The Buddha partook of his last meal, a meal of spoiled meat given to him by a blacksmith names Chunda. Chunda placed the meat into the Buddha's alms bowl (Buddhist monks are mendicant monks), and out of gratitude the Buddha ate it. The Buddha insisted that no one else eat the meat he ingested, and he made them dispose of it after he was finished. In order that Chunda not feel responsible for the Buddha's illness and impending death, the Buddha called Chunda to his side and told him how grateful he was for the meal.

He then asked the sangha if they had any questions for him, if there was anything yet they did not understand. Right up until the end of his human life, the Buddha served others and thought only of what the sangha needed. But no one came forth to ask any questions. The Buddha then asked if perhaps they were not asking questions for which they needed answers out of reverence for him. If this was the case, he said, they could ask their questions through a friend. When still no one came forth the Buddha knew they were well-versed in his teachings and, as Karen Armstrong tells us in *Buddha,* he uttered his last words: "All individual things pass away. Seek your liberation with diligence." The Buddha died at eighty years old, after teaching the dharma for forty years.

You often see artwork of the Buddha as he is lying down on his side: the reclining Buddha statues. These reclining Buddhas represent the Buddha as he enters Nirvana, on his death.

After the Buddha's death, his body was cremated. The ashes were then delivered to eight different stupas. These stupas would later become the object of much devotion.

In India, Tibet, and Southeast Asian countries, stupas are usually dome-shaped with a center spire. In China, Korea, and Japan they resemble a pagoda. They have traditionally been regarded as places of peace, sending out pacifying energies into their surroundings.

◀ Pagoda

The Followers

The Buddha had taught his students well. His emphasis on self-reliance left the sangha in good shape. He had left behind his teachings, the dharma, and the sangha knew the dharma would guide them if they followed it.

However, shortly after the Buddha's death, one of the newly ordained *bhikkus*, Subhadda, rebelled. He suggested that now that the Buddha was gone—the one who oppressed them by telling them how to do this, how to do that—they had the freedom to do whatever they desired. They had the freedom to choose.

FACT

A *stupa* is a burial monument that stands for the Buddha and his enlightenment.

One of the Buddha's greatest students, the Venerable Mahakassapa, became very upset at Subhadda's statement. He decided that a council should be called to recite aloud all of the Buddha's teachings. He knew well that if they did not establish the Buddha's teachings soon, it would not take long for all to be perverted and lost.

FACT

Upali, a student of another religious teacher, was asked to go to the Buddha and try to best him in a debate about karma. When the Buddha showed Upali he was much the master of the debate, and that his own teacher was wrong, Upali asked to become a student. The Buddha told Upali that he should thoroughly investigate his teachings with an open mind before doing so. Upali was so impressed with the Buddha's openness that he soon signed on.

The First Council: The Council at Rajagriha

Three months after the Buddha's paranirvana, five hundred senior monks gathered together at Rajagriha in what has come to be known as the First Council. Rajagriha was the capital of Magadha, which was one of the four great kingdoms (including Kosala, Vansa, and Avanti) in ancient India. Their hope was that they would be able to establish the Buddhist canon and create the definite teachings of the Buddha.

Ananda and Upali each took on a special task at the council. Ananda, as the longtime companion of the Buddha, was responsible for the recitation of the Buddha's teachings. It was felt that since he had spent so many years by the Buddha's side, he would have heard the teachings most frequently. Upali was given the task of setting forth the rules of discipline for the sangha.

Each of the arhats recited the teachings, examining the words to ensure they were accurate. They recited them over and over again, and each repetition was checked over to make sure they all agreed that it was correct. The meanings and accuracy were debated, and before being finalized, each recitation was approved by the council at large. When the members agreed that a teaching had been captured correctly, they recited it together and it was approved. The First Council lasted seven months.

The members of the council carried the memorized teachings away with them to all parts of the country, wherever disciples of the Buddha were to be found. Thus, the oral tradition of passing on the Buddha's teaching was established and remained so for many hundreds of years. It should be noted, however, that although it would seem great effort was made to orally record the exact words of the Buddha, due to language differences, local dialect variances, and the possible potential for error that exists in all oral transmissions, it cannot be said without doubt that what we have today are the words of the Buddha himself.

Arhat means "worthy one" in Sanskrit. An arhat is one who has attained enlightened mind and is free of desires and cravings. An arhat has nothing more to learn and has absorbed all of the Buddha's teachings.

The Second Council: The Council at Vesali

One hundred years later, the Second Council took place, another assembly of the Buddha's followers. This council was held at Vesali and 700 arhats attended. The Elders of the council felt that certain members of the sangha were taking some of the Ten Precepts too lightly and that there was a general slackening of discipline.

A group of monks put forth a series of changes in the precepts, making them more lax than they had been previously. For example, they felt it was acceptable for the members of the sangha to accept money, and debated the need for the precept that forbade them to use money. The assembly of monks thereby discussed the validity of the Ten Precepts. The dissenting monks, the Vajjians, were outvoted. They refused to give in, however, and seceded from the group of the council of Elders. Thus, Buddhism was divided into two schools of thought: Theravada and Mahayana. The Elders belonged to the Theravada school; Vajjian monks split off to create the Mahayana school. (See more on Theravada and Mahayana in Chapter 10.)

King Ashoka and the Third Council: The Council at Pataliputra

Another 135 or so years passed before another council was held. The need for this council arose as debate was being carried on about both the dharma and the precepts.

At this time, during the third century B.C.E., King Ashoka was ruling a vast empire in India. He had taken the throne in a bloody war and was a ruthless leader with many violent triumphs to his credit. But during the eighth year of his rule, after a particularly gruesome battle, King Ashoka became shaken by his own bloodbath—upward of 100,000 people are said to have been slaughtered—and it set the stage for a powerful change.

King Ashoka was largely responsible for the spread of Buddhism beyond India's borders and its emergence as one of the world's great religions. He practiced tolerance and respect for other religious disciplines, promoted peace instead of war, and established schools, hospitals, and orphanages for his people. He was living proof that it is possible to rule a great nation with kindness and open-mindedness, promoting peace and goodwill.

Ashoka ran into a monk who told the mighty king that he could use his power for good instead of evil. The monk was a Buddhist. Ashoka soon put down his sword and picked up the dharma instead.

He stopped hunting, started meditating, stopped fighting, and started doing humanitarian work wherever he could. Instead of soldiers he had missionary monks, who spread the dharma wherever they could, reaching out past the boundaries of India and into the neighboring nations. He built thousands of stupas and thousands of monasteries throughout the land. King Ashoka inscribed his new beliefs on rocks that can be found throughout India, Nepal, Pakistan, and Afghanistan. These inscriptions would come to be know as the Edicts of King Ashoka and included such promises as moderate spending, proper schooling for children, medical treatments for everyone, promotion of proper behavior; he promised to practice the dharma until the end of time, to always be available—no matter what he was doing—for the affairs of his people; he promoted respect for everyone and all religions . . . and so on.

Because he practiced such spiritual generosity, many less-devoted practitioners entered the Buddhist practice and the purity of the practice was diluted. Ashoka sought to weed out these weak links from the monasteries he had created and called a new council with the genuine, steadfast monks who were left. This council is said to have had 1,000 attendants, the largest council yet.

At the Third Council, the teachings were reviewed and a new, purified collection was set forth. Nine missions of arhats were sent out to spread the dharma into different areas of India and to cross the boundaries into other countries.

The Fourth Council: The Council at Jalandhar

One last council is said to have been held in India in the first century C.E. This council was led by Kanishka, ruler of what is today Pakistan and northern India. King Kanishka loved the teachings of the Buddha and often called the *bhikkos* in to see him to relate the dharma to him.

He soon found that they were not in accord on the teaching of the dharma, and he was very distressed over the differences he heard. At the advice of another, he convened a council to sort out the differences. Five hundred monks compiled a new canon at the Fourth Council. This was the start of the Mahayana scriptural canon: the collection of Mahayana teachings. Theravada Buddhists, however, do not recognize this council.

The Eighteen Schools

During the time of the Second Council, Buddhism started to splinter into different schools of thought. Then, as the dharma spread to other countries and cultures at the time of King Ashoka, different traditions arose that were as individual as the people who practiced them. There arose the Hinayana and the Mahayana traditions. Hinayana was the tradition that spread under King Ashoka.

Hinayana refers to a group of eighteen Buddhist schools, of which only one is currently in existence, Theravada. Mayahana Buddhists, who called their tradition "the Great Vehicle," named the other traditions of Buddhism "Hinayana"—meaning "Little Vehicle"—which is not considered a favorable term by many Buddhists. Today you would not use the word Hinayana to refer to the Theravada tradition of Buddhism.

FACT

Hinayana spread to Burma, Cambodia, Laos, Sri Lanka, and Thailand. Mahayana spread to China, Japan, Korea, Mongolia, Nepal, Russia, Tibet, and Vietnam. The Theravada that survives today was derived from the Elder monks at the Second Council.

Each of the eighteen schools had its own version of the dharma. The Buddha was not a big fan of intellectualizing and rationalizing, viewing speculation as veering off course. One cannot help but wonder what he would have thought of the diversification that was taking place.

The Pali Canon and the Mahayana Scriptures

The Theravada Buddhists believe that another council—which they call the Fourth Council—was held during the first century B.C.E. in Sri Lanka. According to Theravada belief, this canon was written down on palm leaves and was thus passed down to us intact. It is known as the Pali canon as it was written in Pali, as opposed to Sanskrit. Today the Pali canon would translate into several thousand pages of scripture.

The Pali canon contained three sections. Those sections are:

1. Vinaya Pitaka
2. Sutta Pitaka
3. Abhidhamma Pitaka

The Vinaya Pitaka contained the directions for keeping the sangha in order, from daily practices to how to maintain harmony among all the monks and nuns. The Sutta Pitaka contained the collection of the central teachings of Theravada Buddhism, including all the Jataka tales, the Dhammapada, and various discourses. The Abhidhamma (or Abidharma in Sanskrit) Pitaka was an extraordinarily precise and detailed explanation of the principles behind the mental and physical processes of the Buddha's teachings. In Pali, *abhi* means "ultimate" so Abhidharma meant the "ultimate truth," or ultimate teachings. Of course, over time, further works were added to the canon.

The Mahayana Buddhists had their own scriptures, which were written in Sanskrit. These texts included:

1. The sutras (the words of the Buddha): including the Heart Sutra, the Lotus Sutra, and the Diamond Sutra.
2. Shastras: the commentary on the sutras.
3. Tantras: more mystical texts.

As Mahayana Buddhism grew, new texts were added. It is easy to imagine that the Buddha's followers mourned him greatly. However, they had been taught well by their leader and knew that all things come to pass, and everything changes. We might guess that Ananda grieved the most for his cousin and beloved teacher, as Ananda had not yet become an arhat and did not yet understand the true nature of things. The Buddha had prepared his sangha, well, however, and crowds gathered around the great sage to witness his passing and hear his last words. It is said he died with a smile on his face as he passed over to the other shore.

◀ Buddhist temple, India

From the Buddha's death until the third century B.C.E., Buddhism spread across many nations and took on different forms and traditions. It spread from India to Sri Lanka, Burma, Cambodia, Laos, Thailand, China, Japan, Korea, Mongolia, Nepal, Russia, Tibet, and Vietnam. Thanks to the great reformed leader King Ashoka, Buddhism became one of the greatest religions of the world and the teachings were passed down so that we can practice them today, much the way the Buddha practiced them centuries ago.

Although the sangha tried very hard to carefully maintain the integrity of the original teachings of the Buddha, it is probable that what we know now are not the exact words of the Buddha himself. It is hard to imagine that with oral transmission lasting for four hundred years, that perfect accuracy could have been maintained. Eighteen different schools came out of the Second and Third Councils as practitioners differed on matters of philosophy. Today there are different traditions of Buddhism, just as there were so many years ago. But at essence the practice is still the same and the basic principles hold. Ⓔ

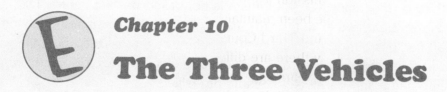

Chapter 10

The Three Vehicles

There are three different vehicles, or schools, of Buddhist teachings, and virtually all sects of Buddhism fall into one of these three schools. As we saw previously, Theravada and Mahayana Buddhism grew out of the early councils as differences arose in practice and principle. So, the three schools of Buddhism are Theravada Buddhism, Mahayana Buddhism, and the third vehicle, Vajrayana Buddhism.

The Diversification of Buddhism

We have seen what the Buddha taught, as closely as we can tell from the sources that have been passed down through the years. There was a strong effort on the part of the early Elders to keep the teaching pure, but diversity was inevitable as different countries, cultures, and people input their own perspectives. Buddhism is not based on one central text, such as the Bible, the Koran, or the Torah. In fact, there was nothing written at all for four hundred years, as the teachings were passed down via word of mouth. So over the years, a multitude of guidelines for practice came into being and Buddhism became diversified.

We say there are three *vehicles* of Buddhism, meaning three schools of Buddhist thought. The word *vehicles* comes from the Sanskrit word *vada,* meaning "ferryboat." If we go back to the image of the river crosser and his raft, we can see that these vehicles ferry us to the opposite shore . . . or enlightenment.

There ended up being three schools of practice and belief as Buddhism evolved over the years, though the Mahayana and the Theravada schools are considered the two main Buddhist vehicles. The third, Vajrayana, is also known as Tantra Buddhism. Technically, Tantra is a part of Mahayana, but we will consider it separately as it deserves a lot of attention.

There is no one authority on Buddhism—there is no pope, no president, no leader of the Buddhist people. There is no central office, no definitive source. Buddhism is alive in many forms, with many voices today. Within the three schools of thought there are Tibetan Buddhism, Zen Buddhism, Pure Land, Yogacara, and more. But all these forms can basically fit within the three vehicles, and some would agree that they could even fit within the two main vehicles—Theravada and Mahayana.

With the rise of Mahayana after the Second Council, a dispute began over what to call the various vehicles. Mahayana Buddhists called Mahayana the "Great Vehicle," meaning it was widespread, designed for the common people as well as monastics. They therefore labeled Hinayana Buddhism (of which Theravada was a part) the "Lesser Vehicle," meaning it encompassed a narrower field. Mahayana evolved out of the general population's desire to take an active part in their religion. The Elders would not tolerate what they considered a dilution of the purity of the teachings by including everyone, so the Mahayanas broke off into their own *yana*. Thus, Mahayana included a greater variety of people, and was labeled "Great Vehicle." Since Theravada meant "School of the Elders," and therefore implied that Mahayanas were less experienced (School of the Novices?), there didn't seem to be a way to refer to either school without offending the other. Whatever the name, however, it all comes up Buddhism.

FACT

In addition to calling the three different schools of Buddhism *vehicles,* you could also call them *yanas.*

How these different schools evolved is a subject open to debate. Many people believe they all go back to the Buddha's direct teachings, but others disagree. However, it is agreed that all forms of Buddhism do share the fundamental belief in the Four Noble Truths. The split of Buddhism into the different vehicles was, all in all, most likely a result of geographical circumstances and change over time rather than any strong argument over differences in practice between the various members of the *yanas.*

Theravada

Theravada Buddhism can be traced all the way back to the First Council, shortly after Buddha's death. Like each of the other vehicles, Theravada Buddhists could claim that they have the most direct line to the Buddha's teachings and, therefore, the purist form of Buddhism. They established the Pali Canon, the teachings that were passed down orally for four hundred years—the first recorded teachings from the Buddha. The Pali language is still used as the primary language for the texts of Theravada Buddhists all these years later.

At the time of the First Council, the arhat, or Elders of the sangha, were displeased with the request that laypeople be included as a representative voice. They felt that allowing laypeople equal representation as monastics would dilute the purity of Buddhism. The path to enlightenment, they believed, was reserved for the monastics, who could practice with no distractions. Mahayana Buddhism was considered too liberal and "for the people."

Theravada stresses education over practice. The monastic life is considered the path to enlightenment, and the monastics focus on education and rules. Practitioners strive to become the arhat—an enlightened person. Students believe they can reach Nirvana through personal effort and moral stringency—that enlightenment is attained by the cessation of suffering, and therefore the cessation of worldly desires. Therefore, a stringent earthly practice of high education and adherence to strict rules was the most direct path to awakening. Theravada Buddhism leans toward realism, rather than mysticism. Mahayana and especially Vajrayana Buddhism tend more toward mysticism and even magic. Theravada Buddhists relied on rationality, rules, and education, while the other vehicles tended toward insight and intuition over rationality. Theravada emphasizes wisdom, scholarship, and intellectual training.

Well awake they arise, at all times,
The disciples of Gautama,
In whom both day and night,
Constantly there is mindfulness on the Buddha.
—Dhammapada

There were two ways that a monk should strive to become an arhat: one was by meditation and insight, *vipashyana-dhura*, and one was by study, *gantha-dhura*. *Vipashyana-dhura* is insight meditation, the practice of tranquility and the quieting of the mind. (Vipashyana is the Sanskrit spelling; Vipassana is the Pali spelling.) *Gantha-dhura* is the study of the Buddhist canon, the scriptures, and the path to knowledge and wisdom. Today the Theravada tradition most likely found in the United States is *vipissana*, or insight meditation.

Mahayana

Mahayana Buddhism is the vehicle most familiar to Americans. Mahayana practitioners wanted to make religion and practice more accessible to the masses. The emphasis in Mahayana is on compassion and intuition, rather than self-discipline and study. Mahayanas believed that Theravada Buddhism was elitist and exclusive. Everyday people, who had work and families, could not practice at the same level as the monastics. Should they therefore be excluded from practice at all? It should be noted that while Theravada Buddhists and Mahayana Buddhists might disagree on who should be walking the path, they both agreed on where the walkers were going and how they were going to get there.

Mahayana has been around since the Second Council, but Mahayana also can argue a direct descent to the Buddha's teachings. Mahayana Buddhists believe they split off from the Theravada tradition in order to reform the teachings and take them back to the purer form the Buddha had originally taught. They believe the Buddha would have promoted the cause of the laypeople as part of the community and therefore believe *they* have the most direct link to the original teachings.

FACT

Manjushri is the bodhisattva of wisdom—he symbolizes the wisdom one needs in order to seek the truth. In artworks depicting Manjushri, he is often portrayed with one hand holding a sword, which is needed to cut through illusion to the heart of wisdom. In the other hand he holds the sacred text of wisdom, the Prajna-paramita Sutra.

Bodhisattvas

Much as the Theravada student strives to become an arhat—a spiritually enlightened individual—so the Mahayana student strives to become a bodhisattva. A bodhisattva is a person who has already attained enlightenment, or is ready to attain enlightenment but puts off his or her own final enlightenment in order to re-enter the cycle of samsara and save all sentient beings. A bodhisattva is the ultimate in compassion, and Mahayana Buddhists believe that enlightenment can be attained not only by striving individually but also by helping others to achieve enlightenment as well.

Bodhisattvas willingly seek to be reborn into the endless cycles of samsara so that they can constantly help others toward their own enlightened state. They need wisdom so that they can discern how to help others toward Nirvana. This extreme level of compassion—loving all beings and all states completely and helping them toward enlightenment—is known as *skillful means*. Inherent within skillful means is wisdom—the ability to discern how to help each sentient being toward enlightenment. Wisdom heart is referred to as *bodhicitta*—the quality that allows them to return to samsara and earthly life to help others toward enlightenment. Therefore, someone who desires to become a bodhisattva will develop and then generate *bodhicitta*. Once *bodhicitta* has been manifested they can be reborn and practice the skillful means necessary to help others.

FACT

Mahayana practitioners believe that the Buddha is still somehow connected to everything, forever helping humans toward enlightened mind—the Buddha represents the ultimate bodhisattva.

Every sentient being has buddha-nature. Discovering your buddha-nature is identical to attaining enlightened mind. Mahayanas believe that buddha-nature appears in three different forms. These bodies are the forms that the Buddha or buddha-nature take. This is known as the Three Body Doctrine of compassion. The three forms are:

- *Nirmanakaya* (physical body): the physical embodiment of buddha-nature; the body in which the Buddha abides in the world.
- *Sambhogakaya* (bliss body): the body that is in the celestial realm; graspable only through meditation.
- *Dharmakaya* (truth, or dharma body): when the Buddha is one with the dharma and is in true-self, absolute reality; graspable only to those who have attained enlightenment.

Reading about Buddhism is a great way to introduce yourself to another way of life. But in order to understand the Three Body Doctrine, the Four Noble Truths, and other Buddhist teachings, the best thing to do is to set yourself down on a pillow and start to practice. Through practice the teachings will make much more sense. Buddhism is something you *do;* it's a religion of action and experience. As the Buddha tells, take nothing on another's word and find out for yourself.

As we have seen, the aspiring bodhisattva strives to generate *bodhicitta,* but also strives for the Six Perfections. These Six Perfections are:

1. Concentration (meditation)
2. Giving
3. Morality
4. Patience
5. Persistence
6. Wisdom

As we can see, the bodhisattva in Mahayana Buddhism is very different from the arhat of Theravada Buddhism. The arhat strives for his own enlightenment and for cessation of his own suffering. The arhat seeks to leave this world behind. The bodhisattva on the other hand, seeks enlightenment so that she can return to the earth to help others along the same course.

Bodhisattvas like Avalokiteshvara and Manjushri became celestial bodies that people could use for devotional practice. This allowed the laypeople to share in the religious life of Buddhism.

Theravada and Mahayana on Emptiness

At the core of Buddhist belief is the notion of Emptiness. However, Theravada and Mahayana Buddhists differ on their relationship to emptiness as well. Theravada Buddhists believe that when one attains enlightened mind, one wakes up to the reality of emptiness in the self. One realizes that the personal self does not have any defined qualities.

In other words, when one wakes up, the self dies.

In Mahayana tradition, when one wakes up one realizes that the *whole world* is emptiness, that emptiness is not just the self but all things, and form and emptiness are the same thing, indistinguishable from one another. Or as it states in the Heart Sutra:

"Form is emptiness, emptiness is from."

Emptiness is not a negative quality. When we speak of the emptiness of existence in Buddhism we do not mean that life takes place in a void. Many Buddhist concepts are described in negative terms, not because the concepts themselves are negative, but because we have no prior equivalent to compare to. Therefore, we speak of what something *isn't,* rather than of what it is. By trying to rule out what is *not,* perhaps we can gain a sense of what is. At the heart of matter, at the center of the universe, everything is empty: it is like nothing we can name, taste, see, touch, hear, or describe. The best way, again, to understand *shunyata* is to practice. Only through practice will you start to comprehend the essence of empty mind.

Differences Between the Two Main Schools

As we saw in Chapter 9, another difference between Mahayana and Theravada Buddhism is the scriptures that each tradition claims. The Pali canon is the library of teachings claimed by Theravada Buddhists and was the first known collection of Buddhist literature. In addition to the Pali canon, the Mahayana Buddhists have an extensive collection of scriptures written in Sanskrit that contain the Buddha's words and more, as translations and additions were made over the years.

FACT

Theravada Buddhists do not as a rule recognize the bodhisattva, but they do believe in Maitreya. Maitreya is believed to be the future Buddha, the Buddha who will appear after the present Buddha is long gone and the teachings have been forgotten. Theravada Buddhists believe Maitreya is currently a celestial bohdisattva and will appear on Earth as the new Buddha in future years.

In summary, here are the differences between the two main vehicles of Mahayana and Theravada Buddhism:

Mahayana and Theravada Buddhism		
	Theravada	**Mahayana**
Ideal	*arhat*	*bodhisattva*
Literature	Pali canon	Pali canon plus scriptures
Political leanings	Conservative	Liberal
Learning	Emphasizes rules and education	Emphasizes intuition and practice
Teachings	No buddha-nature in teachings	Buddha-nature present in teachings
Transmission	South	North

Some well-known schools of the Mahayana tradition of Buddhism are Madhyamika, Yogacara, Pure Land, and Zen Buddhism. Pure Land and Zen Buddhism are covered in later chapters. Now let's take a look at Vajrayana, considered to be the third vehicle.

Vajrayana

Vajrayana Buddhism developed out of the Mahayana school of teachings sometime between the third and seventh centuries B.C.E. It is said that the Buddha practiced this esoteric tradition, but because of its advanced and special nature it didn't evolve into common practice. Vajrayanas believe the Buddha taught these practices through special texts, called tantras, but the tantras themselves didn't come to light until the seventh century.

Vajrayana Buddhists believe their teachings can therefore also be directly linked to the Buddha and that *they* practice the purest form of Buddhism. Because Vajrayana was found predominately in Tibet and stayed there for many years, it is most likely true that Vajrayana remained untouched for a long time. Tibet is a remote country, surrounded by the

Himalayan Mountains, and therefore fairly isolated from the rest of the world; the teachings would have remained unchanged but from within for many, many years. One possibility for Vajrayana is that when Mahayana Buddhism reached into Tibet, it became intertwined with the native folk religion of Bön, and the tantric and magical elements became more pronounced and Vajrayana Buddhism arose.

FACT

Vajrayana Buddhism is also called Tantric Buddhism, "Diamond Vehicle," the "Completion Vehicle," the "Thunderbolt Vehicle," and the "Indestructible Path."

Padmasambhava, a Buddhist monk who arrived in Tibet from India, is considered one of the founders of Vajrayana Buddhism and is credited with developing many of the practices present today.

When we think of Tibet today, we think of the Dalai Lama and his exile from his native country and the expulsion of Buddhism. Centuries after Mahayana Buddhism spread to Tibet we can see the effect of its influence on Tibetan culture, as most of us today think of Tibet as essentially a (until recently) Buddhist nation. Tibet absorbed Buddhism into its culture wholeheartedly. According to Jack Maguire in *Essential Buddhism,* "No other country in history has absorbed this religion so thoroughly and, in turn, invested it with so much native character or so much cultural power. As Vajrayana grew increasingly influential in Tibet, so did the monastery as the focus of daily life, a position it retained until the mid-twentieth century . . . Over time, the monasteries assumed complete political control of the country, giving Tibet a singularly sacred form of government for centuries."

Vajrayana relies heavily on symbol and ritual, and is the most magical form of Buddhism. It relies upon magical deities belonging to a cosmic monastery, and values practice over education, as does Mahayana. However, Vajrayana Buddhism is concerned with attaining enlightenment as are all the other forms of Buddhism discussed here, and differs in the ways the teachings are practiced.

The practices in Vajrayana Buddhism are special and complex. The teachings are designed to bring the student to enlightenment in this lifetime; therefore the practices are intense, subtle, difficult, and enlightenment occurs more quickly than with other forms of practice. The student of the tantric practices has a teacher, called a guru (an enlightened teacher is a *lama*). The practices are often kept secret between the student and teacher, which adds to the mystery and magic around the tradition.

The practices of Vajrayana revolve around a spiritual "toolbox" that contains such items as: mandalas, mantras, *yidam*, mudras, and *vajras*.

Mandalas are maps of the spiritual world. They are usually represented in artwork as a graphic of a symbolic pattern. The pattern is usually in the form of a circle with intricate designs within. The patterns are representative of the sacred place where the Buddha or deity abides. They are used for contemplation and meditation and are designed to awaken spiritual potential.

Mantras are mystical incantations whose repetitions contain the potential for magic and spiritual connection. By repeating a mantra one can clear the mind, purify speech, and connect to the spiritual. The most famous mantra is, of course, *Om mani padme hum*.

Viewing the written mantra is also just as powerful as the incantation. You can also spin the written form of the mantra around in a prayer wheel, which is believed to have the same beneficial properties as the incantation and the viewing of the written form.

QUESTION?

What or who is a Dalai Lama?

The Dalai Lama is considered to be the present incarnation of the bodhisattva Avalokiteshvara. The third great leader of the Geluk lineage of Tibetan Buddhism was given the title Dalai Lama (Great Leader) and was deemed to be the physical manifestation of the compassionate bodhisattva. The present-day Dalai Lama is the fourteenth Dalai Lama.

Prayer wheels, also called *Mani wheels* by the Tibetans, are mechanical devices for dispersing spiritual blessings. Prayer wheels look like two wheels with an axle in between them. The top of the prayer wheel is one wheel and the bottom is the other. Paper with the mantra printed on it many times over is rolled around an axle of the wheel in a protective container. You can spin the wheel round and round, spreading the message out on the wind. Some wheels are portable, with a handle, and some are much larger and stationary.

Yidam are meditational deities. The Tibetan spiritual world contains a very large number of spiritual powers, both men and women, who appear in Tibetan art very colorfully and with much fanfare. They are all different manifestations of the Buddha. Some of the *yidam* are actually wrathful deities. The tantric masters subdue these demons and they then go into the service of the Buddha.

◀ At practice

A **mudra** is the formation your hands take when meditating. The formation is deeply symbolic and often relates to a particular deity. A common mudra is the cosmic mudra:

The dominant hand is held palm up on your lap. The other hand is placed on top of the dominant hand so that the knuckles of both hands overlap. The thumbs touch lightly so that you are forming a circle.

The *vajras* are symbolic, ritual objects such as a bell or dagger.

The student in Vajrayana Buddhism is called the *chela*. The *chela* is initiated into his practice by his guru. The guru and the *chela* must be suited to work together if the teaching arrangement is to work well. The *chela* is given a mandala of his prescribed *yidam*. He is then made to perform many feats, such as more than 100,000 prostrations and numerous repetitions of mantras. This extreme mind-body-speech involvement is said to be an excellent practice for clearing the mind for meditation.

In Vajrayana Buddhism there are different levels of tantra at which one can study. There are programs for the less intelligent, the medium intelligent, the very intelligent student, and the extremely advanced student. Like Mahayana Buddhism, the emphasis is on being enlightened so that you can help all sentient beings.

These are the three main vehicles of Buddhism and all are still alive today. There are many different types of Buddhism within these traditions, but each of these schools can fit into one of the *yanas* herein. All Buddhists follow the Eightfold Path as laid out in the Four Noble Truths. All strive to attain enlightenment, either for themselves or for others.

Vajrayana is the most magical, ritualistic form of Buddhism, and Theravada is the most conservative. Tibetan Buddhism in general is covered in a later chapter. Buddhism started in India with the enlightenment of the Buddha, who then transmitted his teachings to his students, who carried the message of the Buddha's practice to other countries. Buddhism was starting to spread throughout the world and would eventually end up in the West, where it would have a powerful Eastern impact on a very Western world.

Chapter 11

The Spread of Buddhism

Buddhism spread quickly within India as the Buddha and his disciples traveled around the country introducing the teachings to the population. The power of his message and the proof of its value were evident as thousands joined him on the path to enlightenment. It didn't take long, however, before Buddhism was to spread beyond the borders of India, moving into Southeastern Asia and the Indian subcontinent, and then beyond.

Sri Lanka

However, before long Buddhism in India was to suffer. The Islamic Mongol invasions and the resurgence and strengthening of Hinduism were to take a toll on the Buddhist population. By the thirteenth century, Buddhism was substantially weakened in India and all but disappeared. Fortunately, it was to take a stronghold in other parts of the world, thriving in other countries.

Nalanda, the world's most ancient seat of Buddhist learning, flourished in India from the fifth century to the twelfth century B.C.E. Buddhist teachings drew scholars, artists, and healers from many different Asian countries and religious traditions. Nalanda was known for its emphasis on merging intellect and intuition, and was founded in the Mahayana tradition.

Remember that monks were mendicants—they had no possessions or property. They traveled by foot, begging for money and lodging, mingling amongst the native people while performing compassionate acts to further themselves along the path toward enlightenment. As they traveled they spread the message of the Buddha's teachings and convinced people—through attraction rather than self-promotion—that the Path was a good way to live. Their passage through south Asia was one way in which Buddhism started to spread across the continent.

And King Ashoka was another of the primary reasons for the spread and growth of Buddhism—he was often the man behind the missionaries. Once he undertook the teachings and practice himself, he quickly realized the power of the message and sent his own missionaries beyond his borders. Ashoka was a powerful and respected man and his representatives were generally well received in the countries they sought out.

King Ashoka had cast his eye toward the south and decided to send his son, the monk Mahinda, over to the beautiful tropical island Sri Lanka as a missionary. Mahinda was well received by King Devanampiyatissa, the king of Sri Lanka, and they held many enthusiastic and energetic conversations about the religion that had so completely changed Ashoka.

Captivated by such engaging exchanges, the native king asked Mahinda to bring a branch of the Bodhi Tree over to his country so Sri Lanka could have a piece of history. And so Mahinda sent for his sister, Sanghamitta, who soon left India for Sri Lanka, bearing the gift her brother had requested. A grateful King Devanampiyatissa planted the branch on the grounds of the Mahavihara—the first and largest monastery set up in the city of Anuradhapura. To this day there are bodhi trees in Sri Lanka considered to be relatives to the original branch brought over by Sanghamitta.

Sri Lanka embraced Buddhism and shortly it was thriving in the small nation. Sometime around 100 B.C.E., it was here that the Pali scriptures were written down on palm leaves and filed away as recorded history during the Fourth Council. Some four hundred years later, in the fifth century C.E., a Buddhist monk by the name of Buddhaghosa left India for the beautiful island. Buddhaghosa wrote a detailed examination of the Tripitaka, a commentary on the Pali texts, called Visuddhimagga (Path to Purity). It is still widely read today and is considered the great treatise of Theravada Buddhism. Buddhaghosa means, in Pali, "Voice of Enlightenment." He was also known as The Great Translator.

During the fourth century C.E., the Buddha's tooth was brought over to Sri Lanka with great fanfare. To this day there is a celebration centered around the Buddha's tooth. It is preserved in the city of Kandy in the Temple of the Tooth Relic. Daily rituals revolve around the venerated tooth; it is a much revered and celebrated artifact.

FACT

Sri Lanka used to be known as Ceylon. On May 22, 1972, the country officially became the socialist Republic of Sri Lanka, when the assembly adopted a new constitution. Ceylon wasn't the only country to undergo a name change: Myanmar was once called Burma and Thailand was long ago known as Siam.

Over the years Sri Lanka struggled to keep Buddhism alive and vital. But time brought struggles to the small island, and Buddhism was eventually challenged by European colonialism and invasions of the

Portuguese, the Dutch, and the British. Efforts to convert the natives to Christianity were exerted but the Buddhists hung on, even importing *bhikkos* from India to retain and fortify the presence of Buddhism. Buddhism prevailed and today Sri Lanka is considered one of the few predominantly Buddhist countries.

However, whether or not Sri Lanka remains primarily Buddhist is to be seen. There is, and has been for the past nineteen years, a war raging in this exquisite tropical island just south of India. Nearly half a million civilians are trapped between the opposing forces of the Tamil Tigers—the minority force in Sri Lanka—and the Singhalese Buddhist state.

The Tigers want to create a separate Tamil nation in the north and the east of Sri Lanka and claim discrimination from the Singhalese, who make up more than 14 million of the country's 19 million inhabitants. Buddhism here has been severely tested. The Temple of the Tooth was recently attacked.

When the native monks were asked what they regarded as the single most important thing anyone could do to help secure peace, the answer was meditation. They believe, as the Buddha believed 2,500 years ago, that meditation is the single most fundamental tool of transformation. For the Buddhist monks in Sri Lanka, the path is clear: Follow the Buddha to the end of war. Peace talks are taking place for the first time in six long years. In the meantime, meditate.

Mahinda had so much success with Buddhism in Sri Lanka that he was asked by 500 women if they could join the order. When Mahinda's sister, Sanghamitta, arrived, she soon thereafter founded the first order of Buddhist nuns in Sri Lanka. These nuns were known as *bhikkunis*.

Burma

From Sri Lanka and India, Buddhism continued its march across the Asian continent. Monks from Sri Lanka left their beautiful, tropical home to spread the teachings abroad, having a powerful impact on such other countries as

Burma, Thailand, Laos, Vietnam, and Cambodia. These southeastern transmissions were mostly found to be of the Theravada tradition. Today, 85 percent of the population of Burma (now Myanmar) is Buddhist.

Buddhism originally came to Burma via trade with the people of India and via monks from Sri Lanka. With the aid of Sri Lankan monks and supporters, Buddhism was able to establish a firm foothold.

FACT

The Buddha's body parts are not only to be found in Sri Lanka. Eight hairs said to once belong on the Buddha's head are enshrined in Rangoon's Shwedagon Pagoda.

Originally the predominant form of Buddhism was Vajrayana Buddhism, but by the year 1044 C.E. the powerful Burmese king Anawrahta sponsored Theravada monasteries and changed the country over to a largely Theravada-supported nation. Anawrahta built monasteries, stupas, and shrines all over the capital city of Pagan, and the city soon became a center for Buddhist study and practice.

Buddhism flourished in Burma for many years, but ran up against a large threat with the British invasion of the nineteenth century. Today Theravada Buddhism continues to flourish. There are more than 50,000 monasteries to be found and fully 88 percent of the population considers themselves Buddhist.

Thailand

Buddhism is said to have first appeared in Thailand among the Mon people in the third century B.C.E. The Mons left China about 2,000 years ago and settled in both Thailand and Burma. They are believed to be the first settlers in Thailand. Once established, they soon encountered other peoples arriving from the north. Many small kingdoms were subsequently established across the land, each vying for power over another. It is likely—considering the first settlers were originally from China—that some Chinese Buddhist influence was possible. However, Buddhism is generally considered to have appeared in Thailand from India and not from China.

FACT

Thailand is one of the few countries that has never been colonized. Its kingdoms resisted the influence of the French, British, and Dutch, and Thailand was able to remain independent.

By the thirteenth century, missionaries from Sri Lanka were able to convince the king of Thailand, Ramkhamhaeng, to convert to Buddhism. Pali was established as the religious language of Thailand and Theravada Buddhism firmly took root, where it thrives to this day.

Cambodia, Laos, and Indonesia

From India, Buddhism spread to the East and South.

Cambodia

Cambodia was affected by Indian influence early in its history and Mahayana Buddhism took a foothold with its people. Early Cambodian history is not well documented, so it is not until the ninth century that we know Buddhism was favorably viewed there. Kings of the Khmer, who were dominant in Cambodia, started to build large temples and monasteries.

Then at the turn of the twelfth century, King Jayavarman VII came into power. He was a devout Buddhist and Mahayana Buddhism became the dominant religion of the kingdom under his influence. Neighbor Thailand was soon to have a strong effect, however, and by the end of the thirteenth century Theravada was predominant. When communists took control of Cambodia in the 1970s they tried to eradicate Buddhism and nearly succeeded. Today Buddhism is attempting to re-establish itself but political unrest continues.

Laos

Similarly, in Laos Buddhism was probably also introduced by the Khmer. Later, it was heavily influenced by Thailand and thusly became Buddhist in the Theravada school. Communists also tried to rid Laos of

Buddhism in 1975, but it has largely remained and fully 60 percent of the population is considered to be practicing Buddhists.

Indonesia

The first Buddhists arrived in Indonesia sometime in the first century C.E. from India. It is believed that Buddhism spread here through Ashoka's missionaries as well. Both Theravada and Mahayana Buddhism were prevalent, though Mahayana eventually took hold in the eighth century C.E. In the nineteenth century, the largest Buddhist shrine in the world was revealed on the island of Java. It is known as Borobudur, and this monumental stupa was most likely built at the end of the ninth century by Hindu kings as a central sanctuary of the Buddhist religion. Until recent history, Borobudur was mostly covered and just a small portion was visible above the surrounding earth and forests. It was restored just two hundred years ago. This enormous temple is said to be a mandala, a representation of the cosmos, erected by practicing Tantra Buddhists.

▲ Borobudor, Java, Indonesia

Northward Bound

Mahayana Buddhism was spreading northward from India as Theravada was spreading throughout the south and southeast. Vajrayana Buddhism headed straight up to Tibet and took a fast hold of that isolated mountainous country. Mahayana Buddhism was welcomed in China, Japan, and Korea. But before we take a look at how Buddhism entered these various countries we need to look at how it got there. And so we turn to the Silk Road.

The Silk Road

Silk was a hot commodity in the ancient world and everyone wanted to have some. Therefore, in the second century B.C.E., a path developed across Asia that allowed the passage of silk from one country to another. This road, which came to be known as the Silk Road, was just north of India and west of Tibet. Parts of Afghanistan, Pakistan, and northwestern China would form this route today. A hotbed of international trade arose in this area, and the 6,000-mile road passed through it all.

The road went in each direction as silk went one way and gold and silver went the other.

Early Chinese tradesmen started to hear of the wonderful teachings coming out of India and curiosity in Buddhism was aroused in China. And then in the third century B.C.E., on this very road went King Ashoka's missionaries, headed northward from India to spread the teachings of the Buddha.

China: Pure Land and Ch'an

As Chinese interest in Buddhism grew, a need for texts was established. Translators arrived from Central Asia and Buddhist teachings were slowly translated into the Chinese language. Buddhism slowly flourished in China as new texts were brought into the country and translated so the locals could learn. By the seventh century, different schools of Buddhism arose in China. The two most prominent schools were the Ch'an and the Pure Land schools. Ch'an Buddhism would come to be known in the West and Japan as Zen Buddhism.

Ch'an and *Zen* both mean "meditation." Ch'an is the Chinese word; Zen the Japanese word. Today, in the United States it is more common to see the word Zen used than the word Ch'an, but both can be found.

Bodhidharma Enters China

It was early in the sixth century C.E. Emperor Wu of China was a devout student of Buddhism. He had built many temples and translated many sutras and considered himself well versed in the teachings of the Buddha. When he heard that Bodhidharma, a renowned Buddhist monk, had arrived in China, he requested a meeting with the Indian monastic. In reference to the great works he had done in the service of Buddhism through the construction of monasteries and translation of core texts, Emperor Wu asked Bodhidharma, "What merit have I accumulated for all my good to Buddhism?"

"None," Bodhidharma replied.

Then Emperor Wu was shocked; this contradicted everything that Emperor Wu thought he knew about Buddhism. It was a common belief that good deeds added up to merit points in Buddhism. Giving food to a mendicant monk was considered good karma and advancement on the path to enlightenment. Especially if the monk you gave to meditated well and was a good student. He considered himself knowledgeable about Buddhism and wanted to engage Bodhidharma in conversation. He became defensive and decided to test the newcomer. "What is the meaning of enlightenment?" he asked.

"Vast emptiness, nothing sacred," Bodhidharma said.

This, too, must have confused the great emperor. This was not in line with his beliefs and he did not understand what it meant. Emperor Wu then asked in frustration, "*Who* are you?"

And Bodhidharma replied, "I don't know."

Bodhidharma was unable to show Emperor Wu the value of his teachings. Emperor Wu did not understand what Bodhidharma was telling him. Bodhidharma symbolizes a serious commitment to meditation practice and the concept of emptiness. He was the founder of Ch'an in

China. The Ch'an school of Buddhism was all about keeping Buddhism simple. It included none of the bells and whistles of the Vajrayana school of meditation but at its heart was the desire to get down to basics. Ch'an, or Zen, Buddhism promotes the belief that meditation is the direct route to enlightenment—and with meditation buddha-nature arises.

Bodhidharma left the frustrated emperor and made his way up the mountains to Shaolin. It was here in a small cave that he meditated for nine years straight, facing a blank wall. Legend has it that he became frustrated with himself for falling asleep, so he cut off his eyelids to ensure he didn't fall asleep again. Artworks depicting Bodhidharma often show him with eyes wide open.

FACT

While Bodhidharma was at Shaolin Temple, he found the monks there to be in terrible physical conditions. He helped them with their meditation practice and also helped them get back into top physical condition. It was here at Shaolin Temple that the Shaolin Kung Fu was born.

Ch'an Buddhism had started in China. Bodhidharma became the first Chinese patriarch, starting a transmission of Ch'an from one person to another, from mind to mind, until the present day, just as the Buddha passed the teachings so many years before.

Pure Land Buddhism

The other main school of Buddhism to start in China around the same time was called Pure Land. This school of Buddhism, unlike Bodhidharma's Ch'an, did believe in a system of merits and also promoted the idea that there is more than one Buddha—the Buddha we are familiar with being the Buddha that resides over the realm we occupy.

They also believe that this realm has many different fields, the best being that of paradise, or Pure Land. Pure Land Buddhists believe in a paradise after death. Amitabha, the Buddha of Infinite Light, is host there. If we invoke the name of Amitabha (or in Chinese, Namo Amito-fo) we will be reborn into Pure Land. This doesn't mean you actually die and are reborn, it means you are reborn into the buddha-nature of your own mind. Pure Land exists in your mind as well as after death. Pure Land in your mind is the place where enlightenment takes place; it is not enlightenment itself.

Therefore, in Pure Land Buddhism, if you invoke the name of the Buddha you invoke the reality of Pure Land. This practice was obviously less rigorous than the Ch'an practice and found widespread acceptability. One could be reborn into a paradise here at any time, and also after death. All you had to do was recite the Buddha's name over and over, and paradise is yours. The ability to attain Nirvana was found within Pure Land, so your job was to get to Pure Land and then the rest would take care of itself once you arrived. There were no impediments to enlightenment once you attained Pure Land, so much of the work of practice was alleviated.

So Pure Land relied on three basic elements:

1. **Faith:** one must have absolute trust and confidence in the power and wisdom of the Buddhas.
2. **Vows:** one must vow to be reborn.
3. **Practice:** one must practice nianfo (remembrance) and remain mindful of the Buddha at all times.

Pure Land Buddhism is popular in the West today.

Japan

Toward the end of the twelfth century, Ch'an (Zen) arrived in Japan. The samurai warrior spirit was thriving in Japan, and the rigors of Zen practice were welcomed by the Japanese. There are two classes of Zen that arose in Japan. The first was called Rinzai and was brought back from China by the Japanese monk Eisai. Eisai's student Dogen brought the second class of Zen to Japanese shores from China. This school of Zen was called the Soto school. The two schools of Zen are covered in much greater detail in a later chapter.

Both schools of Zen emphasized the importance of seated meditation.

Over many years, the Soto school became larger than the Rinzai school in Japan (today, it might be as much as three times as large), though both schools are still very prominent. The strictness of practice in the monasteries historically inhibited many people from practicing Zen. But as Zen headed West in the twentieth century, this would no longer be the case.

There was another Buddhist tradition to arise in Japan. Nichiren (early thirteenth century), a Buddhist monk, was the founder of this school, which came to bear his name. Nichiren studied the Lotus Sutra and came to believe it was the embodiment of Truth. He believed that by reciting *Namu-myoho-renge-kyo* (Glory to the Lotus Sutra) one could evoke all of the wisdom contained in its verses.

Tibet

Monks headed over the footpaths of the Himalayan Mountains and up into the remote and isolated Tibet, taking their Buddhist practices with them. They reached Tibet and began to spread the teachings, as so many others were doing all over Southeast Asia. But it wasn't until the seventh century, when the king of Tibet, Songtsen Gambo, wed two women—one a princess from Nepal and the other a princess from China—that Buddhism flourished in Tibet. Both of Songtsen's new wives were Buddhist and it wasn't long before the king became very interested in Buddhism himself, sending representatives from Tibet over to China and India to learn more about it.

Life is a series of spontaneous changes. Don't resist them—that only creates sorrow. Let reality be reality. Let things flow naturally forward in whatever way they like.

—Lao-tzu

He became convinced of the benefits of the Buddhist lifestyle and soon had a strong faith. He built many temples and encouraged the growth of Buddhism among his people. Eventually translations were made and the Mahayana scriptures were soon read in the Tibetan language as well. Buddhism remained a prominent part of life in Tibet until the 1950s, when Chinese communists took over the country with violence.

Korea

Buddhism arrived in Korea in 372 C.E. At that time shamanism was the native religion and Buddhism was to eventually blend in with shamanism—a religion based on nature worship and the belief in a world of gods, demons, and ancestral spirits—to create Korean Buddhism. Shamanism promoted a belief in three gods: the god of the mountains, the hermit god, and the god of the seven stars. Korean Buddhism blended the belief in these gods into the teachings of the Buddha, and Korean Buddhism bloomed.

◀ Tibetan Buddhist mask

Pure Land and Son (Korean Zen or Ch'an) also found their way to Korea and took root there. Son emphasized the meditation practice over text study, and eventually nine different Son schools emerged in Korea, which were called the Nine Schools of Son.

Today about half the population of Korea is Buddhist, though Buddhism has deep roots in the community and many others incorporate Buddhist practices into their lives, regardless of religious affiliation.

QUESTION?

What percentage of the world's population is Buddhist?
Today it is estimated that approximately 6 percent of the world's population is Buddhist. Christianity weighs in with the largest percentage of adherents at 33 percent, and Islam comes in second at 18 percent.

Buddhism spread quickly all over Asia and was soon well on its way to becoming a world-class religion. Theravada Buddhism flourished in Sri Lanka, Cambodia, Laos, Thailand, Myanmar, and Bangladesh. Mahayana Buddhism had deep roots in Tibet, Japan, China, Korea, Vietnam, Indonesia, and Nepal. It wasn't long before Buddhism in all its forms spread its net wider, eventually ending up halfway around the world on the shores of the United States.

The East Today

Today, the top ten countries with the highest number of Buddhist practitioners are:

1. Thailand
2. Cambodia
3. Myanmar
4. Bhutan
5. Sri Lanka
6. Tibet
7. Laos
8. Vietnam
9. Japan
10. Macau

Although the countries with the greatest number of Buddhists are all in the Eastern hemisphere, Buddhism has made great inroads in the West. In the past fifty years, Americans and other Westerners have been increasingly interested in this peaceful and harmonious practice. Writers, philosophers, artists, and teachers have spread the word of Buddhism all over North America and Europe. Refugees from Tibet have brought Buddhism into the public eye and the Dalai Lama tirelessly works with the hope of returning to his native Tibet and giving the land back to its people. Emigrants from Asia have brought their practices westward and introduced new ideas and a new way of life into the hearts and minds of Americans and Europeans. Buddhism might be new to the West but it is spreading rapidly and is welcomed openly by those searching for a new way to live.

Chapter 12

Tibetan Buddhism

There aren't many people who are un-aware of the plight of the Tibetans in recent history. The Dalai Lama and his supporters—including American celebrities like Richard Gere—are frequently in the news, so most people have a passing acquaintance with what has been happening in Tibet for more than fifty years.

In the News

The Himalayan country of Tibet was an independent nation until the Chinese invasion in 1949. Since then, the Tibetans have not raised a hand against their oppressors, as they believe in the practice of nonviolence. His Holiness the Dalai Lama, the current leader of the Tibetan government-in-exile people, uses activism in nonviolent forms to bring the status of this country in crisis to the attention of the world's political leaders in the sincere hope that the Chinese government will be stopped and their forces will withdraw from Tibet.

FACT

There are about 120,000 Tibetans living abroad, most of them in India.

The Tibetan crisis has brought international attention to this isolated, mountainous country. Awareness and interest in Tibetan Buddhism and Buddhism in general has subsequently increased greatly in recent years, although no world leaders have to date come to the rescue of this nonviolent civilization. Tibetan Buddhism is a unique form of Buddhism; let's take a look at how it evolved and what makes it special.

Buddhist Origins

Tibetan Buddhism is unique in the Buddhist practices in that Tibetans believe that there are multiple Buddhas living everywhere among them. They believe that Shakyamuni Buddha is the premiere Buddha of this era but he is by no means alone. They believe that the Buddha lives among us in many different forms, and any person at all can attain Buddhahood.

As we saw earlier, one of the earliest showing of Buddhist interest was by Songtsen Gambo, an emperor of Tibet in the mid-seventh century. Songtsen Gambo tried to convert Tibet from a militaristic society into a peaceful, more monastic society. He developed an interest in Buddhism and wed his two Buddhist wives who brought Buddhist texts and teachings into Tibet. His team began to translate the Sanskrit texts into Tibetan and thus a written Tibetan language was born. But Buddhism wasn't to remain strong for long, and its popularity waned before returning to strength in the eighth century, principally due to Padmasambhava.

Padmasambhava

Padmasambhava, a Buddhist monk, originally brought Buddhism to Tibet from India in the eighth century. He was considered by Tibetans to be an example of a living Buddha—a fully attained Buddha who lives among the people. The native religion at the time Padmasambhava arrived was Bön. Bön was a shamanistic religion, and practice included prophecies, rites, sorcery, sacrifice, and a belief in the interdependence of humans and nature. Bön rituals and ceremonies revolved around the priests and priestesses, who were believed to possess supernatural powers. Tibetans tended toward deifying elements of the natural world, such as mountains, and believed in a world of gods who inhabited all types of space from the underworld to the heavens above.

Tibetans live at great altitudes, many inhabiting the land at an average of 14,000 feet. It takes a special kind of body to adjust to life at such height, so much of the population was born into the land since acclimatization was extremely difficult for those not native. The climate and the isolating location bred a population of resilient citizens, and their history—both recent and ancient—speaks of their strength and their deep attachment to their cultural and spiritual beliefs.

Tibet was a nation of militaristic power with many different kingdoms spread across the Tibetan plateau. It was believed that the seven ruling kings had descended from heaven on a ladder and therefore their kings were divine. They practiced their shamanism and believed the shamans could move as intermediaries between the divine origins of the kings and the people of the earth. Their belief system was based on magic, multiple deities, and ritual. In order for someone to come in and wow this populace, that person would have to be a great charismatic teacher capable of teachings that would impress upon them his power over nature, life, and death. And so came Padmasambhava.

Padmasambhava, with the help of his twenty-five disciples, helped to build the first monastery in Tibet, at Samye. He helped to translate many of the Buddhist scriptures into Tibetan, and educated the populace in Buddhist teachings, traveling around the country, transforming the country from a fighting country based on militarism into a peaceful, spiritual people. Padmasambhava strived to do an inside job on the Tibetan people—changing them internally, spiritually, so that their warring external life would fall away. He was largely successful at making significant changes in the internal life of Tibet's population.

FACT

Legend has it that Padmasambhava was born sitting on a lotus blossom in the middle of a lake. He was born enlightened and knew the true nature of the world from his very first moments. He became a Buddha, and was then reborn on Earth in various incarnations; he showed up in Tibet as Padmasambhava in the eighth century.

This peaceful spirit and age of education and growth would continue in Tibet until the ninth century when Tibet entered a dark age and Buddhism was suppressed. Many of the teachings were kept alive during this dark time by the twenty-five disciples who passed down the teachings. Eventually the seeds of knowledge that were planted by Padmasambhava were to bloom and Buddhism would establish itself as a major force in Tibetan culture.

The Six Traditions of Tibetan Spirituality

Historically, there are six traditions, or schools, of Tibetan spirituality. Four of these schools are considered the principal schools. The six traditions are:

1. The Bön tradition.
2. The Nyingma tradition (the Old Ones).
3. The Bound by Command school (Kadam).
4. The Sakya tradition.
5. The Transmitted Command school (the Kagyu tradition).
6. The Virtuous school (the Gelug tradition).

The four principal schools are: Nyingma, Sakya, Kagyu, and Gelug.

The Bön Tradition

The Bön tradition is alive today and getting stronger after a long period of virtual invisibility in Tibet during the eighth to the eleventh centuries. However, there has been a revival, and Bön is supported today by His Holiness the Fourteenth Dalai Lama. The Bön community has been successful in establishing monasteries in India and Nepal. It is an integral part of Tibetan culture and history, and the Tibetans strive to preserve Bön customs.

The four other traditions of Tibetan spirituality are all Buddhist and combine elements of all three vehicles of Buddhism—Theravada, Mahayana, and Vajrayana—while leaning heavily on the Tantra practices that became so popular in Tibet. They trace back to the different gurus, or lamas, who started the lineages.

The Nyingma Tradition (The Old Ones)

The Nyingma tradition of Tibetan Buddhism traces its roots back to Padmasambhava, and is the oldest school of Tibetan Buddhism. The Nyingma tradition has origins in Bön as well as tantra and has many magical and mystical elements of practice. Padmasambhava mixed both Bön with Tantra Buddhism (with all of their magical forms and multiple deities) and came up with a very unique form of Tibetan Buddhism.

It is believed that Padmasambhava found his disciples unready to experience the full disclosure of his knowledge, so he hid hundreds of teachings from them, to be revealed in the future to teachers more prepared for the knowledge he had to impart. Subsequently, teachers through the years have revealed these hidden treasures to their students to aid in their enlightenment.

There are nine paths to enlightenment in Nyingma, six based on the sutras, and three based on the tantras. Nyingma is based on the practice of Dzogchen—a practice of meditation that presupposes the existence of the buddha-nature and strives to allow it to manifest.

Dzogchen has fairly recently become very popular in the United States as a meditation practice.

▲ Pagoda

FACT

Atisha wrote *Lamp for the Path of Enlightenment* for the Tibetan people, to answer the questions they had about practice and show them all of the Buddha's teachings—distilled from sutras and tantras—in a short guide that simplified direction for practice. These teachings on the stages of the Path were known as *lam-rim*. *Lamp for the Path of Enlightenment* is still used in practice today.

The Bound by Command School (The Kadam)

The Bound by Command school traces its roots back to Atisha, a monk who taught in Tibet starting in 1040 B.C.E. Atisha was born Chandragarbha to a royal family in Bengal. He was renamed Atisha, which means "peace," by a Tibetan king.

Atisha brought to Tibet a synthesis of the three major vehicles of Buddhism. His coming initiated the era of the Second Transmission of Buddhism to Tibet, seminal for the Bound by Command school of

Tibetan Buddhism but also for the Virtuous school and Transmitted by Command school.

Atisha was also known as one of the living Buddhas among the Tibetan people. He promoted the premise that the teachings of the guru, the lama, should be held above all else as the lama can demonstrate the living nature of the teachings and directly show the student how to practice. The teacher could choose the specific practices that would benefit the specific student.

The Bound by Command school of Tibetan Buddhism did not last long. It was considered too strict for the Tibetan people, prohibiting intoxicants, money handling, sexual relations, and travel.

"Insight" is fully explained as knowing
The Emptiness of intrinsic nature,
In comprehending that Aggregates
and Sense bases and Elements do not arise.
—*Lamp for the Path of Enlightenment*

The Sakya Tradition

Founded in 1073 by Khön Könchok Gyelpo, the Sakya school took its name from the monastery of the same name in central Tibet. Sakya means "Gray Earth." The Sakya tradition, which developed out of the earlier Nyingma teachings, has been preserved to the present day through the unbroken succession of the heads of the Khön school. The Khön lineage is hereditary, but does not pass directly from father to son, but rather indirectly from uncle to nephew. The lineage holders of the tradition pass down the transmission of the Path and Fruit (*Lam-dre*) teachings. The Path and Fruit teachings synthesize the teaching of the sutras and the tantras, and are designed to bring the student to enlightenment in a single lifetime.

The Sakya tradition continues to this day. The current head of the Sakya school is the forty-first in the lineage and practices in exile from Tibet.

The Transmitted Command School
(The Kagyu Tradition)

The Transmitted Command school of Tibetan Buddhism can trace its roots back to two Indian masters: Naropa and Tilopa. These masters were skilled in advanced yogic practices. The emphasis in the Transmitted Command school has been and still is on practice and mysticism rather than academics. Kagyu tradition has some of the more familiar names in Tibetan Buddhism if we trace its long lineage back. Naropa taught Marpa and Marpa took the teachings back to Tibet with him where he continued to practice as a layperson.

Marpa in turn passed the teachings on to his most famous student, Milarepa (1052–1135 C.E.), one of the most popular figures of all time in Tibetan Buddhism. Milarepa started out as a dark figure in history—he was a black magician bent on revenging his widowed mother and sister who were being mistreated by relatives—but became a poet and a supremely powerful yogi who mastered self-knowledge and achieved liberation. He was legendary for his mystical powers but ultimately achieved the greatest feat of all when he completely turned himself around, with Marpa's aid, and went from a black sorcerer to living in the purest light of all—Nirvana.

Among Milarepa's disciples was Gampopa, who wrote *The Jewel Ornament of Liberation.* Gampopa received the Six Yogas of the Naropa from Milarepa as well as the practice of Mahamudra (simplistically, a meditation practice), and then combined them into one lineage—Dakpo Kagyu. The Dakpo Kagyu school then gave rise to four additional schools. One of the most successful of these schools, the Karma Kagyu school, is still going strong today and is passed down through the reincarnations of the Karma Kagyu teachers.

The Six Yogas of Naropa is one of the tantric practices unique to the Transmission by Command school. It is a system of advanced tantric meditation passed down by Naropa that represents the completion stage teachings. Mahamudra practice is explained according to interpretations of sutra and tantra—with the goal being direct understanding of buddha-nature. Mahamudra was an effort to get back to the basics of meditation practice much like Ch'an or Dzogchen. Each of the schools within Kagyu tradition approach Mahamudra differently.

The Virtuous School (The Gelug Tradition)

The Virtuous school could be called the reform movement of Tibetan Buddhism. Started by Tsongkhapa in the fifteenth century, Gelug can be traced back to the Bound by Command school and was greatly influenced by the teachings of Atisha. Tsongkhapa reiterated the emphasis that Atisha had made on the monastic traditions and the importance of the guru. Tsongkhapa was extremely well educated in various schools of Buddhism and engaged in extensive meditation practices as well. He did it all—prostrations, meditation, incantations, scriptures, monastic study, ethics, and more. He founded the Ganden Monastery in 1409, which was later divided into two colleges. He died at the age of sixty but left behind a legacy that has lasted to this day. The emphasis in the Gelug tradition is on monastic and academic study. Few masters, if any, are laypeople. Monks who train in the Gelug tradition receive advanced degrees in Buddhist philosophy and thought.

FACT

The word *dalai* means "ocean" and can be traced back to Mongolian origins. *Lama* means "teacher" or "wisdom." Therefore, the title *Dalai Lama* could be translated as "Ocean of Wisdom."

The Dalai Lamas come from the Virtuous school of Tibetan Buddhism and have been the spiritual and secular leaders of Tibet ever since. However, the Dalai Lamas are not the heads of the Virtuous school itself. The Dalai Lamas receive training in many if not all the Tibetan schools of Buddhism and the leader of the Virtuous school is the abbot of the Ganden monastery.

Common Threads

All of the principal Tibetan traditions of Buddhism have more in common than not. The energy behind Tibetan Buddhism is the spirit of Avalokiteshvara, the bodhisattva of compassion. The Tibetans belief that anyone can attain enlightenment and the individual should help all sentient beings toward the Ultimate Path is the bedrock of Tibetan spiritual culture. All schools derive mostly from the Mahayana vehicle and all mix native and tantric elements into their practices, though the tantric elements are extremely strong.

The role of the guru (or lama) in Tibetan spirituality is key, especially when it comes to the more sophisticated tantric practices, for which a student needs very attentive guidance. Another element of Tibetan Buddhism that is weaved into the very fabric of their society if the mantra *Om mani padme hum*. It appears everywhere: It is on the lips of all Tibetans, on the walls of buildings, on prayer flags, in art, in jewelry, in stonework, on prayer wheels. The mantra captures the spirit of the path and the magical nature of Tibetan Buddhism.

The Quest for the Dalai Lama

The Dalai Lama is regarded by Tibetans as one of a succession of fourteen incarnations (to date) of the bodhisattva of compassion, Avalokiteshvara. The original Dalai Lama came out of the Gelug or Virtuous school of Tibetan Buddhism. This third teacher in the Gelug lineage appeared as the incarnation of the compassionate bodhisattva and was subsequently named the Dalai Lama, or Ocean of Wisdom.

For as long as space endures, and for as long as living beings remain, I, too, abide to dispel the misery of the world.
—The Dalai Lama

The current Dalai Lama was born on July 6, 1935, to a family of poor farmers in the province of Amdo in Tibet. His eldest brother, Thubten Jigme Norbu had already been recognized as a reincarnation of a high lama, Taktser Rinpoche, so it was unthinkable that the small child would also be singled out when he was just three years old. The Tibetan government had sent out a party to search for the next incarnation of the Dalai Lama. A series of clues led them to the province of Amdo and the home of the small boy. The thirteenth Dalai Lama had died in 1933 and while his body was in its period of sitting in state, the head had been found to have mysteriously turned toward the area near Amdo—this was just one of the clues that sent the party on its way.

Once the search party had narrowed down their focus, they found the Dalai Lama. The small boy is said to have immediately recognized one of the monks and when handed some of the thirteenth Dalai Lama's possessions as a test, he is said to have cried out, "It is mine!"

The three-year-old child was taken away from his family to be trained and prepared for his role as the fourteenth in the long succession of Dalai Lamas. He was eventually reunited with his family and began his intensive education and training. At the age of fifteen, with the Chinese invasion threatening the horizon, the Dalai Lama was formally made the leader of Tibet. The young leader tried to secure the assistance of Great Britain and America but was turned down. Tibet was going to have to face the might of the huge Chinese government alone. On March 17, 1958, the Dalai Lama consulted with the Nechung Oracle and was instructed to leave Tibet. For nine years the Tibetan people had tried to hold back a full-scale invasion of the Chinese government, but in the winter of 1959, the Dalai Lama knew it was time to go. On a winter's day General Chiang Chin-wu of Communist China invited the Dalai Lama to see a Chinese dance troupe—the invitation stipulated that no Tibetan soldiers were to go with the Dalai Lama and his bodyguards should remain unarmed. The people of Lhasa became upset as the news spread and soon a mob of tens of thousands of citizens surrounded the palace where the young leader resided. The Dalai Lama, disguised as a soldier, slipped through the crowds and fled his homeland.

The first thirteen Dalai Lamas were:

1. Gedun Drub (1391–1474)
2. Gedun Gyatso (1475–1542)
3. Sonam Gyatso (1543–1588)
4. Yonten Gyatso (1589–1616)
5. Ngawang Lobsang Gyatso (1617–1682)
6. Tsang-yang Gyatso (1683–1706)
7. Kezang Gyatso (1708–1757)

8. Jampel Gyatso (1758–1804)
9. Luntok Gyatso (1806–1815)
10. Tshultrim Gyatso (1816–1837)
11. Khedrup Gyatso (1838–1856)
12. Trinley Gyatso (1856–1875)
13. Thubten Gyatso (1876–1933)

The current Dalai Lama, the fourteenth, is named Tenzin Gyatso.

Contemporary Tibet

There is an international interest in Tibet today. This nation has been held captive and tortured by a foreign power since 1959. The leaders of the free world have done nothing to aid Tibet and in fact continue to do business with China, the oppressor. The Chinese government insists that Tibet is now and has been for 700 years an integral part of China and that the matter is an internal affair, not an international concern.

When the People's Republic of China defeated the small Tibetan army in 1949 when it first crossed into Tibet, it subsequently imposed the Seventeen-Point Agreement for the Peaceful Liberation of Tibet on the Tibetan government in May 1951. The agreement was signed at gunpoint and Tibetans do not recognize its validity. However, the 40,000 armed Chinese troops were convincing.

FACT

According to the exiled Tibetan prime minister Samdhong Rinpoche, approximately 7.5 million Chinese have been transferred to Tibet from China since 1949. The total population of Tibetans living in their country stands at six million. The Chinese influx has more than doubled the population of Tibet.

By the end of the Tibetan uprising in 1959, more than 80,000 Tibetans were dead and the government-in-exile was established in Dharamsala, India. Native Tibet has been devastated by the loss of its people and the environmental impact of the invasion. Deforestation, overpopulation, mining, and pollution have all added up to a negative impact on the ecosystem of this Himalayan country. March 10 is now a national Tibetan holiday called Uprising Day.

The Buddhist history of Tibet is colorful and diverse. Tibetans forged their own kind of Buddhism that is unique and intense. Tibetan Buddhism in different forms has found great popularity in the United States. There are many monasteries and study centers set up for various forms of Tibetan Buddhist study all over the country. One of the most well-known teachers of Tibetan Buddhism to emigrate to the United States was Chögyam Trungpa.

He fled Tibet at the age of twenty in 1959. In 1970 he moved to the United States and established his first American meditation center. He started Naropa University—the first Buddhist-inspired university in North America. There are more than 100 meditation centers throughout the world that were founded by Chögyam Trungpa. He was a prolific author and was responsible for bringing many great teachers to the United States from Tibet. Although he died in 1987, he left a legacy of study and education that continues strongly to this day.

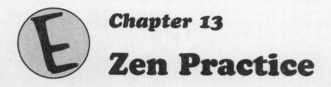

Chapter 13

Zen Practice

Zen Buddhism began back in China with Bodhidharma during the sixth century. In China it was called Ch'an, in Korea it was called Son, in Japan it was called Zen. We will go by the name of Zen from here on. What did Bodhidharma mean when he said, "vast emptiness, nothing sacred"? What exactly is the nature of emptiness?

Beginner's Mind

The aim of Zen practice is enlightenment. Zen practice is all about self-realization, awakening to the absolute truth of reality. In other words, it is understanding reality, what really exists, not what you invent with your ego, your fear, and your notions. Zen is the here and now. *This* moment. This moment just as it occurs, just as it is. Zen is something you experience intuitively. It is not about your rational, intellectual thoughts. In fact, your rational, intellectual thoughts are obstructive when it comes to Zen practice. Now that you've spent your life trying to hone your logical, rational mind you will have to quiet it and put it to rest to find your true nature.

We have, throughout our lives, constructed an idea of who we are. Ask yourself, *Who am I?* And you might come up with answers such as "I am kind, I am fearful, I am a lawyer, I am successful, I am a mother, a son," etc. Zen is being in the moment without the *I* construct, the *me* we have created for ourselves. It is existing in the moment with no thought, no ego, bringing nothing to the table. We achieve this realization of emptiness through Zen meditation.

Body and mind of themselves will drop away and your original face will be manifested. If you want to attain suchness, you should practice suchness without delay.

—Dogen, on *zazen* practice

Shunryu Suzuki, in *Zen Mind, Beginner's Mind,* tells us that beginner's mind is most helpful for Zen practice. Having no preconceived notions, and the willingness to be open to new experiences, is a wonderful gift. If you can bring your beginner's mind to your Zen practice the world will begin to open to you in wonderful ways you never dreamed possible. And if you experience moments of enlightened mind, you will recognize something you will realize you have always had, and somehow lost. Finding enlightened mind is like going home, and Zen practice is one of the pathways home.

Zazen

The heart of Zen practice is *zazen*. Zen *is zazen* and without *zazen* there is no Zen. *Zazen* is seated meditation, and the total concentration of mind and body. *Zazen* can be described to you with words, but the words are not *zazen* and you will not have experienced *zazen*. You can study, discuss, and read about *zazen* but that is not *zazen*. That is study and practice and reading.

Sitting

You have everything you will ever need right now to practice *zazen* but if you want some paraphernalia, you can get a cushion to sit on (round meditation cushions are called *zafus*). Your *zafu* can sit on a *zabuton* to protect your knees from the floor (a *zabuton* is a rectangular cushion that goes beneath the *zafu*). Put on some comfortable clothing and take off your shoes. Sit with your legs crossed, in lotus or half lotus position if you can. Put the *zafu* underneath you and sit forward on the *zafu* so that your knees are touching the ground.

You can also put the cushion between your legs and kneel with the majority of your weight resting on the cushion so your legs don't fall asleep. This is called sitting *seiza*. If neither of these positions works for you, you can always sit in a chair with your back straight and your feet on the floor. Make sure you are in a quiet space with no distractions such as televisions, radio, or other people who are not practicing.

FACT

Lotus position: Sit on the floor with your legs stretched out in front, slightly apart. Place your right foot on your left thigh with the sole facing up. Your right knee should now rest on the floor. Take your left foot and place it high on your right thigh with the sole facing up. Your left knee should now rest on the floor. This may be difficult at first but your legs should relax into it with some practice.

Keep your spine as straight as possible and the top of your head pointed toward the ceiling. Rest your hands in your lap, palms up, with one hand cradling the other. Touch your thumbs gently together. You can also rest your hands palms up or palms down on your thighs. Your lips touch lightly and your tongue can gently touch the roof of your mouth. Make sure you are relaxed and your shoulders are not tense and tight. Your eyes can be open or closed. If open, try to relax them and loosen their focus.

Set a time limit for your meditation and perhaps use a bell or a timer to indicate when time is up. You can start with very short periods, such as ten minutes, building up to longer periods of sitting as you continue practicing.

FACT

Bowing in Zen practice is a show of respect. In bowing, we pay respect to buddha-nature. When we bow in Zen, the bow is always accompanied by *gassho*. *Gassho* means "to place the two palms together." We place our palms together in front of us and bow from the waist.

When your timer goes off or your sitting time is over, be careful that you do not jump to stand up. Often your legs can go quite dead in the beginning of your practice and if you stand up quickly you might fall over. Take your time, shake out your legs, and then stand slowly. Bow to the cushion.

Breathing

In beginning *zazen* you will pay careful attention to the breath. You will be doing breath meditation. Now breathe in through your nose and out through your nose. Breathe from your diaphragm and feel it rise and fall with your breath. Let your breathing fall naturally, in and out, in and out. Now start to count your out breaths. Breathe in, breathe out, count "one." Breathe in, breathe out, count "two." Continue doing this until you notice that you are no longer concentrating on the counting but instead your mind has started to wander and you are thinking of pizza, or work, or what else you should be doing, or perhaps how silly this is.

Acknowledge the thought, let it go, and go back to the breath. In and out, one. In and out, two. Continue to do this until the bell rings. You will notice how hard it is to bring the mind back to the breath. Our minds are like unruly monkeys jumping from tree to tree. Sitting practice helps you train the monkey, and eventually make him still.

Being Present

It is important to acknowledge your thoughts as they come up and then to let them go. Do not attach to your thoughts. If you do attach to a thought, when you become aware that you have been thinking instead of concentrating on your breath, bring your mind back to the breath as soon as you can.

You are learning to be present in the moment. Do not judge the moment—that would be thinking about the moment and not being in the moment. Nothing bad is usually going on right in the moment. Few of us are being tortured right at this moment. If we can learn to live a moment at a time, fully aware and alive in each moment, completely focused on the moment at hand, our lives will be transformed and we will know the nature of the truth, of reality. We do not suppress our thoughts while we are sitting; we merely watch them and let them go.

Sit still. Do not move. This may seem impossible at first, but the more you move the more you will want to move. Sit through the pain, the discomfort. Sometimes the physical pain can be quite powerful. Sit through it. No one to my knowledge has of yet died from sitting still. You will soon start to see how much we wiggle around to get away from the moment. How much of our activity is designed to distract and escape from dis-ease. Sit still as a mountain. *Be* a mountain.

Walking meditation is called *kinhin*. *Zazen* is often broken up with a period or periods of *kinhin* to stretch the legs and give them some relief. The walking meditation is very slow and the steps are usually synchronized with the breath so that you step with the in-breath and step with the out-breath.

Group Practice

Practicing with others is important in Zen because maintaining a solitary practice can be very difficult. The sangha is key to Zen practice. The sangha usually meets in the *zendo,* a large hall or room where *zazen* is practiced. When a group gets together to practice, certain rules must apply to ensure that order and the quality of practice is maintained. Each practice group might have its own agenda of practice and there might be some variation. Some of the practices used by a sangha might include: walking meditation, a dharma talk given by the teacher, tea service, sutra recitation, and bowing. Lighting of incense might be part of the session as well as small seated rest breaks.

When the Student Is Ready

It is said that when the student is ready, the teacher appears. Although at the heart of Zen is the realization that you have everything you will ever need already, the student/teacher relationship in Zen is also a very important element of practice. A teacher will guide the student through the various stages of practice, helping the student toward enlightenment.

Zen is transmitted from face to face, from person to person. A teacher will have become a teacher through the transmission of Zen from person to person.

The teacher in Zen is called the *roshi.* The roshi does not try to affect the lives of his or her student outside of Zen practice. The roshi is not a therapist or counselor. The roshi guides the student through *zazen,* and along the path to self-realization.

Teisho is not a lecture or a sermon. It is more of a presentation of insight to the students. Often the subject of a *teisho* will be a koan or koans.

A private encounter with the teacher during a *zazen* session is called *dokusan.* In *dokusan* the teacher will gauge the student's progress and do what is necessary to encourage the student to continue. When the teacher gives a talk to the group it is called *teisho*.

Zen Transmission

The transmission of Zen from one person to another, from mind to mind, has been the tradition since Bodhidharma showed up in China so many hundreds of years ago. Bodhidharma was sitting in a cave at Shaolin in the mountains of China. One day the Hui Ko showed up outside and begged Bodhidharma to teach him how to tame his mind. Bodhidharma continually refused to help Hui Ko.

Hui Ko persisted until Bodhidharma said to him, "How can you hope for self-realization with a shallow heart and an arrogant mind?"

Hearing these words, Hui Ko, standing in the raging snowstorm, took out his sword and cut of his arm to show his willingness.

Hui Ko proved his sincerity. When Bodhidharma asked him, "What do you want me to teach you?"

Hui Ko replied, "I want peace of mind."

"Where do you find your mind?" asked Bodhidharma. "Bring it to me and I will pacify it."

"When I look for my mind I cannot find it," said Hui Ko.

"There! I have pacified your mind," said Bodhidharma.

And so in that moment Hui Ko attained enlightened mind.

This is an example of mind to mind transmission. Bodhidharma was the first Zen patriarch. Hui Ko was the second. And so Zen was passed from mind to mind until the present day.

FACT

Dogen was the founder of the Soto lineage of Buddhism in Japan. Dogen taught a way of sitting called *shikantaza*, which means "just sitting," nothing else—no breath counting, no koan practice at all. *Shikantaza* means that sitting *is* enlightened mind. You don't sit to become enlightened, you sit to enjoy your enlightened mind.

Koan Practice

As you sit and your practice deepens, you go through different stages. A koan is a tool that helps you move through these stages toward enlightened mind, or as one Zen master said, "It is the place where truth is." During our meditation practice we reach a stage known as *samadhi*. *Samadhi* is a deep and focused meditation wherein concentration is effortless but complete absorption has been attained. Koan practice is done in the *samadhi* state.

The most famous koan is "What is the sound of one hand clapping?" Koans are puzzles that cannot be answered with the rational mind, but must be answered intuitively. To access the answers to koans one must develop his or her sitting practice.

The Student/Teacher Relationship

Students are normally assigned a koan in *dokusan*. Koans should never be discussed with other students and should always be a private matter between the teacher and student.

The student tries to answer the koan when she meets with the teacher. Answers are usually not verbal, but can be. They are not yes/no, this/that answers. When the answer is known by the student, it will be apparent to the student how to convey the answer to the teacher.

This kind of individual instruction has been a part of Zen practice from the beginning and can be traced back to the Buddha. The relationship between the teacher and student is not to be taken lightly and is of a very intimate nature. The teacher is helping the student toward true self-realization, so only the truth can be spoken between them. The relationship is symbiotic as the teacher imparts knowledge and skill to the student and the student shares his beginner's mind with the teacher. The teacher also needs someone to practice with, for practice never ends. The Zen teacher is compassionate and has enlightened wisdom that the student longs to share. If you can find a Zen master to study with, the compassionate and wise nature of the teacher can awaken a faith in practice.

The teacher helps the student give away everything he has: his ego, his misguided ideas about reality, his very thoughts. The mind is cleared of the debris of a lifetime and a new way of living emerges.

Sesshin

A *sesshin* is basically a meditation retreat. *Sesshins* vary greatly in length, from a weekend to several weeks or more. *Zazen* is usually practiced for seven to ten hours a day, broken with *kinhin,* work practice, rest periods, *teisho,* and food. The *sesshin* members rise before dawn and do *zazen* before breakfast. They end the day with *zazen* as well. *Dokusan* is held anywhere from one to three times during the day.

Most of the movement in practice happens during a *sesshin. Sesshins* are the optimum time to work on koan practice as the teacher encounters are most helpful and provide encouragement to a flagging spirit. *Sesshins* are extremely difficult and rewarding. But they are wonderful opportunities for practice in a safe environment with no distraction except for your own monkey mind.

Mu

One of the koans most frequently assigned to newcomers to Zen practice is Mu. Mu gained fame from the story of Joshu.

A Zen master said to Joshu, "Does a dog have buddha-nature?" Joshu replied, "Mu!"

Mu is a negative symbol in Chinese meaning, "no-thing."

FACT

Joshu Jushin was a renowned Zen master of the T'ang period in Chinese history. He is best known for his Mu koan but appears in many of the koans that have been handed down to us. He was known for his wisdom with his students and for the dharma debates he engaged in with Zen masters all over China.

While the rational mind might get excited by such koans as "What is the sound of one hand clapping" or "What is your face before your parents were born?" Mu can leave one cold and uninspired. Perhaps its success as the most frequently assigned koan comes from just this. It is impossible to come up with a rational answer for Mu. The student takes Mu into *zazan* practice and, while sitting, instead of concentrating on the counting of breaths, the student must answer the question, "What is Mu?" The answer can only be found in sitting and working on the koan. The teacher helps the student move through Mu toward the answer to the koan.

Work Practice

We can practice Zen in our everyday lives. Don't leave Zen on your cushion every morning; take it on the bus, in your car, into work! However, taking Zen out of the *zendo* is not an easy practice. People push on the bus, they criticize at work, they honk at us in cars. It is easy to lose our equilibrium and our tempers. Our Zen practice can slow us down and keep us in the moment. A traffic jam can be a wonderful opportunity for practice.

When we see a red light . . . we can thank it, because it is a bodhisattva helping us return to the present moment . . . We may have thought of it as an enemy, preventing us from achieving our goal. But now we know the red light is our friend . . . calling us to return to the present moment where we can meet with life, joy, and peace.

—Thich Nhat Hanh

Zazen is *more* than seated meditation. It is portable and you can apply the mindfulness of *zazen* to your work whether it is farming your land or crunching numbers. Mindfulness in our work environments is essential to practice. People tend to think that Zen is a quiet, static practice. Zen is life and life involves activity. You can take Zen with you into the activity. Work is filled with actions. Be mindful of each action as you complete it. Do not get ahead of yourself but concentrate completely on the task at hand.

Apply the principles of seated *zazen* to your work. Concentrate wholly on what you are doing. When your concentration starts to wander, acknowledge your distraction and let it go. Bring your mind back to your work. Cut down on the unnecessary talking and noise . . . and breathe.

You should take your practice with you into everything you do. Vietnamese Zen Master Thich Nhat Hahn gives us mindfulness exercises in his wonderful book, *The Miracle of Mindfulness*. Here are a few of his suggestions that you can use during the day:

- Measure your breath by your footsteps.
- Count your breaths.
- Set aside a day of mindfulness.
- Half-smile.
- Follow your breath while having a conversation.

Strive to become mindful in every part of your life. When you are eating, eat. When you are walking, walk. When you are making love, make love. When you are cooking, cook. Be there in the moment each and every moment. The moment is all you have. *This* moment.

◀ Monk working on mandala

Zen Study and Liturgy

Zazen is the heart of Zen practice and there is traditionally little emphasis on text study, or as Bodhidharma said, "no dependence on words and letters, a direct pointing to the human mind." This does not mean that Zen practitioners should ignore the sutras, but it does mean there should be no attachment to them. The Heart Sutra and the Lotus Sutra are two of the sutras commonly studied and recited by Zen practitioners.

Liturgical practice is another element of Zen. Liturgy is experiential in nature, and hard to qualify. Liturgy is used in Zen practice in daily monastic life and in *sesshin*. Liturgy is used to introduce transition, such as a meal *gatha*. Recitation of liturgy can also be a time of group activity in a practice that is mostly solitary.

Zen practitioners are part of the Mahayana vehicle of Buddhism. As such, they aspire to be bodhisattvas. Every bodhisattva resolves to realize the Four Great Vows. The Four Great Vows are:

- Sentient beings are numberless: I vow to save them.
- Desires are inexhaustible; I vow to put an end to them.
- The dharmas are boundless; I vow to master them.
- The Buddha Way is unattainable: I vow to attain it.

The early Buddhists were scientists of the mind. They came up with specific practices that would encourage the mind to unfold and open to the nature of reality, like a flower opening to the sun. Each practice, whether it is *zazen,* mantras, liturgy recitation, or koan practice was designed by these scientists to aid you along the path toward enlightenment. These practices have been proved and refined over thousands of years. Zen is a very basic, bare bones practice. It attempts to strip practice down to the essentials so emptiness can be experienced. Other forms of meditation will be examined in the following chapter. Ⓔ

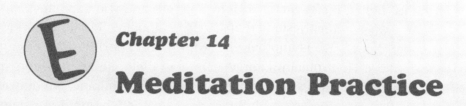

Chapter 14

Meditation Practice

Meditation is an elemental part of Buddhism. The various schools of Buddhism approach meditation differently. Zen meditation, *vipashyana* meditation, walking meditation, mantra meditation, Tibetan meditation . . . there are many different techniques to meditation. The goal is to still our minds. Whatever way you choose, you're on the path and that's what matters!

Why Meditate?

Meditation can transform your life. It can reduce stress and anxiety, help you to sleep better, energize you, slow you down, make you more patient, get you in touch with how you feel both emotionally and physically, provide a quiet space in your day, and much more. And of course, in Buddhist belief, it can reveal your true nature and you can attain Nirvana.

At a weekend meditation retreat at Zen Mountain Monastery in Mt. Tremper, New York, I heard Abbott John Daido Loori Roshi speaking about *zazen*. He told us that at Mt. Tremper they often had visitors from the outside. People frequently came in to see the building, which was awarded recognition as a historic landmark in 1995 by both the state of New York and the nation.

The monastery, a turn-of-the century building erected by a Catholic priest and Norwegian craftspeople, is nestled among acres of fields and forest in the Catskill Mountains. The visitors often ask if they can watch a *zazen* session, if they can stand quietly and witness the meditation. Abbott Daido told us he always says no. *Zazen* may look peaceful on the outside, but inside it can be anything but peaceful for the one who is sitting. Picture a calm lake, the water completely still, like glass—a wonder of serenity. But underneath those still waters all sort of activity goes on with all kinds of life movement. It is much the same with meditation. It might look like stillness on the outside, but getting to the stillness on the inside takes some work.

In addition to the benefits mentioned above, the Abhidhyan Yoga Institute lists these benefits to meditation, among others:

1. You can further develop intuition.
2. You will realize the difference between reality and illusion.
3. You will remain calm in any situation.
4. You will learn how to enjoy life.
5. You will learn the nature of impermanence.

Meditation is transformative and best of all does not take that much time. If you can set aside twenty to twenty-five minutes a day you can begin to make changes in yourself that will affect the quality of the rest of your life. Sit still and see what happens!

▲ Reclining Buddha

What You Will Need: Supplies

Of course you don't actually need any supplies to meditate, but traditionally many Buddhists have things that accompany their meditation routines, from altars and incense, to cushions and bells. Here are some supplies you might want to consider:

- A meditation cushion
- Incense
- Timer, bell, or Tibetan singing bowl
- Altar
- Altar cloth
- Candles
- Flowers
- Devotional objects
- Prayer beads

Buddhists call their meditation cushions *zafus*. Zen practitioners traditionally have round *zafus* and Tibetan practitioners usually have square *zafus*. The *zafu* can be placed on a *zabuton,* which is a large, flat, square cushion that protects the knees from the floor.

Traditionally incense is burned for the duration of the meditation. Incense can be used as a timer for meditation sessions. Once the incense is burned, the time is up. This could be one of the original uses for incense. Incense also covered those unpleasant body odors found in prolonged meditation sessions, and helped keep flies out of the *zendo*. Most teachers would probably not say that incense promotes the ability to attain enlightenment, but the senses are aroused by the smell of the incense and there are those who do consider it to play a factor in increased sensitivity to enlightenment. It does smell good and that can be good enough reason to use it.

An altar is used for several reasons. First of all, repetition, habit, and ceremony play a large part in meditation practice. The altar is a visual reminder of the importance of practice. It is an indicator of faith in practice. And an altar sets the stage for the awakening of the senses: gazing at the Buddha, smelling the incense, bowing or doing prostrations . . . all combine to form a relationship with the practice itself.

I practice meditation
To subdue the dragon of desire.

—Wang Wei

If possible, it is a good idea to have the altar in a room you will use for no other purpose. If not possible, the altar can be in a corner of a room that can be accessed for quiet times. No unexpected activity will disturb the practice. The Buddha statue and its place holder can be placed in the center of the altar. The Buddha is placed on the altar so your attention can be focused on the Buddha and his teachings. Dharma implements (such as bells, *vajra*) can be placed to the side of the Buddha. The incense and incense holder can be placed in the center of the altar. In order to ensure that your incense sticks remain upright, you can place rice in the bottom of the incense holder until you have enough ash from the incense to allow the sticks to stay upright. Flowers can be placed to the side of the altar. Flowers symbolize the nature of impermanence. The candle can also be placed to one side. The candle symbolizes the light of truth brightening the darkness of delusion.

You put the timer or Tibetan singing bowl by your *zafu* and strike the bell when the meditation begins. The sound of the bell striking reminds you to clear your mind. You can follow the sound of the bell with your mind and start your meditation.

Tibetan singing bowls traditionally come with a striker and a silk-covered cushion to rest the bowl on. They come in a variety of sizes from quite small to large. You can use a Tibetan singing bowl to mark time, as an alarm, a timer, or to hold your incense sticks.

Prayer beads and devotional objects can be placed on the altar and prayer beads should be held during meditation. Prayer beads traditionally came from the Bodhi Tree. A typical strand of prayer beads would have 108 beads on a strand. The person who is meditating could run her hands over the beads as she repeated *Oh mani padme hum,* using the beads to keep track of the number of repetitions. Different schools of Buddhism use different meditation items. Tibetan Buddhism tends toward more meditation tools, while Zen focuses on the basics.

Posture

In virtually all Buddhist meditations, you are required to take a specific posture. Meditation is the integration of mind and body. It is not just about your mind—it is very much about the unification of both mind and body. Chapter 13 covers the basic meditation positions and posture. The lotus position is most recommended as it is a very stable position and after your legs learn to adjust to the position it tends to be the most comfortable. Thousands of years of thought have gone into this, so even though it might seem crazy, it is eventually the most comfortable position to take for many. Try one of four positions for your meditation: lotus, half lotus, Burmese-style, or seated in a chair with back straight and feet firmly on the floor.

No matter how you are sitting, your back should be straight and your head should be pointing straight up to the sky. Your lower back should be curved inward and your upper back should be curved outward so that your back is an S shape. Shoulders should be back and your chest should be able to expand comfortable on your in-breath. Your ears should be directly over your shoulder so your head is held erect. Your chin is tucked in and your eyes are either closed or focused loosely on the ground in front of you. Your hands can be in the classic mudra discussed in the last chapter or rest lightly on your thighs. If it helps, do light stretching before getting into your meditation position. Sometimes limbering up helps.

Keep your mouth closed and the tip of your tongue lightly touching the roof of your mouth. Relax your shoulders and your face. But final, specific meditation instruction should come from your teacher.

The Breath

You obviously already know how to breathe, but sometimes during meditation you can feel as if you are struggling for breath. Just keep breathing in and out, in and out, and you will be fine. Familiarize yourself with your breath. Let your breath lead you like it does all day long without you even thinking about it. Suddenly, when sitting with nothing else to do, you can be overwhelmed with a desire to take control of your breathing. Let the breath take care of itself. Breathe in, breathe out.

Center your attention on your *hara*. The *hara* is located two inches below your bellybutton and is the spiritual and physical center of your body. Take deep breaths, letting your belly fill out as you breathe in, and then breathe out, watching your breath as it goes.

Focus your attention on your *hara* and keep breathing. Imagine that the breath comes in and goes down to your *hara*, then comes out from there again, back up into your nasal passages and out your nose. Meditation is about watching the body, watching the breath, watching the thoughts, and letting them go. It is not about controlling anything. Let go.

What if anxiety or physical pain overwhelms me while I am meditating? What should I do?

If you start to feel very uncomfortable while meditating, focus your attention on your breath. Breathe in, and then on the out-breath push the pain away. This way you will get some respite from the pain or anxiety on the out-breath. Continue to do this and the pain or anxiety should start to dissipate. Remember, nobody dies from sitting still.

Techniques

There are different techniques for meditation. *Zazen,* or Zen meditation, was covered in the previous chapter. Two other types of meditation are *shamatha* meditation and *vipashyana* meditation. *Shamatha* means "calm abiding" and *vipashyana* means "insight." *Vipashyana* is therefore also called "insight meditation." Most Buddhist traditions encourage a combination and unification of meditations instead of promoting one over the other.

Shamatha Meditation

Shamatha meditation techniques involve concentration on one thing in particular whether it be your breath or the sound of rain. "Calm abiding" means sitting with one's breath, or other point of concentration, gently sitting with the focused attention while keeping thoughts and emotions at a distance. The benefits of one-pointed concentration are many. Our minds are like monkeys jumping from tree to tree in the forest. Having the skill of one-pointedness is having the ability to control the jumping monkey. You can make great progress in any undertaking you choose if you have the ability to focus diligently on the task at hand. People who can practice one-pointedness also can be still while so many people, especially today, seem to have great difficulty remaining still and sitting with themselves for any length of time. What's so bad about sitting with yourself?

Shamatha meditation gets you to focus on one point but not with undue exertion, but calmly and quietly. *Shamatha* is stopping and becoming aware.

Vipashyana Meditation

As compared to one-pointed concentration, *vipashyana* meditation—insight meditation—is a more open awareness. Thoughts and feelings are watched and studied. Penetration of the nature of existence, the true nature of things, will lead to understanding impermanence, suffering, and the nature of emptiness.

When thoughts arise while meditating, try to stay away from the *I*. Just note your thoughts and say (not aloud), "thoughts" or "thinking, thinking." Try not to say to yourself, "*I* am thinking," "*I* am having thoughts," "*My* legs hurt." "Hurting, hurting," or "pain, pain" will keep you in the observation and help keep the small self at bay.

You can use *shamatha* to move into *vipashyana* meditation. Once your mind is still and calm, and you have the ability to watch that which arises in your mind, you can start to penetrate the nature of that which arises. Once the monkey is quiet and has stopped jumping from tree branch to tree branch, you can watch where your mind wanders off. If your mind is perfectly still, you can abide with your breath. If your mind wanders off, just observe where it goes. When you do catch your mind wandering away, say to yourself, "thoughts" and let them go. Acknowledge the thoughts, then let them go. Or say, "thinking" or "mind wandering" and let the thoughts go. Sometimes you will get caught up in the thoughts quickly and forget to observe them. Instead, there's that monkey again, jumping crazily around the forest. As soon as you notice the monkey is up and at it again, try again to still him and return to the breath.

Your monkey wants to judge everything. This is good. This is bad. Feet are dead: bad. Bird singing: good. Practice nonjudgment. Feet dead. Birds singing. Stay in the moment and experience the world without the judgment. Just observe, just watch.

Compassionate Meditation

Compassion, generosity, open-heartedness, and loving-kindness are all wonderful qualities to acquire. Why not meditate on compassion or loving-kindness for yourself and for others?

Metta is a natural occurrence in the world. I can see that my dog has *metta.* He is openhearted and loving. If it's a natural occurrence in the world, then you have it inside you, too. Meditate on *metta,* and cultivate it toward yourself and toward others. In *The Complete Idiot's Guide to Understanding Buddhism,* Gary Gach tells us that "metta opens your heart, to yourself, to those around you, even those you hate, and to the whole world. Begin by opening your heart toward yourself. If you can't be kind to yourself, who can you be kind to? So begin by thinking kindly of yourself. As you do so, say to yourself, 'May I be well,' and visualize yourself as being well. Send yourself the gift of metta. Then move on to wishing 'May I be happy,' and picture a happy you. Then, wishing, 'May I be peaceful,' envision yourself at peace."

Then do the same for others in your life: your friends, your parents, your sangha, your workmates, your enemies, your friends, and all sentient beings.

FACT

Kathleen McDonald is the resident teacher in the Foundation for the Preservation of the Mahayana Tradition. She is a Tibetan Buddhist nun, ordained in 1974. In her book, *How to Meditate,* she refers to the interdependence of mind and body and recommends the seven-point posture, paying careful attention to the positioning of legs, arms, back, eyes, jaw, tongue, and head.

Another meditation that focuses on compassion is called *tonglen—* sending and receiving.

Pema Chödrön writes about *tonglen* in *When Things Fall Apart. Tonglen,* she tells us is "designed to awaken bodhicitta, to put us in touch with genuine noble heart. It is the practice of taking in pain and sending out pleasure and therefore completely turns around our well-established habit of doing just the opposite." The way to practice *tonglen* is to breathe in suffering—your own suffering, the suffering of others, those with disease, with heartache, with pain—and breathe out wellness and kindness and direct it toward others, toward yourself. Breathe in pain, breathe out wellness. Breathe in hatred, breathe out love. In this manner you cultivate *bodhicitta* and awaken a compassionate spirit inside yourself.

Mantra Meditation

Mantras are often used as meditation devices by Buddhist. A mantra is basically a sound vibration. A silent and constant repetition of a sound, a phrase, or syllables can help to clear the mind of the debris of thoughts and feelings, and focus the attention. Distractions fall away as the mind is concentrated on the repetitive calling. You can use a specific mantra for a specific spiritual purpose or you can use the mantra in a general way for focusing the attention and clearing the mind.

Different vehicles of Buddhism tend toward using different mantras:

Mantras		
Pure Land	**Tibetan**	**Nichiren**
Namo Amito	*Om mani padme hum*	*Namu myoho renge kyo*
Glory to Amitabha	Jewel in the Lotus	Glory to the Lotus Sutra

For example, according to Gen Rinpoche, *Om mani padme hum* is associated with Avalokiteshvara, the bodhisattva of compassion. This mantra has six syllables. Each of the six syllables is said to aid you in the perfection of the six *paramitas* of the bodhisattvas. The six paramitas are: generosity, ethics, patience, perseverance, concentration, and wisdom. Chanting the mantra *Om mani padme hum* will help you master these six perfections. Mastering these six perfections will help you to become a more compassionate person.

Mantra is actually Sanskrit for two words: "man" and "tra." *Man* can be translated as "mind" and *tra* can be translated as "deliverance."

The mantra is also associated with the six realms of existence: the god realm, the titan realm, the human realm, the animal realm, the realm of the hungry ghosts, and the hell realm. Emotions corresponding with these realms can also be relieved, such as jealousy, desire, and hatred.

FACT

Gen Rinpoche left Tibet in 1959, when the Chinese oppression forced him out. He eventually made his way to India, where he joined His Holiness the Dalai Lama and some of his other teachers. In 1971 the Dalai Lama asked him to begin a program for westerners at the Library of Tibetan Works and Archives in Dharamsala. He spent the remainder of his life teaching Buddhism to westerners in the United States, New Zealand, and Australia.

Walking Meditation

Zen walking meditation, *kinhin*, was covered in the last chapter, but walking meditation is not peculiar to Zen practice. Walking meditation is a wonderful complement to seated meditation, mindfulness, or mantra practice. Walking meditation is a way to practice mindfulness while moving around the world we inhabit. If you leave your meditation on the floor with your zafu you won't make as much progress as you will if you take it with you into your day.

Because walking meditation proved so beneficial, the Buddha and his disciples used it in their practice all the time. In Thailand walking meditation is such a fundamental part of practice that a Walk is built into each meditation center for the monks' use. There are obvious physical benefits to walking meditation as well, as the legs get stretched and the blood gets pumping. Sitting can be tough on the body and surprisingly exhausting. Walking meditation can rejuvenate the mind and the body. Walking helps the concentration, digestion, promotes physical fitness, and rejuvenates the body—all the while still practicing mindfulness!

Mindfulness

Mindfulness also extends to all vehicles of Buddhism and is not only relevant in Zen practice. In *The Greater Discourse on the Foundations of Mindfulness*, the Buddha set forth the practice of mindfulness for his students:

> *There is, Monks, this one way to the purification of beings, for the overcoming of sorrow and distress, for the disappearance of pain and sadness, for the gaining of the right path, for the realization of Nirvana—that is to say the four foundations of mindfulness.*
>
> *What are the four? Here, monks, a monk abides contemplating body as a body, ardent, clearly aware and mindful, having put aside hankering and fretting for the world; he abides contemplating feelings as feelings . . . ; he abides contemplating mind as mind . . . ; he abides contemplating mind-objects as mind-objects, ardent, clearly aware and mindful, having put aside hankering and fretting for the world.*

Seated meditation is the beginning of mindfulness but we must carry our mindfulness into all that we do. As the Buddha tells us, we must be aware of our bodies in all that we do when we do it. When we walk we must feel ourselves walking. Be mindful of our walking. What are our feet doing? What are our shoulders doing? Feel your body. Few of us truly inhabit our bodies today and many of us go to great lengths to get outside of our bodies by overeating, suppressing our feelings with food, drugs, alcohol, and more. Reside in your body and pay attention to what it tells you. Practice mindfulness with everything you do. When eating, eat. When dressing, pay attention to what the arms do, the hands, the head. When using the toilet, be present. When swallowing, pay attention to the swallow. What does your throat do? What about your tongue? Do you know what it truly feels like to eat something? When you are driving your car, are you driving your car? Or are you putting on makeup, looking at a map, talking on the phone, listening to music? When you shift gears, shift gears. When you turn left, turn the wheel and notice your hands, your body, the feel of the wheel. Be mindful!

If you are mindful of your feelings you can get some perspective on them. When you are angry, know that you are angry. How does it feel to be angry? Do your shoulders tighten? Does your stomach hurt? Does the heart race? Be mindful and pay attention to each of your emotions as they arise. Use your mindfulness meditation to see from where the emotions arise. Be mindful of pain. What is pain and how does it feel? Acknowledge the pain and do not try to get away from the pain. If you abide with the pain it will leave as you abide with it.

As you are mindful of the mind itself you know that all states of the mind are exactly what they are. Prejudice is prejudice. Kindness is kindness. Know you are tired, you are excited, you are anxious. Know your mental state and be mindful of it all day long. Know the hindrances to your practice of mindfulness: be aware of fatigue, ill-will, anxiety, doubt, and desire.

Take your meditation practice with you to work, to school, to work out, to lunch, to the bath, to the garden. If you are mindful in everything you do your practice will improve immeasurably. Of course, it is difficult to be mindful all the time. We talk on the phone as we wash the dishes, we rush through the dinner to get to our reading. We rush through our reading to get out the door. We rush our lives away. Be mindful of your life and *live* the moments of your day. If you can be mindful for just five minutes outside your seated meditation every day, it will make a difference in your practice and your life. Wake up!

When in sitting meditation there is agitation of thought, then with that very agitated mind seek to find where the agitated thought came from, and who it is that is aware of it. In this way pressing forward as to the location of the disturbance further and further to the ultimate point, you will find that the agitation does not have any original location, and that the one who is aware of it also is void.

—*Zen and the Ways*, Trevor Leggett

The art of meditation is a way to wake up to the world. We can learn new ways to see our troubles and our pain and bring true wisdom to our life. As American *vipashyana* teacher Jack Kornfield tells us in *A Path with Heart,* meditation is like training a puppy. We sit the puppy down and tell him to stay, but the puppy immediately gets up and runs away. So we sit the puppy back down again and tell him to stay. And the puppy runs away. Sometimes he runs away and poops in the corner, sometimes he runs away and creates another mess. So it is with our minds. We tell our minds to sit still and our minds are off to the races and we have to start over and start over and start over.

Meditation practice is not easy. It is frustrating, painful, time-consuming, irritating, and sometimes it feels almost unbearable. Sometimes the last thing in the world we feel up to is sitting still with ourselves. But once we start sitting, we get glimpses of the no-self who is sitting and we slowly start to realize the delusion of self. And slowly our true nature will become visible, and the nature of all things will peek out. Slowly, slowly, with much dedication, much toil, and much joy, we wake up.

Chapter 15
Nirvana

The Eightfold Path leads straight to Nirvana. And Nirvana seems shrouded in mystery and confusion. You may have many questions about Nirvana, such as: Is this all smoke and mirrors? What exactly is Nirvana? Is all this trouble really worth it? So let's take a look at what all this is about—including what some of the great Buddhist teachers and writers have had to say.

Extinguishing the Fires of Desire

The Buddha outlined the Four Noble Truths—the truths that have been passed down to us over the course of 2,500 years—at the Deer Park so long ago. He told us that the Third Noble Truth was the cessation of suffering, and the cessation of suffering is Nirvana: "This, oh *Bhikkhus*, is the noble truth of the cessation of suffering: It ceases with the complete cessation of this thirst—a cessation which consists in the absence of every passion with the abandoning of this thirst, with doing away with it, with the destruction of desire." And then the Buddha goes on to tell us that with the realization of this knowledge he had found the key to Nirvana. The cessation of suffering could be attained by following the Eightfold Path, and since Nirvana itself was the cessation of this suffering—the extinguishing of all desire—Nirvana could be obtained by any who followed the path.

Nirvana literally means "extinguished" or "blown out."

When craving ceases, Nirvana is uncovered. Nirvana can be attained only by letting go of everything and seeing that letting go of everything is true freedom.

We experience fear at the idea of letting go of everything, fear and defensiveness. We want to protect that which we have, that which we believe in, even though we are told that to protect what we have is to crave what we have, and that craving is causing us to suffer. The path to Nirvana is an experiential path. It must be experienced to be understood.

You cannot think your way into Nirvana or think your way into dropping your small self. You cannot see beyond the world you know so well without following the Eightfold Path. Perhaps there are other ways to attain Nirvana, but the early Buddhist teachers made a science out of studying the mind and the ego. They found a surefire way of letting go—whether in happens in this lifetime or another—and they passed it down for us to share.

Nirvana is letting go of the Three Poisons: craving (or greed), hatred, and ignorance. Imagine no hatred, no ignorance, and no greed. Imagine never wanting anything, never wanting *for* anything. Nirvana extinguishes the Three Poisons. Someone who has attained Nirvana is free of these delusions and attachments. Absolutely free. Nirvana extinguishes the burning fire of desire, hatred, and ignorance.

No Place

Nirvana is not a place. It is not somewhere you go, such as the grocery store or the theater. It is not an out-of-body experience or somewhere you float away to after death. It is not something you earn by being good or practicing virtuous behavior. Nirvana is there all the time if you want to experience it. It has always been there and it will always be there. Nirvana is the cessation of suffering and it can be yours if you want to try to attain it. The Buddha was not hiding a magical place from his students, nor promising the unattainable. If it is possible to stop suffering in all its forms, it is possible to attain Nirvana.

The Dhammapada, the collected sayings of the Buddha, in Chapter 14: The Awakened One, says:

> *But who to the Buddha, Dharma,*
> *And Sangha as refuge has gone,*
> *Sees with full insight*
> *The Four Noble Truths;*
> *Misery, the arising of misery,*
> *And the transcending of misery*
> *The noble Eightfold path*
> *Leading to the allaying of misery*
> *This indeed, is a refuge secure.*
> *This is the highest refuge.*
> *Having come to this refuge,*
> *One is released from all misery.*

The highest refuge (Nirvana) is the refuge where one is released from all misery, all suffering: the cessation of suffering.

▲ Wheel of life

Although we can try very hard, there are really no words that can *adequately* describe what Nirvana is. It would be like describing clouds to a blind person. We must experience Nirvana ourselves through our own practice and insight. It is easier for people to speak of what Nirvana is *not,* than what it is. Scriptures have referred to Nirvana as "supreme bliss," however. But when we hear the words "supreme bliss" we start to create our own picture of something like paradise. And each of us has our own picture of paradise. Maybe your paradise is a place with green grass and tulips, prancing dogs and a gentle breeze on a sunny, soft day (oops, that's mine), or maybe it's of complete and utter peacefulness and love, floating on clouds. Nirvana is not something you have seen on television; it is not an *idea* about peace.

Nor is it nothingness. As John Snelling writes in *The Buddhist Handbook,* "One classic misconception is to see Nirvana as some kind of nothingness. This is to fall prey to the mistaken view of annihilationism (complete nonexistence), which is twinned with the equally mistaken view of eternalism (that something may exist forever). Nirvana lies beyond both existence an nonexistence."

FACT

John Snelling was General Secretary of the Buddhist Society from 1980 through 1984. He was also editor of the Society's journal, *The Middle Way,* which is reputed to be the most widely circulated Buddhist periodical in the West, if not the world. He was the author of *The Buddhist Handbook, The Elements of Buddhism,* and numerous other books and articles. He died in 1992.

What the Buddha did for his students and what his students passed on to the next generations was the verification that something existed beyond what was known at that time: that there is "an unborn, unoriginated, unmade, and unconditioned." He verified the "unborn, unoriginated, unmade, and unconditioned," and because he did so he verified that there was escape from the born, originated, made, and conditioned. There was escape from rebirth, from suffering. And he told us how to go about seeing it for ourselves.

In the movie *The Matrix* a group of people have discovered that their lives are an illusion. They discover that instead of living the lives they thought they were living—working, making love, eating, walking, reading—they were actually lying in a machine-sustained world being fed dreams of their lives. Once they "woke up" to the true reality of their situation they could escape the machines and live a new life. This can be seen as a metaphorical example of what we perceive as our lives and the reality of Nirvana. The real world was always there, but the group of people could not see it as they were stuck in their illusion. Once they broke out, they realized the other world, the real world, was always there, always within grasp. And they aimed to free the rest of the world from their delusions of life. Much like the Buddha. They just needed to get the tools to free themselves from their delusions.

The destruction of lust, the destruction of hatred, the destruction of illusion, is called Nirvana.

—*The Book of the Kindred Saying*

Nirvana in This Life

There are different kinds of Nirvana, such as Nirvana in this life and Nirvana after death. As we know, the Buddha attained Nirvana in this life at age thirty-five as he sat under the Bodhi Tree. Though the Buddha's experience was transformative, does it mean he never experienced suffering again in his entire life, even though he lived until he was an old man? No, it does not.

Nirvana, as we can see by the Buddha's own words, is the cessation of suffering and the realization of "an unborn, unoriginated, unmade, and unconditioned" state. In order to be those things forever more (not born, no origins, not made, no conditions) it would have to mean that the Buddha did not suffer ever again in his lifetime and beyond. It would mean he never again felt pain when he was hurt, or felt the desire for the sun on his face. But the Buddha was still a human being, and it is inevitable that a human being will be subject to some form of suffering. Therefore, it must be seen that Nirvana—for those of us who are living—is a state that is entered into and then left behind. It can then be re-entered into, and then exited once again.

What does "unborn, unoriginated, unmade, unconditioned" actually mean? It means there is no beginning and no end, no creation, and no conditions to existence. It means the world never began nor will it end. It means there is no hot, no cold, no wet, no dry, no space, no time, no pressure. These things are beyond our current comprehension, as we cannot grasp the unborn, unoriginated, unmade, and unconditioned with our small minds.

If Nirvana is entered into, left, and re-entered, than the state of being unborn, unoriginated, unmade, and unconditioned can be attained here on Earth, but not forever more until death. Through continual practice of the steps laid out by the Buddha it is possible to experience the state of unborn, unoriginated, unmade, and unconditioned here on Earth intermittently, but not continually forevermore until life as we know it is extinguished. It is important to note that Buddhists consider enlightenment on Earth equal and not inferior to enlightenment after death; it is just not ever-present.

Nirvana is described in both negative terms (it is common in Buddhist literature to describe Buddhist states in negative terms, as there is often nothing similar to which to relate them—therefore we resort to what something is *not*) and positive terms, though the negative terms following do not correspond to the positive terms, and vice versa:

Nirvana	
Negative Terms for Nirvana	**Positive Terms for Nirvana**
Unborn	Farther shore
Unoriginated	Wholly radiant
Emptiness	Bliss
Unmade	Cooling
Deathless	Calming
Unconditioned	Joyful
Cessation of suffering	Timeless

Theravada Buddhists believe in four stages of enlightenment before the final stage of Nirvana is gained. As Jack Maguire tells us in *Essential Buddhism,* first one becomes a "stream-enterer" and is enlightened but not as powerfully as an arhat might experience enlightenment. The stream-enterer will still be reborn, though not as frequently as someone who has never been enlightened. A "once-returner" experiences a more powerful enlightenment than a stream-enterer and may return for only one more rebirth. A nonreturner will not be reborn again and will go on to become an arhat. An arhat is the final stage and attains Nirvana.

Mahayana and Vajrayana Buddhists believe in stages of enlightenment as well. Sudden, quick flashes of insight into the nature of oneself is called *kensho,* which literally means "seeing one's nature." People who are practicing regularly can have *kensho* experiences at any stage of their practice. *Daikensho,* or *satori,* is a more powerful and all-encompassing, final enlightenment experience that leads to Nirvana. Satori experiences usually come after many years of dedicated practice.

The Arhat

Arhat means "worthy one" in Sanskrit. The arhat enters enlightened mind and escapes the pain and suffering of eternal rebirth, never to be reborn in any form again. Delusion is gone. Desire is gone. Suffering and pain in all forms are gone. "To such a one, travels in samsara there are not," The Dhammapada tells us of the arhat. "Of such a one pacified, released by proper understanding, calm is the mind, calm his speech and act."

During life the arhat will experience the state of Nirvana, entering and re-entering over time. Practice must be maintained even for the arhat, so the arhat will continue to walk the steps of the Eightfold Path throughout his or her life. In early Buddhist history, arhats were the preeminent disciples of the Buddha and were the patriarchs of the sangha after Shakyamuni's death.

FACT

While the Buddha was alive he picked out sixteen arhats to be the guardians of his teachings, protecting them until the coming of the next Buddha—Maitreya. These sixteen arhats (eighteen in China, as the Chinese added two more) are often depicted in Buddhist art. Supposedly the arhats would live indefinitely in their own paradises, waiting for the arrival of Maitreya.

Bodhisattvas

The bodhisattvas postpone eternal enlightenment in order to stay in the realm of samsara and help others to attain enlightenment. Through the development of *bodhicitta*—wisdom heart—the bodhisattva learns how best to help the student. It is the Mahayana belief that Nirvana and samsara are the same—even though the bodhisattvas are reborn they retain their enlightened status. Therefore, Nirvana can be found within samsara and it follows that enlightenment and life are the same. Enlightenment can be found in each moment. Enlightenment is, in fact, residing in the moment. For the bodhisattva, if the moment is experienced fully, there is no suffering, no desire, just the moment, and therefore the moment is Nirvana. It is this way that meditation was seen as experiencing Nirvana. The Theravada Buddhists believed in the system of the arhat, while the Mahayana Buddhist believed in the bodhisattvas. A Buddha has achieved full and perfect enlightenment. A Buddha has unique powers that enable him or her to use skillful means to free human beings to awaken themselves. Arhats are fully awakened but do not have the level of powers that a Buddha has attained. Bodhisattvas aspire to become Buddhas. A bodhisattva believes the path to Buddhahood is through the postponement of his or her own final enlightenment (paranirvana) until all the requisite qualities are perfected that would make the bodhisattva a Buddha.

Nirvana after Death

When the Buddha died he had his final Nirvana—paranirvana. What happens to an enlightened person after death? Does he get "blown out," "extinguished" as the Theravada Buddhist believes, like the arhat? Or does he still exist after death? The Buddha never answered this question. When asked about the possibilities of life after death he said asking such questions was like getting shot with an arrow and needing to know what make of arrow it was and where it was made before having someone pull it out of your body. In other words, there was so much to do at hand that asking questions—perhaps questions with no answers—was a waste of time, precious time you could be using to practice. You could die before you ever received the answers to such questions.

Besides, if the result of diligent practice is awakening to the fact that there is no self, then why would we expect to find a self after death when we found there was not a self in life? Ultimately we have no way of knowing until we get there. The answer to the question of what happens after death is beyond our comprehension.

The Buddha emphasized the importance of personal experience in practice, so perhaps he considered that he just didn't know the answer to what happens after death and would find out soon enough himself. As we all will.

> Nirvana is also known as enlightenment, thusness, buddhahood, enlightened mind, *daikensho*, awakening, and *satori*.

Embracing the reality of impermanence is an essential step on the path to enlightenment. In fact, there are directed meditations on death and impermanence. In Thich Nhat Hanh's book *The Miracle of Mindfulness*, he directs readers to meditate on the skeletons of their own bodies, envisioning the decomposition of flesh, and the disintegration of the very bones of the body. "See that your skeleton is not you," he writes. "Your bodily form is not you. Be at one with life. Live eternally in the trees and grass, in other people, in the birds and other beasts, in the sky, in the ocean waves . . . You are present everywhere and in every moment."

Whatever happens after death, Buddhists see death, as Karen Armstrong writes in *Buddha,* as "the supreme state of being and the final goal of humanity."

Nirvana versus Heaven

Nirvana is not Heaven. The Christian Heaven is a place of ultimate joy, where fulfillment is absolute. The Christian Heaven is a state in which one has the most powerful of all desires satisfied—the desire for God. In Heaven a person maintains a body and soul and the personal identity continues forever, in absolute joy and satisfaction. And finally, in Heaven one resides alongside God, forever in his grace.

Nirvana, on the other hand is a state noted by the absence of all desire. The body is gone, there is no soul, and there is no personal identity that continues forever.

In Nirvana, one disappears into the very essence and become one with the essence—you can call this God or true nature or the truth.

A brief comparison follows:

Heaven	Nirvana
Eternal soul	No soul
Reside with God	Disappear into God
Ultimate desires are fulfilled	Desires disappear
Eternal body	No body

There are heavens in Buddhist cosmology and these are wonderful places to be reborn where you can reside for very long periods of time, hundreds and hundreds of years. However, the ultimate attraction is Nirvana, and Nirvana can only be reached from the human form. Therefore, even though the Buddhist heavens are wonderful places to abide in, they are not the places from which one can reach Nirvana. Nirvana can only be reached from the human state, and therefore the human state is the most desirable state to inhabit.

FACT

Nirvana is often described as a "cooling" down. During the Fire Sermon, the Buddha said, "*Bhikkus,* all is burning!"—our desires set us on fire and only Nirvana will cool us down." In Christianity, Hell is illustrated as a fiery place of unbelievable heat and suffering. In Buddhism, fire is associated with desire and our own private hell. In Christianity, Hell comes after life. In Buddhism, sometimes hell is life.

What the Teachers Say about Nirvana

There are truly no words to describe Nirvana, but that doesn't mean we cannot try. Without some kind of grasping at an idea of what we are striving for it is hard to summon the faith to continue practice. Finding an enlightened teacher is a wonderful way of creating or affirming faith. This is what some of the great teachers and writers of Buddhism have had to say about Nirvana:

The Buddha: Nirvana is "the extinction of desire, the extinction of hatred, the extinction of illusion."

Walpola Rahula, *What the Buddha Taught:* "Nirvana is definitely no annihilation of self, because there is no self to annihilate. If at all, it is the annihilation of the illusion, of the false idea of self."

The Dalai Lama, *The Path to Tranquility:* "Enlightenment is the ending of rebirth, which means a complete nonattachment or non-identification with all thoughts, feelings, perceptions, physical sensation, and ideas."

David A. Cooper, *Silence, Simplicity, and Solitude:* "In many ways, the process of enlightenment is clearing away the thoughts, beliefs, and ideas that cloud our ability to see things as they really are in their pristine form."

B. Alan Wallace, *Tibetan Buddhism from the Ground Up:* "All we need to do is unveil our own nature, and we will find an inexhaustible source of wisdom, compassion, and power. It is nothing we need to acquire, from anywhere or anything. It has always been there."

Suzuki Roshi, "Enlightenment is not some good feeling or some particular state of mind. The state of mind that exists when you sit in the right posture, is, itself, enlightenment."

D. T. Suzuki, *Radiant Mind:* "Satori may be defined as an intuitive looking into the nature of things in contradistinction to the analytical or logical understanding of it. Practically, it means the unfolding of a new world hitherto unperceived in the confusion of a dualistically trained mind."

FACT

D. T. Suzuki was a Buddhist scholar, prolific author, and a philosopher of religion. He was instrumental in spreading Zen in the West. He died in 1966.

Samuel Bercholz, *Entering the Stream:* "Even at night the sun is shining, but then we can't see it because the earth is in the way, and probably our pillow also. The Buddha explained that behind the cloud cover of thoughts—including very heavy clouds of emotionally charged thoughts backed up by entrenched habitual patterns—there is continual warm, bright, loving intelligence constantly shining."

Dogen: "A person who gives rise to a real desire and puts his utmost efforts into study under a teacher will surely gain enlightenment."

Bodhidharma, *The Zen Teachings of Bodhidharma*, translated by Red Pine: "To attain enlightenment you have to see your nature. Unless you see your nature all this talk about cause and effect is nonsense. Buddhas don't practice nonsense. To say he attains anything at all is to slander a buddha. What could he possibly attain? Even focusing on a mind, a power, an understanding, or a view is impossible for a buddha. A buddha isn't one-sided. The nature of his mind is basically empty, neither pure nor impure. He's free of practice and realization. He's free of cause and effect."

Sixth Patriarch, *T'an-ching* in *The Way of Zen* by Alan Watts: "In this moment there is nothing which comes to be. In this moment there is nothing which ceases to be. Thus there is no birth-and-death to be brought to an end. Wherefore the absolute tranquility of (of Nirvana) is this present moment."

Enlightenment is a process. It can happen in flashes of insight but it grows out of our daily practice. We are either moving toward wisdom, through practice, or away from wisdom as our practice falters. Wisdom wanes as practice wanes. Nirvana is something we can work toward by practicing mindfulness and compassion.

But ultimately, there are no words to describe Nirvana, as it is beyond what we can know in our current state of being; it is beyond the conditioned states in which we abide. It is a state to be experienced, not talked about. For when we try to talk about Nirvana we talk about our own personal experiences and we talk about it through the vehicle of our smaller self, so in a sense our description of Nirvana becomes subjective. But Nirvana is spaceless, timeless, endless, accessible everywhere, and beyond all phenomena. As Ch'an master Mumon Ekai said, "It would be easier for a mute to explain his dreams." Ⓔ

Chapter 16

Ceremony and Celebration

Buddhists don't just sit around on pillows all the time meditating. They are out among the Christians, Jews, Hindus, atheists, agnostics, Muslims, and the rest of our world living their lives as well as their religions. This chapter looks at some of the ceremonies you can find in the Buddhist world, as well as some of the things the Buddhists might be celebrating.

Pilgrimages

A pilgrimage is a trip to a shrine or sacred place. A pilgrimage is much more than a holiday with a spiritual destination, but often changes the traveler in an irrevocable way. The Buddha made pilgrimages all over India, traveling from place to place, spreading his teachings. Today you can walk in the Buddha's footsteps and follow his path. If you are interested in experiencing some of the sacred places in the history of Buddhism you will have many to choose from.

A few of the more interesting pilgrimages are covered here—the four holy sites of Buddhism—but this coverage is hardly comprehensive. You can also visit Sri Lanka, Myanmar, Bhutan, China, Taiwan, Tibet, Thailand, Vietnam, Japan, Korea, and more. The Buddha himself may not have left footsteps in these countries, but Buddhist culture and history is rich and there are many wonderful places to experience.

Now might not be the best time to visit Sri Lanka. The Sri Lankan group Liberation Tigers of Tamil Eelam (LTTE) has been on the State Department list of foreign terrorist organizations since 1997. The U.S. government has issued travel restrictions to Sri Lanka. To check on travel advisability for U.S. citizens anytime, or to check on conditions in Sri Lanka specifically, go to the U.S. Department of State Travel Warnings Web site (listed in the bibliography).

FACT

The four holy sites of Buddhism are: Lumbini, the Buddha's birthplace; Bodhgaya, the site of enlightenment; Sarnath, the site of the First Sermon; and Kushinagara, where Buddha reached paranirvana.

Nepal

Nepal, the birthplace of the Buddha: What better place for a Buddhist pilgrimage? The Buddha was born in Lumbini, which is now in Nepal, where Vajrayana Buddhism is prevalent. Legend has it that Queen Maya was on her way to visit her parents when she gave birth to Siddhartha Gautama in Lumbini, Nepal. Places of interest to visit in Lumbini include

Lumbini Garden, which contains the Ashokan Pillar and the image of Queen Maya (Maya Devi); Puskarni, the sacred pool; Sanctum-Sanctorum of the Birthplace; and the Buddhist Temple. The Ashokan Pillar was erected by King Ashoka in homage to the Buddha and contains an inscription dedicating the site to the Shakyamuni. The image of Maya Devi is inscribed into a pagoda-like structure. The image itself is in bas-relief and pictures Maya holding onto the baby Buddha who is standing on a lotus petal. Puskarni is the sacred pool in which it is said that Maya bathed the baby Siddhartha soon after he was born. Sanctum-Sanctorum is the holiest of places in the garden—within the Sanctum-Sanctorum is a stone slab that marks the exact spot the Buddha was born. Also of interest is the nearby Buddhist Temple. And not too far from Lumbini is Kapilavastu, where Siddhartha's father, King Suddhodhana had his palace.

Kushinagara is the site of the Buddha's death. It is here in the Sala Grove that he reached paranirvana and passed into death. Places of interest in Kushinagara include the Nirvana Stupa, built over the spot where the Buddha died; the Makutabandhana Stupa, which marks the place of the Buddha's cremation; and a large stone reclining Buddha, housed in the Nirvana Temple.

These, Ananda, are the four places that a devout person should visit and look upon with feelings of reverence. And truly there will come to these places, Ananda, devoted monks and nuns, laymen and laywomen, reflecting: 'Here the Tathagata was born! Here the Tathagata became fully enlightened in unsurpassed, supreme Enlightenment!

—The Buddha

Sadly, the current situation in Nepal is not all that travel friendly. Just a few years ago it was a wonderful, peaceful, and safe place to visit but the recent Maoist insurgency in Nepal has increased dramatically. No American travelers have to this date been hurt, but things could change rapidly, so check the U.S. State Department's Travel Warnings before booking passage to Nepal.

◀ Swayambhunath, "The Monkey Temple," Kathmandu, Nepal

India

There are many equally wonderful places to visit in India. There is Bodhgaya, where Siddhartha sat in meditation under the Bodhi Tree and attained enlightenment. In the place where Siddhartha sat now sits the magnificent Mahabodhi Temple. You can also see a cave where Siddhartha practiced asceticism and the village of Uruvela, where the young Siddhartha broke his fast after attaining enlightenment.

Also a wonderful place to visit is Sarnath, several miles from Varanasi, where Buddha gave his First Sermon in the Deer Park—the turning of the Dharma Wheel. Sites of interest in Sarnath include Ashoka's Pillar (which used to have the Lion Capital on top of it that now resides in the Sarnath Museum), the ruins of the Mulagandhakuti, and the enormous Dharmek Stupa—a tower that dates back to the fifth or sixth century.

To the east is the modern Mulagandhakuti Vihara, which is said to house the original relics of the Buddha in the silver casket within. The casket was recovered from the ruins of the first-century temple. The temple has beautifully painted walls that depict the Buddha's life story. The Sarnath Museum is also not to be missed as it contains some of the greatest treasures of Indian Buddhist art. There is also an interesting archaeological museum and the remains of a monastery of the third century B.C.E.

FACT

One of the more well-known Buddhist pilgrims was Hsüan-tsang, a monk from eighth-century China who traveled vastly throughout central and southern Asia and spent many years in India and Sri Lanka studying Buddhism. Hsüan-tsang spent sixteen years in India on a pilgrimage. He studied at Nalanda University and visited all the important Buddhist pilgrimage sites.

Also of interest in India is Rajgir, the home of Vulture Peak, site of many of the Buddha's teachings.

It should be noted that at the time of this writing, the U.S. Department of State had lifted restrictions in India, but still recommended that Americans avoid travel to all border areas between India and Pakistan, including those regions within the border states of Gujarat, Punjab, and Rajasthan, and in all of the states of Jammu and Kashmir.

Giving It Away: Engaged Buddhism

The bodhisattva vows to help others to wake up—sacrificing his or her own paranirvana for the benefit of others. This spirit of giving is a large part of being a Buddhist—cultivating an open heart and practicing "random acts of kindness" as they say. In *Peace Is Every Step,* Thich Naht Hahn writes, "When I was in Vietnam, so many of our villages were being bombed. Along with my monastic brothers and sisters, I had to decide what to do. Should we continue to practice in our monasteries or should we leave the meditation halls in order to help the people who were suffering under the bombs? After careful reflection, we decided to do both—to go out and help people and to do so in mindfulness. We called it engaged Buddhism. Mindfulness must be engaged. Once there is seeing, there must be acting. Otherwise, what is the sense of seeing?"

So, Engaged Buddhism is getting out there and making the world a better place; it's connecting with other people and forming relationships. It's giving it away so you get it back. Once a Buddhist, through diligent practice, sees clearly that nothing is independent, that everything is connected, it becomes difficult to sit back and do nothing. "If anyone is hurting, I too am hurting" becomes the philosophy of the Buddhist. In fact, volunteering—helping other people—begins to seem a little selfish as so much is gotten back in return.

There are small ways to give and there are large ways to give. Practice both in your daily life. You can volunteer with an organization that helps the sick or the dying, such as Hospice or a cancer camp for children. You can work at a local homeless shelter, giving out meals or just listening to the residents who desperately need to be heard. You can donate your time to a shelter for battered women, an orphanage, or reading to children at your local library. You can smile at a stranger, talk to someone who needs a friend; you can *always* be a friend to those who need one. You can take time out for prisoners, the sick and suffering at your local hospital, a senior citizen center, or work with animals, such as saving strays from being euthanized.

You can also practice Engaged Buddhism by working toward promoting peace in the world. Buddhist Peace Fellowship is the oldest socially engaged Buddhist nonprofit organization in the United States. There is an environmentally aware group called Earth Sangha that encourages the practice of Buddhism as an answer to the global environmental crisis. There are gay and lesbian fellowships, women's support systems, Tibetan rescue groups, and more. There are as many ways to help as there are varieties of people in the world, so put out your hand, lend a smile, and roll up your sleeves. Celebrate life by improving the quality of someone else's life. Check in with your town center or your local library for information on volunteering in your community. You might find a happiness you never imagined in the joy of serving others.

Tea Ceremonies

Most Westerners think of tea as a pick-me-up, an after-meal beverage, or something with which you can sit back and relax. Most of us serve our tea in a cup with a bag and maybe a garnish of lemon and honey or a little bit of milk and sugar. In Zen Buddhism, tea is a ritual. Once you experience tea the Zen way, you will never look at a cup of tea quite the same way. Tea is ceremony itself.

FACT

Tea was originally used as a medicine, not a beverage. It was not only taken internally, but externally as well. Rubbing some tea in paste form on joints was thought to alleviate joint pain.

The tea ceremony is called *Chanoyu*. It translates into "hot water for tea." *Chanoyu* is based on the principles of respect, harmony, purity, and tranquility. If we could bring these qualities into our everyday life, our lives would be filled with utter peace. Everyone in the tearoom is equal, and great respect is paid to each person present. Everything in the tearoom matters, from the air you breathe to the flower arrangement to the actual space it is served in—everything must contribute to the enjoyment of each moment of the tea ceremony.

The rules for the tea ceremony are to be exactly followed. Each moment matters and the sequence of events is laid out rigidly. The ceremony flows, but there is meaning in every gesture and each moment is to be savored: the tea ceremony is the way of life itself. It captures the essence of Zen: life in the moment, with each moment lived fully and with great attention. In this regard, the tea ceremony is a mindfulness meditation. It is a moving meditation, practiced while in deep samadhi. The repetition and rigidity of action allows the you to enter a deep meditative state as you know each movement coming your way. As you perform each part of the ceremony you do so with utter mindfulness, paying careful attention to each and every movement. When you whisk, you whisk. When you pour, you pour. When you drink, you drink.

In *The Book of Tea* by Okakura Kakuzo, the author tells us that there are actually schools of tea. These schools can be classified as Boiled

Tea, Whipped Tea, and Steeped Tea. We in the West would fall into the latter category. Caked tea is boiled, powdered tea is whipped, and leaf tea is steeped.

In the liquid amber within the ivory-porcelain, the initiated may touch the sweet reticence of Confucius, the piquancy of Lao-Tzu, and the ethereal aroma of Shakyamuni himself.

—Okakura Kakuzo

Vocabulary

First we introduce the vocabulary of the tea ceremony so you can familiarize yourself with it. The tea ceremony takes place in the *chashitsu*—a room designed for the tea ceremony. This room is usually in the tea house itself, which is usually within the gardens. Here are some other words you will want to familiarize yourself with:

- *Sayu*—hot water with which to make tea.
- *Furo*—brazier (a pan for holding hot or burning coals).
- *Chabana*—tea flower arrangement.
- *Fukusa*—a cleansing cloth, usually a square of silk, folded into a triangle, which hangs from the host's sash.
- *Kama*—a container for boiling water (kettle).
- *Kashi*—sweet candy snack.
- *Mizusashi*—container for cold water.
- *Chawan*—tea bowl.
- *Chakin*—napkin.
- *Chashaku*—scoop for tea.
- *Chaki*—tea container.
- *Kensui*—water waste container with *futaoki* (lid rest).
- *Hishaku*—water ladle.

In order to have a tea ceremony, you will also need the tea and the charcoal for the fire.

Procedure

The guests are greeted by the host and ushered into the tearoom. The guests take their seats and the *kashi* is served and eaten. The *kama* has been set on the *furo* so that the water can boil. Then the host brings items necessary to start preparation of the tea. First he brings over the tea bowl containing the wiping napkin, the whisk, the tea scoop, and the container holding the tea. He then brings over the waste water container, which holds the lid rest and the water ladle. The lid rest should be placed near the kettle with the water ladle on top of it. The lid rest is used to hold the lid of the kettle and is usually made of green bamboo. Now the host is ready to start preparations.

▲ Thangka (see Chapter 18)

The host takes the *fukusa* and wipes the tea scoop and the tea container. This is done with intense concentration as the host's focus on meditation increases. This cleansing gesture signifies to the guests that everything is clean and the host cares about the cleanliness and purity of his service. Taking the ladle in hand, he scoops hot water out of the kettle and pours it into the tea bowl, and the whisk is then rinsed in the water. The water is then poured into the waste water container, the bowl is cleaned with the wiping cloth, and the cloth is put back in its place. Now the tea can be made.

QUESTION?

Where did tea originate?
According to several sources, tea is thought to be nearly 5,000 years old. It is said that a Chinese emperor—Shen Nung, who was a scholar and herbalist—discovered tea in 2737 B.C.E., when a wind gust blew some tea leaves into a kettle of boiling water. The English are traditionally known for being big tea drinkers, but they have only been drinking tea for 350 years!

The tea used in the tea ceremony is powdered tea, so it has to be whipped. The host picks up the tea container in his left hand and the scoop in his right, and puts three scoops of tea into the tea bowl from the tea container. The water ladle is filled nearly to the brim with hot water, and enough water is added to the tea to make a paste. More water is added as necessary to get the correct consistency for the tea. The tea is briskly whisked, and then the host picks up the tea bowl and places it on top of his left palm. He holds the right side of the bowl with his right hand, then turns it twice away from himself, a full turn of the wrist each time, so that the front of the bowl is facing away from the host. Then the tea bowl is placed in front of the guests, and the first guest picks up the bowl and holds it the same way.

The first guest to pick up the bowl will turn to the next guest, *gassho,* and offer the tea bowl. The guest will bow back and decline. Then she will *gassho* to the host, pick up the bowl and hold it in the same way. She raises it a little bit while bowing again to show gratitude, then turns the bowl toward herself. She then drinks from the side of the bowl.

She wipes off the bowl with her thumb and finger and then turns the bowl back to the front. She admires the craftsmanship of the bowl—tea bowls are a work of art and the choosing of the tea bowl is part of the beauty of the ceremony—and returns the bowl to the host, turning it so the front of the bowl faces the host. Before she returns the bowl, she can ask questions about the bowl, such as "Where was this bowl made?" and "Does this bowl have a name?" The host pours water into the tea bowl, swirling it around to cleanse the bowl, then pours the water into the waste water container.

The process is repeated for the next guest. When the last guest has had tea, the host cleans the tea bowl with the cold water and reverses the process. In the winter and spring months, a *ro* (a sunken hearth) is used instead of the *furo,* which is used the rest of the year so that the tearoom does not get uncomfortably hot.

This is a bare bones explanation of the tea ceremony, and some of the finer points have been glossed over. For instance, the tea guests are often served light snacks, such as cakes or figs, and conversation often takes place throughout the ceremony. If you are interested in learning more, you can often take classes on tea ceremonies at a university in your area, or perhaps visit a monastery for instruction. Also see the bibliography for resources on the tea ceremony.

FACT

To illustrate the difference in calendar years we can look at the Thai calendar. Calendars in Thailand are calculated from the Buddha's death. The Buddha died in 543 B.C.E., so therefore the year 2003 in Thailand is 2546.

Holidays

A Buddhist likes to celebrate as much as the next guy, and while there might not be a Buddhaclause, there are many traditions and celebrations worth noting. However, dates of holidays vary from country to country and the different vehicles and traditions of Buddhism celebrate different festivals and holidays. For example, the Mahayana Buddhists honor different bodhisattvas throughout the year. However, because the holiday dates change depending on which country you are in and which calendar is being used (for instance, the Japanese do not use the lunar calendar, but use the Gregorian calendar), a listing of holidays is provided but frequently not the time of year they might be celebrated.

The Buddhist Festival

A typical Buddhist festival day starts off with a visit to a local monastery. Food is very often taken as an offering for the monks, who in return might give a dharma talk. While at the monastery, visitors might affirm the Five Precepts, pray, and meditate.

The monasteries and various local Buddhist organizations will perform acts of generosity (called *dana*) within the community, such as visiting and providing for those in need, freeing caged animals, donating blood, providing transportation, medical care, and so on. Laypeople will commit acts of merit, such as feeding the poor or helping the needy. In the evening a visit to a stupa often takes place, where practitioners make three walking circles around the stupa to signify respect for Buddha, sangha, and dharma.

Sampling of Celebrated Days

This listing is by no means exhaustive. There are many days of celebration and festivities in a Buddhist calendar year, but here are some of the more important ones. The most important holiday of the year in Buddhism is Buddha Day. On Buddha Day, which usually falls on the first full moon in May (but as mentioned above changes from country to country), the birth, death, and enlightenment of Shakyamuni Buddha is celebrated. Buddha Day is also called Vesak, which is the Indian month Buddha Day falls on.

Buddhists have a Buddhist New Year celebration. However, it is not usually celebrated on the first day of January. Different traditions have a different time of year to celebrate the New Year, again depending on their calendar. For example, Theravada Buddhists will celebrate the New Year in April. People in Cambodia, Laos, Myanmar, Sri Lanka, Thailand, and parts of Indonesia will all be observing with festivals and sometimes water fights (if you're in Thailand and you are a tourist, watch out!—you might be a special target for good, but wet, fun). Mahayana Buddhist countries tend to celebrate the New Year in January, and in Tibet in February.

▲ *Om mani padme hum*, a meditation

Here are some other Buddhist celebrations:

* Birthday of Maitreya, the coming Buddha.
* Magha Puja Day (Sangha Day).
* Birthday of Avalokiteshvara.
* Asalha Puja Day (Dharma Day): marks the turning of the Dharma Wheel (or First Sermon).
* Ploughing Day: celebrating the day of Buddha's first moment of awakening—when he was a child sitting in the fields watching the plowing.
* Ullambana Day (Ancestor Day): celebrating the time period where the gates of hell open and ghosts visit for fifteen days.

There are of course, many other celebrations and ceremonies in a Buddhist's life. Birth and marriage will be considered in the next chapter, as well as rites of passage, and how Buddhists handle deaths in the family.

Practical Matters: Know Thy Neighbor

So what if you want to have your Buddhist friend over for dinner? Are there any practical restrictions you should be aware of? Well, for one, there's a good chance your friend might be a vegetarian, so you might want to ask if he or she eats fish, dairy, eggs, or flesh of any kind. Also, don't expect your friend to imbibe along with you. He or she will not partake of any alcoholic beverages, so bar-hopping after the meal is pretty much out of the question.

Also you might want to keep in mind that a Buddhist strives to live the Middle Way. Gluttony of any sort is not living life in the moderation. A Buddhist will try not to overindulge no matter how wonderful the repast in front of him or her. So if your dinner guest declines a second helping, don't take it too seriously. Also know that it's very possible if you do serve meat to a vegetarian Buddhist, your guest just might eat it anyway. Don't get upset if you discover this later. You guest might be practicing equanimity and nonattachment. (E)

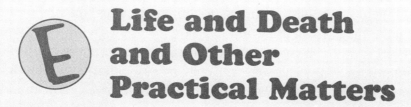

Chapter 17

Life and Death and Other Practical Matters

Children, education, marriage, aging, and death are as much a part of Buddhist life as they are a part of any of our lives. But we can see from the history of Buddhism and the teachings of the Buddha that not much about the rituals surrounding these times of our lives has been mentioned.

Children and Practice

Babies are not born Buddhist in Buddhism. Parents train their children in the dharma, teaching them the skills of meditation and mindfulness, the ethical precepts, moral codes, and so on. The children will take refuge in the Three Jewels when and if they decide to do so. There is no passing of the religion through the parents to the children, as in some of the other great religions of the world.

There is no baptism or naming ceremony, no monastic intervention in the birth of the baby whatsoever. Family is very important in Buddhist life but as there is no central Buddhist office, church, or higher authority, Buddhism does not have much to do with family ritual. Families are a secular matter and not a matter of monastic relevance. Everything falls to the individual and each person's enlightenment is his or her own responsibility. But Buddhism nonetheless infiltrates the daily life and spirit of the Buddhist family as the family practices together.

QUESTION?

How old should a child be when starting a meditation practice?
Young children have trouble sitting still. Forcing them to sit still for long periods of time is probably an exercise in futility or unnecessary punishment. However, as they age into preteens and young adults, you can always ask them to join your seated meditation practice, starting out with very short periods of time.

Children can be wonderful teachers of the dharma. They—more than most people—have the ability to live life in the moment, and they can bring us to mindfulness very quickly as well. A child's temper tantrum can be a key time to practice. A screaming, kicking, frustrated baby can push us to be mindful and loving when perhaps we would like to scream and kick back. A child's joy in the world is inspiring and children as well as animals can be powerful teachers in the household. A dog is so happy to see its owner every single morning. As soon as the household rises from bed the dog is wagging its tail, licking and wiggling, excited to begin a new day. Each day also holds great wonder for a child and we can learn from this openness and welcoming attitude. A child sees everything as new. We can learn to see the world again through watching our children and our pets experience its wonders. They teach us to be mindful.

FACT

The Buddha had a son named Rahula (which interestingly enough means "fetter" in Sanskrit). Although Siddhartha left his family when his son was an infant to search for the spiritual truth, he did return soon after his enlightenment and welcomed Rahula back into his life. Rahula followed in his father's footsteps and eventually became a fully ordained monk.

Children also teach us the daily lesson of impermanence as they grow before our very eyes, changing on a daily basis. From cradle to crawling, babbling to talking, they teach us to let go and live in the present, relishing the day as each one falls away.

As Buddhism moved West the problem of how to simultaneously maintain a meditation practice and raise a family became a pressing issue. Where could parents find the time to dedicate to their practice if they had young children to care for? As James William Coleman tells us in *The New Buddhism,* Western Buddhist centers have not done a satisfactory job of providing for children so their parents can practice. Some have offered limited child care to encourage parents to practice, but even those are few and far between.

Parents come up with creative solutions, such as sharing child care time with other families who practice. But as Buddhism moves away from monastic focus and laypeople get more and more involved with Buddhist monasteries and centers, a solution will have to emerge that frees up parents to practice and concurrently satisfies them of their children's well-being.

Rites of Passage

All spiritual traditions have their rites of passages such as bar mitzvahs and confirmations. Buddhism is no exception, but traditions vary from school to school and country to country.

According to Gary Gach in *The Complete Idiot's Guide to Understanding Buddhism,* in Thailand and Myanmar young men become monks as a rite of passage and live a monastic life for at least three months, while Tibetan children are given a herd of yaks to take care of. In the West programs are being developed for children as Buddhism comes of age in this part of the world and children become an active part of the Buddhist community.

Education

Although you don't meet American children who are going to "Buddhist" school as you do children who are going to Catholic schools, Buddhism has always had a strong foundation and history in encouraging education. At the very heart of Buddhism is mind-to-mind transmission and the profound relationship of the student with his or her teacher. The Buddha himself encouraged his disciples to find out everything for themselves and to take no one else's word for the truth—to pursue education for themselves. He believed the truth is to be found in personal experience. So Buddhism at its very bones encourages education and the search for truth. It is an educational system aimed at helping us to learn about our own buddha-nature and gain wisdom in our lives.

When Buddhism reached China it became apparent to the Chinese government officials that Buddhism had much in common with the prevalent tradition of Confucianism. A ministry was soon after created that was in charge of Buddhist education in China. So there was a Confucian educational system as well as a Buddhist educational system. The Buddhist educational system took off and spread across the country quickly. Within the Buddhist learning centers—the temples—one could find books on all different traditions, and not just on Buddhism. The monks encouraged learning that went beyond Buddhism and the Buddhist educational system began to take over the traditional educational system in China.

Buddhist educational facilities provided educational opportunities across Asia. That tradition continues in the West to this day. Today, Naropa University in Boulder, Colorado, is based on Nalanda University, the ancient Indian university. The mission statement of Naropa University affirms its intention to promote awareness of the moment through intellectual, artistic, and meditative disciplines; create and foster a learning community that reveals wisdom; cultivate communication; stay true to the origins of the original Nalanda University; encourage integration of modern culture with ancient wisdom; and remain nonsectarian and "open to all." The Buddhist educational system seems to be as alive today as it was thousands of years ago.

▲ Inside a Buddhist temple

Visiting Monasteries

When laypeople visit monasteries they often wonder how they can be respectful and what behavior is expected of them. Although many people are curious as to what goes on in a Buddhist monastery and would like to speak with the monks or watch a meditation session, they are afraid they will be pestered for donations or pressured to "convert."

However, you could say that Buddhism, like twelve-step programs, is a program of attraction rather than promotion. Buddhists do not try to convert others to Buddhism. They might speak enthusiastically of their personal practices if asked, but it is highly unlikely that you would be solicited for money or anything else at a monastery or through mail, e-mail, or other means. A small donation might be suggested at certain monasteries, much like a museum will have a suggested donation box in the admission area. However, taking human nature into consideration, nothing is impossible.

FACT

If you visit a monastery it is customary to take a small offering, such as a bouquet of flowers or an offering of food.

Most monasteries welcome visitors and most visits are free of charge. Classes, retreats, and lectures might charge something to cover meals, lodging, and instruction. Weekend or week-long retreats might also charge a nominal fee to cover expenses. Some monasteries have stores where they sell art, meditation supplies, and clothing to help generate money to support the monastery. Most sitting sessions will be free of charge. Check the Internet for a monastery near you if you would like to visit and you can probably find information on the site that will put you at ease before you visit. Call ahead or e-mail with any questions you might have.

Marriage

Buddhism has long been silent on the subject of marriage. There are no great romantic figures in Buddhist history, as there are in other great religions. There are no Samsons and Delilahs, no Muhammads and Khadijahs. In Buddhist countries marriage is considered a secular affair and therefore there is no turning to your monk or religious figure for a marriage ceremony. Perhaps this is due to Buddhism's strong monastic tradition. However, it is common for couples to turn to a monk for a blessing after their civil ceremony has been performed.

In the United States, a Buddhist monk, lama, or other Buddhist officiant can perform a marriage ceremony, depending on the laws of the state. Check your local marriage laws to verify that a Buddhist officiant is allowable before doing so. However, as there are not Buddhist marriage ceremonies within the Buddhist tradition, you might make up your own ceremony with the input of a Buddhist monk, Zen priest, teacher, or similar religious figure. If you do decide to create a marriage ceremony, make sure you adhere to local marriage laws and cover all the necessary requirements for your state. A Buddhist blessing on a civil ceremony is still a lovely alternative.

In a Buddhist wedding ceremony the couple might affirm their commitment to the Three Jewels of Buddha, dharma, and sangha. They might vow to support each other on the path toward enlightenment. But two Buddhists getting married will have a different outlook than perhaps a typical Western outlook toward romance and marriage. The Buddhist will consider him- or herself essentially alone on the path toward enlightenment. There is no ideal of two halves becoming a whole. Each person moves down the path alone with the company of the other, but it is up to the individual to live the precepts, to practice the ethical principles of Buddhist life. Buddhism does not encourage marriage or discourage marriage but it will lend advice on how to live a good married life.

If on the path you don't meet your equal, it's best to travel alone. There's no fellowship with fools.

—Dhammapada

In most Buddhist countries, marriages are arranged by the parents of the bride and groom. The parents are thought to have more life experience and be better judges of a good partnership for their children. The marriage is also seen as a co-joining of two families, so the parents want some control over the future of their family.

The Buddha left his wife and his son and hit the road in an effort to end suffering and find release from the pain of old age and loss. Buddhists could be said to view romantic love as suffering as all desire leads to suffering. But Buddhist marriages can be filled with compassion and friendship and a pure devotion to the other person. Living the precepts will ensure a household of ethical strength, honesty, and faithfulness. A couple sharing a Buddhist practice can know true intimacy and friendship and a bond as strong as any other. However, if one were to wonder if the Buddha was against marriage you would only need to turn to the Maha Mangala Sutra (the Blessings sutra), which tells us that: "To support one's father and mother; to cherish one's wife and children, and to be engaged in peaceful occupations—this is the highest blessing."

Buddhism and Sex

It's not difficult to figure out that sex wasn't high on the Buddha's list of things to do with your spare time. According to the Four Noble truths, desire is suffering and the way to end suffering is to end desire. Naturally, sexual desire would fall into this category. However, as Buddhism changed and spread, the attitudes toward sex ranged from conservative to liberal and back again. The monastic tradition in Buddhism encouraged celibacy—sexual activity for a monk or nun would be distracting. Though, as history tells us, not all monks and masters agreed that sex was forbidden fruit.

FACT

Zen Master Ikkyu, who lived from 1394–1481, was an eccentric and mischievous Zen monk. He frequented brothels and wine houses, saying (according to John Stevens in *Lust for Enlightenment*), "Follow the rule of celibacy blindly and you are not more than an ass. Break it and you are only human."

The ideal of the arhat was based on a life of celibacy and devotion to practice. For many years the tradition in Buddhism was for monks and nuns to remain celibate for life. However, as Buddhism spread and laypeople became more involved in practice the emphasis on celibacy shifted in some traditions and practice. While remaining celibate can certainly free a person's energy—energy that could then be devoted to practice—it wasn't always convenient or practical for people to forgo a sexual life. As we have seen with the recent scandals in the Catholic Church, celibacy in religious life might not be working out all that well.

The Asian ideal of a celibate monastic didn't weather the journey West very well. When Buddhist teachers increasingly headed West in the mid part of the twentieth century, they found an America where sexual freedom was the new game in town. Getting people to restrict themselves in a time of newfound liberation was not easy and not feasible. But impermanence is a fact of life—the sixties and seventies ended and the eighties brought AIDS awareness and a tendency toward sexual conservatism once again.

There is not a standard set of sexual behaviors that all Buddhists would agree upon. For instance, Zen teachers in the United States are often married with families. And some Tibetan monks are celibate while others practice tantric sex. Tantric sex takes sexual activity and transforms it into a spiritual practice where the partners practice meditation while engaging in sexual behavior. Tantric sex is a ritual thought to bring about strong states of awareness and to heighten practice. However, it is supposedly reserved for those who are extremely advanced in their practice. The sexual activities themselves are shrouded in secrecy, although many books on the shelves of your local bookstore will purport to teach you the secrets of tantric sex.

The precept is clear: Do not engage in sexual misconduct. However, it is ultimately up to the individual to define what constitutes sexual conduct for him- or herself.

Women in Buddhism

Like most of recorded history, the early years of Buddhism report few stories of women. The Buddha's mother is mentioned but she died soon after Siddhartha was born. He was then raised by his aunt, his mother's sister, Prajapati. In fact, it was Prajapati who, after the Buddha's enlightenment, went to Shakyamuni and asked him if the women could also join the sangha. She was refused by Shakyamuni but persisted, asking a second time, and then a third. But Shakyamuni was unmovable and denied his good aunt's request.

Prajapati cut off her hair and donned the yellow robes of the mendicant monks. She followed the Buddha and pleaded with him to allow women to become members of the sangha.

It wasn't until Ananda interfered on Prajapati's behalf that the Buddha finally relented, saying, in answer to Ananda's questions, that although he did believe women were equal to men as regards to the ability to attain enlightenment, practical matters kept him from agreeing that it was a good idea to allow them into the community. However, he did say yes and women were subsequently permitted to give up their worldly lives and enter as members of the sangha. Five hundred women joined Prajapati, including Yasodhara, the Buddha's abandoned wife. However, the women were given eight rules they had to follow that separated them from the monks and made them subordinate to their male counterparts.

FACT

Buddhism also has its darker side. Chögyam Trungpa, the famous Tibetan founder of the Naropa Institute, was the center of a sexual scandal, which extended to his dharma heir, Osel Tendzin.

All religions are products of their time and Buddhism could be as sexist as the next, but the Mahayana texts support the Buddha's statement that men and women were equally equipped for enlightenment, and most traditions in Buddhism have included nuns *(bhikkunis)*. But Buddhist literature portrays the difficulties the men had accepting the women as part of monastic life. Women were portrayed as seductresses and unclean creatures—most likely due to men's unfulfilled sexual drives and inability to stave off lust and desire. But women struggled in Buddhism as they have struggled in most other religions. For many years and in many traditions in Buddhist history women were proclaimed to be equal in theory but were in fact subordinate in practice. Theravada was the hardest on women, followed by Mahayanan, and finally Vajrayana, where many of the tantric deities were women. As late as 1979, Irish-American Maureen "Soshin" O'Halloran wrote home to America to tell her family that she was the first woman ever admitted to Toshoji Temple in Japan.

In the West today a great percentage of the teachers of Buddhism are women. Great teachers such as Pema Chödrön, Charlotte Joko Beck, Sharon Salzberg, and Maurine Stuart have strengthened the halls of centers and monasteries, lending their wisdom to the growing community of women who practice. There is little sexist language to be found in modern Buddhist Zen centers, few male-dominated hierarchies, and no gender specific god. The journey to equality has not been completed, but Buddhism has come a long way for women.

Death

We don't deal well with death in the United States. There almost seems to be a belief that we can escape death: It is not a highly developed part of our culture and our psyches. Our death rituals are inadequate compared to other countries—often after a sudden death we are at a loss as to what to do, how to proceed—and we tend to shy away from talking about death as if it is something to be hidden and swept under the carpet—as if we can get away from death by ignoring its presence.

Buddhism asks us to consider our death daily. Our meditations on impermanence are meditations on death. Buddha used to encourage his disciples to sit with the dead, with the rotting and decomposing corpses, so that the nature of impermanence would be understood and experienced. In Zen we would be told to "Die on the cushion."

Buddhism encourages us to face death as a part of life. Tibetan Buddhism has the Tibetan Book of the Dead, which is a study of death and the stages one goes through.

The Tibetans believe there are forty-nine days between lives, forty-nine days in which the living read from the Tibetan Book of the Dead to help the dead gain insight and move away from the attachments of the body.

Buddhism teaches us that we die every day, moment by moment. Things come up and they pass away. The moment is here, and then it is gone. A wonderful dinner is in front of us, then eaten, then gone. The date you were waiting for so eagerly comes and then passes. Your child grows right before your very eyes. Your puppy is a 100-pound watchdog before you know it. Spring turns to summer to autumn to winter. Death is change, and we face change every day. Buddhists see death as just another transformation. Impermanence is the nature of the world.

Sleep itself is like death. We disappear into the night and wake up a new person. Our moods come and go. Our troubles rise and fall, as do our happinesses—all of it a meditation on death and transformation. Buddhists believe that if they are aware and in the moment when death comes to take them they will be open to enlightenment and might be better prepared to move ahead into final enlightenment or to progress on the bodhisattva path.

The Buddha started his search for the truth after having an encounter with death. As he saw the sick and dying outside his palace gates, and a corpse being carried through the streets, he realized that all that was beautiful comes to an end and death is inevitable. This realization was the catalyst that sent him out into the world in search of the truth and in search of a way to transcend what he saw as suffering.

FACT

The Bardö Thodol (the Tibetan Book of the Dead) was passed down orally for centuries. It was first put into written form by Padmasambhava in the eighth century C.E.

If we live with the deep knowledge of our impending death, the moment becomes precious and the day becomes filled with wonder. So many people when given the news of terminal illness say they realize the joy of life as soon as the reality of death becomes clear to them. Working with the sick and dying can bring this truth home to us on a daily basis. Death meditation practice can be a powerful way to keep us aligned with the present and alive in the moment, aware that everything can change.

And so we can see that the practices in Buddhism remain steady from birth through death. Buddhists, Muslims, Christians, Jews, and every person from every religion shares the commonality of birth and death. Buddhism stresses how everything is connected and we are all the same. Buddhism preaches tolerance and educates children to be open-minded.

As we look at the life practices of Buddhists we are apt to see more common threads than differences when comparing it to other belief systems. At heart all of our life practices are the same—to live our lives in the present, to live them well and honorably, to teach our children values that reflect honor and compassion, and to learn how to love. And, finally, to learn how to die gracefully, to help one another die with dignity.

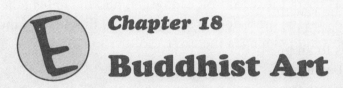

Chapter 18

Buddhist Art

All of the great religions have inspired some amazing works of art. Christianity inspired Michelangelo to paint the ceiling of the Sistine Chapel. Islam spawned exquisite mosques with tile work that can take your breath away, such as the work in the Taj Mahal. Buddhism has also inspired some beautiful artwork. From architecture to *thangkas*, mandalas to statuary, Buddhist art can be found all over the world.

Art Practice

Buddhist art is approached the same way everything in Buddhism is approached—with whole body, mind, and spirit. There is no separation between artist and art—the artist is the work of art and the work of art is the artist. To perceive separation in artist and art is to use the mind and once the mind is used, the small self is engaged and the enlightened mind is gone. When the artist does a sand painting, the artist *is* the sand painting and the sand painting is the artist. No division exists.

> When you paint Spring, do not paint willows, plums, peaches, or apricots, but just paint Spring. To paint willows, plums, peaches, or apricots is to paint willows, plums, peaches, or apricots—it is not yet painting Spring.
>
> —Dogen

Architecture

The beginning of Buddhist architecture can be traced by to King Ashoka in the third century B.C.E. Ashoka built great stupas and pillars in tribute to the Buddha. Two of the most famous pillars are the one at Sarnath that used to house the Lion Capital and the one in the Lumbini Gardens. Both are mentioned in Chapter 16. There are more incredible works of Buddhist architecture than can be listed here, but some of the more outstanding ones deserved special mention. Among the great works of Buddhist architecture are the various stupas and the cave temples of Ajanta.

Stupas

The Buddha died in 543 B.C.E. and his remains were quickly taken for custodial protection by King Ajatasattu of Magadha, India. According to legend, the king divided the remains into eight portions and gave each piece to one of eight different kings to protect and cherish. Each king was directed to build a stupa to house the remains, and these stupas were erected all over India and present-day Nepal.

When the Buddha was cremated, rulers from various kingdoms came quickly to reclaim the relics of his body. Arguments ensued but a Brahmin named Dona was quick to quell the disagreement. His clever speech convinced the kings to divide the relics between them and build stupas to honor the holy Buddha.

King Ashoka was thought to have opened up seven of the eight stupas and relocated the relics of the Buddha to structures that he subsequently had built. The Hill of Sanchi, one of the most well-known Buddhist stupas, is one of Ashoka's most famous creations.

The Hill of Sanchi is a group of Buddhist monuments. The foundation was laid by Ashoka but was later damaged, rebuilt, and added to over the centuries. When two of the stupas on the Hill of Sanchi were excavated in the nineteenth century several of the relic caskets were recovered. Today relics of the Buddha are scattered and appear in China, Burma, Sri Lanka, India, and elsewhere—fingers, teeth, hair, and bone have all been preserved. Three stupas at Sanchi have been recovered.

Another of the greatest works of architecture in Buddhist history is the Borobudur Temple, a Buddhist work of stone wonder standing in the gardens of Java, Indonesia. The size of the temple is awe-inspiring, with nearly 200,000 square feet of lava rock. The temple is composed of six rectangular terraces. The top of the structure contains three more circular terraces and a spire stupa forms the top. The temple is thought to have been the Buddhist cultural center in the seventh and eighth centuries.

It is a massive structure overlooking the misty mountains and green valleys of Java.

Believe it or not, the whole structure is in the form of a lotus, the symbol of Buddhism.

It also represents the Buddhist cosmos, with realms of Desire, Form, and Formlessness depicted from bottom to top. The lowest level of the structure has 160 carved panels illustrating the joys and horrors of life in the Realm of Desire. There are more than 1,400 scenes in all from top to bottom, with ninety-two Buddha statues for each direction. The structure is a marvel of devotion and endurance. Borobudur has been used for devotional practice for centuries—one can walk around the terraces while meditating, walking clockwise until you reach the top.

The Cave Temples of Ajanta

In Western India you can find the cave temples of Ajanta. These "caves" are actually man-made structures carved out of living rock. Hsüan-tsang, the famous Chinese Buddhist pilgrim who traveled in India for sixteen years, first wrote about the Ajanta caves in the eighth century C.E. The caves were originally used as dwelling and meeting houses for Buddhists. Frescoes decorate the cave walls. There are approximately thirty such temple caves, some created as early as 200 B.C.E., and some as late as the seventh century. It is not known who painted the brilliantly depicted scenes from the Buddha's life and from the Jataka tales, but they are on a large scale with wonderful colors and lines. The caves were rediscovered by the British in 1817.

FACT

There are 547 Jataka tales, which are children's stories that tell of the Buddha and his disciples and their past lives as humans as well as animals. They are moral tales, helping the reader to understand karma, forgiveness, and similar Buddhist life themes. The tales were transmitted orally for centuries and are believed to be a part of the original Pali canon.

Buddhist Statuary and Images

The image of the Buddha is familiar worldwide. The first images of the Buddha appeared during the reign of King Kanishka during the first century, greatly influenced by the Hellenic art coming out of Central Asia. The Buddha image conveys serenity and calm. The proportions of the Buddha are always ideal. Though there is some variation in measurement and scale from school to school and country to country, most Buddha images have the following characteristics.

- The top of the Buddha's head has a raised area that symbolizes enlightened mind.
- The hands and the feet are equal in length and scale.
- The nose is long, straight, and noble.
- There is a mark in the center of the forehead—the Eye of Wisdom.
- The ears are elongated.

Buddha images portray grace and great beauty. One of the most famous Buddha images is Wat Pho: The Temple of the Reclining Buddha, in Thailand. The gold-plated reclining Buddha is more than 150 feet long and 49 feet high and represents the Buddha's paranirvana. The temple grounds contain more than 1,000 Buddha images scattered around.

◀ Laughing Buddha

Sand Paintings and Mandalas

A sand painting is exactly what it sounds like—a painting in the sand. Sand paintings represent the impermanence of all things. Mandalas, as covered earlier, are maps of the spiritual world. They are usually represented in artwork as a graphic of a symbolic pattern. The pattern is usually in the form of a circle with intricate designs within. The patterns are representative of the sacred place where the Buddha or deity abides. They are used for contemplation and meditation and are designed to awaken spiritual potential.

Sand paintings are often mandalas. They are created by Tibetan lamas to promote healing in the environment or in people. Sand paintings are made with vegetable-dyed sand, flowers, herbs, grains, stone, and sometimes jewels. A platform is laid out and the sand and other materials are placed on the platform over a period of time. The sand painting takes some time to complete and the process is a meditation for the lama creating it. Once the platform is in place the lama will start a healing ceremony that blesses the area. When the sand painting is finished, it is destroyed, representing the impermanence of all things.

FACT

Native Americans are also known for their sand painting mandalas. Many similarities can be found between the Navajo sand paintings and the Tibetan sand paintings. Both contain images of the cosmos in a circular form.

Thangkas

Thangkas are paintings. They are often done on canvas and turned into scrolls, framed in silk, and hung from a dowel. The dowel can be made of wood with decorative metal knobs on the ends. *Thangkas* are also often mandalas. They depict images of different deities, such as the bodhisattva Avalokiteshvara or any of the numerous Tibetan deities. As compared to sand painting mandalas, *thangkas* are a more permanent art form. They are often used as meditative devices and are hung by the altar.

Gardens

Gardening itself can be an act of meditation. Dropping the boundaries of the self seems more possible with hands immersed in earth and head exposed to the elements.

When we garden we connect with our environment in a powerful way. We become intimate with the cycle of life. We notice the change in the seasons and how each season is hard to define—spring starts in winter with buds showing through the snow, and the summer leaves start to fall sometimes as early as June or July. The insects have their own life cycles and agendas, and in watching the earthworms and the ants, we see a larger pattern to life. We see the interconnection of the roots and the soil, the creatures and rain. We eat that which we have grown ourselves and feel connected to the earth in a way we have never known before. Gardening is a meditative act and an affirmation of life.

Who is the fat, laughing Buddha?
The coming Buddha, Maitreya, is usually represented as a fat, jolly, laughing Buddha.

QUESTION?

Sit in a garden and practice breath meditation. Moments of enlightenment come to you as you drop yourself and bleed into your environment. Lose yourself in the sound of the birds, the delicate tapping of the rain on leaves. Hear the movement of water and the swish of a gentle breeze. If we lose our environment, we lose an integral part of ourselves and an opportunity to connect with life in a powerful and transformative way. Anyone who spends time outdoors knows the connection between every living thing on earth.

The earth itself is a work of art—the colors, the textures, the sensory depth.

Japanese gardens are some of the most exquisite gardens to be found. They grace many of our city parks. Their simplicity, stark beauty, and serenity are moving and they inspire peace. For centuries, Japanese Zen masters created gardens out of rocks and sand, raking the sand into patterns that could be destroyed quickly, emphasizing the impermanence of all things. These gardens were used for contemplation. They were often designed to actively aid the monk in meditation. In a dry element garden, movement can be depicted using sand, and rocks can be used to represent mountains or islands in the sand streams. Bridges are a common element in many Japanese gardens as well.

The little things? The little moments? They aren't little.

—John Zabat-Zinn

Haiku

Haiku is Japanese poetry that traditionally follows a pattern of 5–7–5: the first line has five syllables, the second line seven syllables, and the last line five syllables. This is generally a good way for haiku beginners to start but it is not a rigid rule. Instead, it is important that the haiku uses no spare words—no unnecessary words and syllables.

Haikus are written in a moment of inspiration where the small self drops and the poet is in touch with the unity of all things. Haiku is a mindfulness meditation. In order to haiku one must be mindful—and, of course, ready to write things down. Haikus are about everyday life and usually have a nature theme. One of the lines usually contains a word that indicates to the reader to which season the haiku refers, thereby giving it a sense of time and place. Wild plums, for instance, would indicate summer.

Haikus do not usually refer to a participant: in other words—no self. This usually extends to mean no adjectives as adjectives can imply a judge (a beautiful tree implies an opinion, therefore someone who holds the opinion).

Here is an example of haiku from Basho:

> *Winter rain*
> *falls on the cow-shed;*
> *a cock crows.*

Notice that the haiku does not follow the 5–7–5 rule but a similar beat is found: 3–5–3. Haikus are not about being brilliant and pithy. They are strokes of inspiration and honesty coming from the center. Most of all, haikus are reverent and show a belief in the holiness, the sanctity of the small things, of everything. Children love to create haiku poetry, which says a lot about the simplicity and honesty to be found in the haiku.

FACT

Basho is known as a great haiku poet. He was born Matsuo Munefusa in seventeenth-century Japan. In his youth, Basho was a samurai but put down the sword for his poetry. He lived in a hut made of banana leaves, which is how he came by his pseudonym. *Basho* means "banana leaves."

Zen Art

There is a tradition of art practice within Zen. Art arises in spontaneity and manifests the buddha-nature within us. Zen art forms include calligraphy, painting, archery, gardening, flower arrangements, the tea ceremony, swordsmanship, poetry—such as haiku—photography, and various other art forms. Art practice is mindfulness training. The art itself comes out of technical training that is then expressed in spontaneous practice, as the artist tries to divulge himself of *self* and create art from the Big Mind within. Zen art tends to be simple, sometimes stark, and lovely.

The Ox-herding Pictures

The ten ox-herding pictures are a very famous example of Zen realization. The series of ten illustrations portray the mind as it opens toward enlightenment. The ox, an animal sacred in India, represents buddha-nature, and the boy in the illustrations represents the self.

The sequence of pictures usually goes like this:

1. Seeking the ox.
2. Finding the footprints.

3. Catching sight of the ox.
4. Ensnaring the ox.
5. Taming the ox.
6. Riding the ox home.
7. Ox vanishes; self alone.
8. Both ox and self vanish.
9. Returning to the source.
10. Entering the marketplace ready to help.

This sequence of events illustrates in black and white the process of the mind as it opens to true nature.

FACT

The ten ox-herding pictures are attributed to Kakuan Shion, twelfth-century Zen master from China. Early ox-herding pictures have existed but Kakuan Shion is known to have created the entire sequence of ten that has survived to this day.

Calligraphy

Japanese calligraphy is an art form spiritually expressed through Zen. The artist must be in touch with buddha-nature in order to create an expression of enlightenment. The brush stroke must come from a union with the world; no separation must exist—no *I* and *pen*, just the act itself.

Japanese calligraphy dates back to the seventh century, where it was part of art practice and meditation in monasteries. Often, the subject of a Japanese calligraphy and painting would be a koan. One of the most common examples of *zenga* is the open circle, called *enso* (think of the corporate logo for Lucent). The simplicity of the *enso* was particularly popular during the Edo period of Japan in the eighteenth century. *Enso* symbolized enlightenment, emptiness, and life itself. In the series of ox-herding pictures previously mentioned, the eighth step in the sequence (both ox and self vanish) is represented by *enso*.

During the execution of the calligraphy, the slightest hesitation on the part of the artist will cause the ink to blot on the thin rice paper, and the painting, the calligraphy, will be ruined. Technique is learned and perfected over many years before such spontaneity is possible. Since the artist has to be one with his or her art, craftsmanship must be honed over years of training and practice. Where is the beginning and end of the self? Is the tear falling from your eye part of you or part of the table it hits? Is the sweat of your body part of you or your clothing? Once your sweat dries on your clothes, where does it go? Where are the lines that define what is us and what is not us?

We want to eat an orange. We take an orange from a tree and peel it, slowly ingesting it into our bodies. At what point does the orange become part of us? At what point *is* the orange us? The orange breaks down and makes its way through our system. Eventually it will leave our bodies in a much different form than when it went in. At what point is it no longer part of us? So it is with calligraphy and all forms of Zen art. The boundary is impossible to define. There, in fact, *is* no boundary. Just as there is no boundary between the orange and ourselves, the air and ourselves, the earth and ourselves. Nothing is independent of anything else. Everything is dependent. Thusly, once the boundary between art supplies, art, and self are gone the art can be executed.

Flower Arranging

Japanese flower arranging is called *ikebana*. Ikebana evolved in Japan over the course of many centuries. The written history of ikebana can be traced back to the fifteenth century, to the first ikebana school. Many years of training are required before someone achieves the technical necessary to perform ikebana well. Many different ways of fastening the flowers into an arrangement are possible, using various techniques. The essence of ikebana is simplicity and in contrast to Western flower arrangement very few flowers, leaves, and stems are used to achieve the desired effect. Ikebana uses the flowers, the container, and the space around the flower arrangement as part of the artistic impression.

There are different styles of ikebana. Some styles use low containers and the flowers are piled on top. Other styles use tall, narrow vases and the flowers have a tossed-about look to them. Ikebana strives to use seasonal flowers and foliage in a natural presentation. Traditional forms of ikebana used three points to represent the realms of heaven, man, and earth.

The essence of Buddhist art is the practice of the artist. The art itself is an expression of enlightenment and the creation of the art an act of enlightenment. Years of technical study can go into a single moment of expression. From the centuries' old stupas to the Zen gardens of today, Buddhist art surrounds us and teaches us lessons on life. Art can depict the cosmos in a painting or a single moment in a photo. Art can last for centuries, such as the Borobudur Temple of Java, or it can last hours, like a Tibetan sand painting. No matter the outcome of the durability of the art, the essence is in the creation itself.

The ability to drop self, to become one with the act of creation is at the heart of Buddhist art forms. Art in Buddhism is an act of the deepest love and connection with the world around us. Ⓔ

Chapter 19

Buddha and the West

Buddhism changed as it moved from country to country. New vehicles of Buddhism arose to meet the needs of the people it served. As Buddhism swept through India and into Sri Lanka, China, Japan, and westward it took on new characteristics as the people built on the teachings of the Buddha, enhancing the teachings to meet the needs of the day. Life is not static and change is inevitable.

Westward Bound

As Asian immigrants moved to North America they brought their belief systems with them—and so Buddhism showed up on the shores of the United States. The first vehicle to make it West was Mahayana, in the form of Zen. In 1893, the first formal gathering of representatives from the world's religions—both Eastern and Western spiritual traditions—was held in Chicago. It was called the Parliament of the World's Religions and is seen today to be the foundation of the continuing formal dialogue between the world's religions.

From this Parliament let some valorous, new, strong, and courageous influence go forth, and let us have here an agreement of all faiths for one good end, for one good thing—really for the glory of God, really for the sake of humanity from all that is low and animal and unworthy and undivine.
—Julia Ward Howe, the Parliament of the World's Religions, 1893

That year in Chicago, Zen Mater Soyen Shaku spoke for the first time on western shores and Americans opened to the possibilities of Zen. It wasn't until after World War II, however, that Zen attracted a readership in the West. More than any other figure in history, D. T. Suzuki, Soyen Shakyu's student, is credited with opening the West to Buddhism with his wonderful writings on Zen. Suzuki communicated to Westerners the experiential aspect of Zen and explained Zen in a way the left Westerners hungry for more.

The fifties brought a new crowd of Zen enthusiasts with the Beat Generation, with their experimental nature and generous outlook. Soon, Zen centers spread all over the country, and Zen took root.

FACT

Many of the poets and writers of the Beat Generation were Buddhists, such as Allen Ginsberg, Jack Kerouac, Kenneth Rexroth, Gary Snyder, and Anne Waldman.

Soon after, the Chinese moved into Tibet and the Tibetans started to flee their homeland, heading westward, many landing in the United States. The Tibetans planted themselves on U.S. soil, in our cities and our suburbs, and brought with them the colorful and varied forms of Tibetan Buddhism, which stood in stark contrast to the much plainer nature of Zen. And so different forms of Buddhism came West and quickly grew, attracting an American populace ripe for the experiences Buddhism was offering. Nichiren Buddhism, Tibetan Buddhism, Zen Buddhism, Korean Buddhism—the face of Western Buddhism is a varied and colorful one filled with the traditions, beliefs, and practices of all of the faces of Buddhism the world over.

FACT

Rick Fields dubbed D. T. Suzuki "the First Patriarch of American Zen," though he never officially received dharma transmission and was considered a philosopher and intellectual.

Thich Nhat Hanh and Jesus

Perhaps one of the most beloved Buddhist teachers in the West is Thich Nhat Hanh, whose teachings on mindfulness, peace, and religious tolerance have touched the hearts of millions of Westerners. Thich Nhat Hanh was chairman of the Vietnamese Peace Brigade during the Vietnam War and was subsequently nominated for a Noble Peace Prize by Martin Luther King, Jr. His tireless efforts to promote peace and inter-religious tolerance have won him a steadfast and loyal following the world over.

In his book *Living Buddha, Living Christ,* Thich Nhat Hahn, known as Thāy to his followers and friends (*Thāy* means "Teacher"), writes about the similarities between Jesus and Buddha, erasing the lines in the sand drawn hundreds of years ago and every day since by religious intolerance. The spirit of Jesus and Buddha cannot be found in their names, he tells us—cannot be found by only evoking their names as a means of spiritual awakening. The spirit of Jesus and Buddha can be found in practicing the actions they took in their own lives: by becoming a *living* Jesus and a *living* Buddha ourselves. Both men showed us how to live by the actions each took in his own life.

Jesus said, "I am the way." Thich Nhat Hahn points out that Jesus meant that his *life* was the way—not his name.

Believing in Jesus is not enough. Believing in Buddha is not enough. But becoming the kind of person that Jesus and Buddha were is a step in the right direction. When Jesus said, "I am the way," he meant that he could show us the way if we followed his path. Buddha had the same message: "This is the path," he told us. "Use your own life experience and do what I have done and you too will find the way to the truth," the way to God. Find out for yourself.

We are encouraged by this wise Vietnamese Zen master to put down our books and our words and to become an active member of our churches and sanghas. We are encouraged to live in the mindfulness, the compassion that both Jesus and Buddha promoted.

Psalm 46:10 tells us, "Be still and know." Buddha tells us the same. Be still, be mindful, and feel the presence of truth, of God. Love thy neighbor as yourself. Identify, do not compare. Jesus and Buddha both lived simply, we are told. Are we living simply or are our temples and churches acquiring more and more? Jesus did not have possessions; neither did the Buddha. Are we hoarding too much, taking more than our share? Both Buddha and Jesus were available to the people of their time, teaching them and loving them, helping those who suffered. Thich Nhat Hahn encourages us to do the same. Are we available to help others? Are we doing anything to decrease suffering in the world and in our own back yards?

FACT

Thich Nhat Hahn runs a Buddhist monastery in France called Plum Village, which he founded in 1982. When he is not traveling around the world teaching Mindful Living, he teaches, writes, and gardens in Plum Village.

Thich Nhat Hahn works tirelessly to promote tolerance, peace, compassion, and true understanding. He writes that "Buddhism and Christian practice is the same—to make the truth available—the truth about ourselves, the truth about our brothers and sisters, the truth about our situation. This is the work of writers, preachers, the media, and also practitioners. Each day, we practice looking deeply into ourselves and into the situation of our brothers and sisters. It is the most serious work we can do." Thich Nhat Hahn teaches the essence of Zen, but also the essence of all religions. At the center of each religion we practice is the desire for love and true connection, with a higher power—whether we call it the Truth or God or Allah—and with each other.

> Thich Nhat Hahn is my brother. We are both monks, and we have lived the monastic life about the same number of years. We are both poets, both existentialists. I have far more in common with Nhat Hanh than I have with many Americans.
>
> —Thomas Merton

Thomas Merton

Thomas Merton was an American Christian monk, poet, social critic, and mystic. He was born in France, moved to the United States, and became a Roman Catholic at age twenty-three. He eventually became a Trappist monk, which is one of the strictest orders in Catholicism. But something about Buddhism drew Thomas Merton, and in 1968 he found himself on a plane to Asia for a monastic conference. He welcomed the opportunity to learn more about the Eastern religion he felt compelled to study. Merton remained a devoted Christian monk his entire life, but he actively worked for inter-religious tolerance as his appreciation for the Eastern religion grew.

D. T. Suzuki was an influential presence in Merton's life. Their correspondences formed an essay collection called *Zen and the Birds of Appetite*, which was a dialogue about the similarities and differences between Christianity and Zen Buddhism. Merton came to believe that Buddhism and Christianity were completely compatible with each other and that the emptiness found in Zen could be related to the true self and the idea of unknowing found at the heart of Christian practice.

While he was in Asia, Merton met three times with the Dalai Lama and each was very impressed with the sincerity, humanity, and compassion of the other. They were able to give each other an understanding that their vision was perhaps not the only vision of truth, and each had come to the same realizations, had similar experiences from different approaches. Merton had a powerful awakening experience while in Sri Lanka, and believed that Buddhism had given him an ability to practice Catholicism in a very powerful way. He died while in Asia but the dialogue he started has only just begun.

The Western Face of Buddhism

It would appear that Buddhism is one of the fastest-growing religions in the West. But who are all of these new Buddhists? Most likely not everyone who is expressing an interest in Buddhism is calling her- or himself a Buddhist. Book sales and lecture ticket sales do not necessarily mean that everyone is throwing over their own spirituality to adopt Buddhist beliefs whole-heartedly. The truth is that many Americans are taking some of the practices of Buddhism and incorporating them into their own religious traditions. You might find Jews, Catholics, Hindus, and Christians in a *zendo* one night during the week, but come their own holidays you also might find them celebrating at temple or church as well. I know members of my own sangha who periodically skip practice to attend church functions. Women and men seem fairly equally represented as far as Buddhist practitioners are concerned.

FACT

James William Coleman tells us in *The New Buddhism* that Editor Helen Tworkov estimates that about half of the 60,000 readers of *Tricycle: The Buddhist Review* do not identify themselves as Buddhists.

The Dalai Lama has certainly done quite a bit to bring the face of Buddhism into our living rooms. His great compassion in the face of such suffering, his peaceful demeanor regarding his exiled status, his lack of dogmatism, and his projection of kindness draws people to him with curiosity. In a time when so many Americans are unsure how to proceed with their own suffering, the face of someone coping with his or her own personal loss with equanimity and serenity is a great comfort and source of inspiration. Americans want to be happy and content, especially in the face of so much potential loss.

Books, Web sites, television, and the influx of Asian immigrants in the past decades have brought Buddhism home to many Americans. Buddhism is no longer a stranger, and is no longer considered strange. If I tell anyone I am a Buddhist, the reaction I get is usually one of warm curiosity, not fear or judgment.

Actress Sharon Stone is a Buddhist. After achieving a high degree of fame too fast, Stone took some time off from acting to regain her footing. "My practice is Buddhism, but I believe in God." Stone says. She doesn't see any conflict between her belief in God and her practice of Buddhism. However, she does say, "I don't believe in Buddha as my God . . . I believe in the practical ways of Buddhism as a way to live."

The truth is, more and more people are opening their spiritualities to new experiences. In the United States, many people make a distinction between spirituality and religion. Some people do *zazen* to bring them closer to God. *The New Buddhism* tells us the interesting fact that most of the best-selling books that are sold today on Buddhism offer direct advice on how to practice.

American Buddhists come from all religions, they are equally represented by male and female, they are both young and old, are white, Hispanic, black, and Asian. Some are devout and some are merely curious. Some devote their entire lives to practice and some balance it with their other religious beliefs. The new face of Buddhism is the face of America: diverse, curious, and hopeful.

Contemporary Buddhist Literature

Buddhism has had a great effect on contemporary American literature. Go to a bookstore anywhere and you will be hard-pressed not to find a book on Buddhism. The Eastern religion sections of bookstores are overflowing with books on Zen, Buddhism, meditation, yoga, and more.

FACT

One of the most popular books in the United States on Buddhism is *Zen Mind, Beginner's Mind* by Suzuki Roshi, with nearly a million copies in print.

You'd think Buddhism would be hard to talk about with emptiness being a major theme. But nevertheless people make great effort to put down on paper that which has transformed their lives. The popularity of some Buddhist books is amazing. The Dalai Lama's *Art of Happiness* showed up on the bestseller list everywhere. *The Miracle of Mindfulness* by Thich Naht Hahn is another popular book, which appears on bookshelves all over the country.

You can find daily meditation books, calendars, diaries, and quote books with Buddhist themes.

Some of the wonderful writings available in your local bookstore include books by Pema Chödrön, Sharon Salzberg, the Dalai Lama, Jack Kornfield, Albert Low, Alan Watts, Thich Nhat Hahn, Maurine Stuart, Bernard Glassman, Robert Thurman, Jack Maguire, Philip Kapleau, D. T. Suzuki, Shunryu Suzuki, John Daido Loori, Stephen Batchelor, Ayya Khema, Joseph Goldstein, Peter Matthiessen, Joanna Macy, and many more.

A sampling of poets with Buddhist themes include Kenneth Rexroth, Albert Saijo, Anne Waldman, Lew Welch, Allen Ginsberg, Jack Kerouac, Michael McClure, Peter Levitt, Al Robles, Gary Snyder, and Philip Whalen.

From haiku to novel, nature writing to illuminating nonfiction, Buddhism has infiltrated our literature and our lives.

◀ Stone Buddha

The Zen of Everything

One indication that Buddhism is here to stay is that it is showing up in our pop culture as well as in our art and our bookstores. From movies to golf, Zen is everywhere. A recent trip to the bookstore was illuminating as to how far Zen has infiltrated our popular culture. There are tiny Zen gardening sets, Zen calendars, Zen mugs. Titles that had nothing to do with Zen claimed Zen roots. This is the Zenning of America. Zen is in our movies, in our golf game, in our computer literature, and in our landscapes.

Buddhism and Zen have even made it to the movies. Movies like *The Matrix* have Zen themes running through them. Martial Arts films have taken off in popularity, from the Jackie Chan films to the Hong Kong imports. *Seven Years in Tibet* and *Kundun* are both popular movies whose plots concern the Dalai Lama. *Little Buddha,* by Italian director Bernardo Bertolucci, gained widespread release. And what about *Star Wars?* Does *Star Wars* have a Zen theme running through it? What exactly was the Force? ("You must feel the Force around you, here, between you, me, the tree, the rock, everywhere . . .") Sounds very Buddhist, doesn't it? Why is Zen showing up everywhere?

Zen stories inspire us and make us pause, such as this Buddhist parable about living in the moment:

> *A man traveling across a field encounters a tiger. He fled, the tiger chasing after him. Coming to a precipice, he caught hold of the root of a wild vine and swung himself down over the edge. The tiger sniffed at him from above. Trembling, the man looked down to where, far below, another tiger was waiting to eat him. Only the vine sustained him.*
>
> *Two mice, one white and one black, little by little started to gnaw away the vine. The man saw a luscious strawberry near him. Grasping the vine with one hand, he plucked the strawberry with the other. How sweet it tasted!*

We live in a world where it is possible to wake up on a Tuesday morning and watch the World Trade Center buildings fall down. We know that it is imperative to find meaning in our lives now. Americans are *longing* for meaning in their lives. Everything today goes at such a fast pace and life feels as if it is flying by us. We are frightened of missing out on meaning in our lives and as the new millennium came upon us we looked into our hearts for spiritual meaning.

Zen teaches us to live in the moment; it tells us that everything matters, that work matters, that dinner matters, that walking the dog is a work of art. Zen can comfort us and help us reclaim our lives. We can find peace and energy in a run when all we do is run. We can find joy in the dishes when we merely wash the dishes. Zen elevates the mundane into the sacred and gives us the meaning we so desperately search for. But Zen also have timeless messages that translate into other faiths: compassion, faith, truth, suffering. Zen is everywhere because Zen is in everything. It's not silly to talk about the Zen of golf. It's amazing. When you swing, just swing.

Buddhism and Psychotherapy

Buddhism gets along well with Western science, and particularly well with psychology and therapy. At heart both Buddhism and psychotherapy attempt to deal with the same issue: human suffering. Both promote the method of observing your own behavior. Both Buddhism and psychotherapy stress the moment: dealing with life right now, and living up to one's full potential. Both practices take time to mature. The work one does in Buddhism and the work one does in psychotherapy builds on itself, and patience is necessary if either is to be undertaken with any measure of success. In other words, one therapy session or one seated meditation session will not change much—unless of course a curiosity and faith are born that brings one back to the couch or the pillow.

FACT

Mark Epstein and William James are not the only psychologists to recognize the interrelation of Eastern wisdom and psychology. Carl Jung, Sigmund Freud, Otto Rank, Ernest Jones, and others explored the relationship of Eastern thought and practices with Western therapeutic practices.

In meditation practice one sits despite what is happening in life at that particular time and tries to watch the thoughts come and go, repeatedly letting them go until the mind becomes clear and empty. Learning to sit through the rise and fall of thoughts can bring about a profound realization. *I am okay.* Despite the tendency to believe that obsessively thinking about something will actually change anything, the realization dawns that thinking doesn't matter. Whether or not you obsess over the dent in your new car, the car will either be fixed or remain unfixed and the thinking will not change that. In psychology we bring our obsessive thinking (or other problems) into the presence of another, and are guided through the maze of our thoughts until awareness dawns.

With the increase in Buddhist practice in the West came a willingness on the part of psychotherapists to explore the possibilities of using Buddhist practices for therapy.

Mark Epstein, author of *Thoughts Without a Thinker,* is a therapist who practices Buddhism himself. He tells a story about the great psychologist and philosopher William James (1842–1910), who thought that Buddhism would be a major influence on Western psychology. James was lecturing at Harvard when he noticed a Sri Lankan Buddhist monk in the lecture hall. "Take my chair," he said to the monk. "You are better equipped to lecture on psychology than I."

Epstein explains that meditation, often misunderstood to be a retreat from emotional and mental experiences, requires that we slow down so we can examine the day-to-day mind. And, he concludes, "This examination is, by definition, psychological."

A Bird's-Eye View: Three American Buddhist Teachers

American Buddhism has a style all its own. Let's take a look at the teachings of three American Zen masters to see ways in which Buddhism has changed and adapted to its environment. We can trace the roots of these trees of Buddhism all the way back to the Buddha himself, but each has adapted to fit a particular need or strengthened a particular aspect of practice.

John Daido Loori

John Daido Loori Roshi is Dharma heir of Hakuyu Taizan Maezumi Roshi and is the current abbot of Zen Mountain Monastery in Mount Tremper, New York, located in the Catskills. He is president of Dharma Communications and a prolific author. He is founder and director of the Mountains and Rivers Order of associated Zen Buddhist practice centers.

John Daido Loori Roshi teaches the practices of the Eight Gates of Zen. As he says in his book *The Eight Gates of Zen,* "The Eight Gates and the Ten Stages are the ceaseless practice of Dogen Zenji's *Mountains and Rivers*—practice that engages the whole body and mind, that encompasses and fills all space and time." The Eight Gates of Zen practiced at Zen Mountain Monastery are:

1. Zazen
2. Zen Study
3. Academic Study
4. Liturgy
5. Right Action
6. Art Practice
7. Body Practice
8. Work Practice

The Ten Stages referred to by Loori are the ten stages depicted in the ox-herding pictures, discussed in Chapter 18. In addition, John Daido Loori is heading up a large Internet presence to spread the dharma further. See the Zen Mountain Monastery Web site for more information at: *www.mro.org*.

Bernard Tetsugen Glassman

Bernard Tetsugen Glassman is one of America's most provocative Zen teachers and promoters of Engaged Buddhism. In 1982 he founded the Greyston Bakery in New York City. His idea was to start a business that would employ the members of his sangha—allowing them to leave their day jobs—so they could concentrate more fully on their practice and contribute to the practice of Engaged Buddhism. Today, the bakery generates more than $3.5 million per year and employs more than fifty people. In 1993 The Greyston Foundation, a nonprofit corporation, was created to oversee social improvement programs. Profits from the bakery filter through the foundation, supporting its social development work for the poor and afflicted. Greyston helps the homeless, the jobless, provides child care, health care, and living assistance for people with HIV/AIDS. Greyston also provides all of the brownies found in Ben & Jerry's ice cream—their common concern for the environment made them wonderful complements for one another.

When Greyston was established Roshi Glassman (with Roshi Sandra Holmes), then went on to create an order of Zen practitioners devoted to the cause of peace—the Peacemakers Order subsequently emerged. The Peacemaker Community is now an international peacemaking group with members involving the world's five major religions, including organizations (in the United States: Greyston Mandala, Prison Dharma Network, and Upaya Study Center in Sante Fe; StadtRaum in Germany; Mexico City Village, Mexico; La Rete d'Indra in Italy, Shanti Relief Committee in Japan) and individuals worldwide.

▲ A Buddhist stupa

Currently, Roshi Glassman teaches, writes, and travels, giving talks and workshops on practice and peacemaking. He is also studying to become a clown.

Joan Jiko Halifax

Roshi Joan Jiko Halifax is a student of Thich Nhat Hanh, a founding member of the Zen Peacemaker Order, and founder and roshi of the Upaya Zen Center in Santa Fe, New Mexico. She is an author and activist, greatly respected for her work with the dying. Upaya programs include Being with Dying, the Partners Program, the Prison Project, and the Kailash Education Fund.

Being with Dying is a program aimed at helping caregivers work with dying people, and to change our relationship to both the dying and living. A focus of the program is the training of health care professionals who take their work with the dying back to their own institutions where they can teach these practices to other health care professionals. According to the Upaya Web site *(www.upaya.org)*, practices include "perspectives on death and dying, grief counseling, community development, cultural perspectives on death, grief, bereavement, and work with psychological and spiritual issues related to death and dying." The center opens its doors to the public with retreats aimed at caregivers and the terminally or seriously ill, helping them to practice mindfulness, compassion, and honesty.

The Partners Program matches dying people with caregivers they need, complementing the help of hospice workers and medical professionals. The Prison Project offers mindfulness training to inmates in the Mexico prison system, aiming to reduce stress in prison, and The Kailash Education Fund is aimed at providing educational opportunities to some of the poorest children in Nepal.

American Buddhist teachers are bringing the principles of mindfulness, compassion, right action, and right livelihood into our communities and our homes. Their very own brand of Engaged Buddhism is changing the world around them. American Buddhism is a welcome force in our country in confused and frightening times. The generosity of Buddhism can be humbling. And all it takes is practice.

Chapter 20

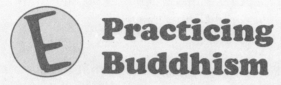

Practicing Buddhism

I t is impossible to capture the essence of Buddhism in words, as it is a program of practice, action, and experience. Picking up a book and introducing yourself to the practice and history of Buddhism is a good start but unless you put the principles into action it remains conceptual and theoretical. In order to truly understand, you must practice the teachings yourself.

No Words

There are no words that can explain what emptiness means, what no-self means, what no-thing means. Buddhists have strived for centuries to convey the meanings of the truths they have discovered using words, images, and actions. Buddhism taps into parts of us that we sometimes don't even know about. Working with a teacher in Buddhism we can stretch ourselves in ways we could never image.

A monk then asked, "Can you say something that transcends the Buddhas and Ancestors?" The Master said, "Sesame flatbread."
— *The Blue Cliff Record*

Learning to reach beyond the words, beyond the gestures, beyond the known is what Buddhism is all about. A book can give you only a tiny, minuscule notion, the smallest trace of a shadow of what it is all about. The ultimate nature of reality, the truth, God . . . call it what you chose . . . it is out there, in here, everywhere. Has always been out there, in here, everywhere. Will always be out there, in here, everywhere, waiting for us to turn on the light and see it. And when we do, we say, "Ahhhh. I can't believe I forgot this. I *always* knew, but I forgot. Yes, this is the way it has always been and this is *home*."

As my teacher always says, Buddhism is a wonderful way to live. It is the greatest gift you might ever give yourself and the most difficult practice you might ever undertake. But who knew sitting alone with yourself could be so very hard?

A wonderful verse on the Way is called "Hsin Hsin Ming" (Verses on the Faith Mind, translated by Richard B. Clarke) by Sengstan. It ends:

Words!
The Way is beyond language
For in it there is
No yesterday
No tomorrow
No today.

There is no better way to say it. Words! The Way is, indeed, beyond language.

How to Start a Practice

If reading this book has convinced you to give Buddhism a try, that indeed is some wonderful news. But practicing alone can be a frustrating and lonely experience, and continuing to practice alone sometimes seems insurmountable, especially in the beginning. Finding a group to practice with is a wonderful gift to give yourself. In the back of this book is a large sampling of American Buddhist sitting groups, monasteries, and practice centers from each state. Investigate a group from this listing or try to find another group nearby.

FACT

Sengstan was the Third Zen Patriarch of China and author of the Verses on the Faith-Mind, written in the early seventh century.

Within the pages of this book are descriptions of the three different vehicles of Buddhism and their offshoots. The vehicles of Buddhism changed as they came West and took on a personality all their own.

Theravada most often shows up on American shores as *vipashyana*. Theravada was traditionally the most conservative of the three traditions of Buddhism and stressed the monastic life more than the others. The Asian Theravada communities in the United States tend to stress study and the precepts over seated meditation. But as Asian immigrants brought Theravada into the country, Americans were also headed over to Asia and were bringing back their own forms of Theravada. *Vipashyana* spread this way and became one of the more Westernized schools of Buddhism here.

Sharon Salzberg, Joseph Goldstein, and Jack Kornfield are three of the most popular and well-known *vipashyana* teachers in the United States. Sharon Salzburg and Joseph Goldstein founded the Insight Meditation School in Massachusetts. Jack Kornfield has a similar organization on the West Coast, the Spirit Rock Meditation Center.

Vipashyana teachers tend to give much guidance to their students and encourage many different types of meditation.

Vajrayana also took firm root in the United States, mostly in the form of Tibetan Buddhism. Chögyam Trungpa Rinpoche was one of the more famous Tibetan Buddhists on Western soil as was Allen Ginsberg.

And finally, Zen, representing the Mahayana vehicle of Buddhism, became firmly established in America. Well-known Zen teachers include Philip Kapleau.

In the United States, *vipashyana* Buddhism tends toward being the less ritualized form of Buddhism of the three. Tibetan Buddhism is the most colorful and most ritualized. Zen tends toward simplicity.

FACT

Jack Kornfield cofounded Insight Meditation Center with Joseph Goldstein and Sharon Salzberg before heading West to start the Spirit Rock Meditation Center. He was first exposed to Buddhism while volunteering with the Peace Corps in Asia. He is one of the most respected Buddhist teachers in the United States and is an author and psychotherapist.

How can you decide which type of Buddhism practice to try? Trust your instincts. Whatever seems to appeal to you most is probably the best way for you to head. There is a rule that people in twelve-step programs tell each other to follow: If you hear the same advice from three people then it's time to follow that advice. If you are getting signals from people or from the world around you to head in one direction, then head that way. Trust yourself and trust the world. It won't let you down. The world is not a hostile place: it is us who erroneously perceive it that way. We bring judgment, fear, and laziness into the world, expecting the world to bring it back to us. Buddhism can open your eyes to the true, loving, compassionate nature of everything. And you will be free.

So start where the trail is heading and take it from there. One type of Buddhism is not better than another. Wherever you can find a starting point is the most wonderful place to begin. Don't worry about the path, the path will take care of itself. Find a center near you and read about it online, in a newspaper or book, request a newsletter from the center, or ask if you may talk to a staff person. Ask whatever questions you need to feel comfortable before showing up in person. You might want to know the kind of people that practice (age, ethnic background, resident, nonresident, etc.), the teachers, if the school is part of a larger organization—worldwide or countrywide—and what the hours of practice are. Do the practice sessions fit in with your work schedule or weekend schedule? Can you reasonably make sits on a regular basis? What is the lineage of the teacher? How long has the teacher been teaching and can you easily understand the teacher (remember, teachers may not be American!).

A common guided meditation practice used in *vipashyana* is called *metta*. *Metta* means "loving-kindness" and the meditation focuses the mind on cultivating feelings of compassion and kindness toward the world.

When you show up at the center for the first time, you can wear comfortable, subdued clothing. Make sure your trousers are loose-fitting and preferably in a dark color. No provocative clothing or wildly colored clothing. Remember, this is a meditative, quiet environment and the less distraction you cause the better off the environment will be. Make an effort to wear clothing that reflects the sobriety of the occasion.

Most places will request that you take off your shoes before entering the *zendo,* so be prepared with socks if the idea of going around barefoot with strangers causes you discomfort. There is usually an area outside the *zendo* or practice area for you to put your shoes. You should leave personal items outside as well. Do not take in backpacks, books, water, purses, cameras, or other extra items. There will most likely be a meditation cushion waiting for you but you can always call ahead to verify.

Remember that the Buddhist community is a community of people who are striving to let go of distinctions, drop judgments, and foster compassion. You will not be walking into an unkind or judgmental situation. To paraphrase Franklin D. Roosevelt, there is nothing to fear except yourself!

Giving Up the Ego

The idea of giving up your ego seems frightening and might even make you feel angry. After all, you are all you have! However, giving up the ego actually comes as a big relief.

You can be truly happy when you are selfless. A common image used in Buddhism to describe our relationship to the universe is the ocean. You are like a wave on the ocean. A wave has a life of its own for the time it is forming, rising, and crashing to shore. Then what happens to the wave? It is, and always was, a part of the ocean. There is no difference between the rest of the ocean and the wave, but the wave appears to have distinctions for the time it is a wave. Things do not have permanent and separate identities. And neither do we. It is an illusion and the good news is . . . you can wake up from this illusion!

Many people enjoy intense, vigorous exercise such as running, bike riding, tennis, or swimming. You will often hear athletes speak of hitting the "zone"—that area of exercise where you can become the running, the biking, the game. It feels like dropping out of yourself and disappearing into the movement. This is a very similar experience to Buddhist practice. The ego falls away and a freedom exists that is absolutely wonderful.

But the question inevitably arises that, if there is no you, then who thinks the thoughts? Who gets enlightened? Who eats the dinner? You will see if you sit long enough that the thoughts do not come from you. You are not the thinker (hence the book title *Thoughts Without a Thinker*, by Mark Epstein). This concept is beyond where you are at the present time. The small self cannot imagine the small self not existing. Just trust that someday—if you practice, you just might know what it means. You just might know the true meaning of *vast*.

Knowing No-Thing Is Everything

Once you can still your mind the entire world is yours and you are the entire world. But once you know no-thing you have truly disappeared. Early Buddhists were scientists of the mind. They studied the mind like we study diseases today. They examined it, wrote about it, noted every little arising and change. As they studied, noted, and observed, they came to know the human mind in a very intimate way. The Zen masters figured out questions to ask that would stimulate our intuitive nature and befuddle our rational mind. They figured out ways to drop the thinking mind that seemed to just get in the way.

◀ Eyes of the Buddha

We can have a lot of gratitude for these early monks who formed a path for us to follow that led nowhere and everywhere, that gave us everything by showing us the intimate nature of emptiness.

This emptiness is *vastness;* it is *unbounded space.* But as we mentioned earlier, it is also completely beyond words and somewhat a waste of paper to try to explain it. Practice Buddhism and try to find it yourself. Gary Gach tells a wonderful story on emptiness.

Some priests and monks from Westminster Abbey were visiting a Japanese Zen monastery. At the sight of a large piece of framed calligraphy they paused. The calligraphy was of the word *no-thing*. One of the monks asked what it meant. Rather than explain the concept to the priests and the monks, their guide just said, "God," and moved on.

Fullness in Emptiness

To discover this emptiness for yourself is to become full like you've never imagined possible. You can be filled with joy at the sound of a bell. You can be grateful for your morning oatmeal and a rainstorm. You can feel true compassion and friendship with another human being. You can want to help others and express the nature of the world in the work that you do. You can tolerate your feelings, want to have a clean and serene environment, you can know energy beyond your dreams.

Emptiness leads to fullness and we can be filled with the essence of buddha-nature. We can drop distinctions, judgments, and see clearly how small our minds have been.

You can want to do seated meditation more than you want to go out to dinner. You can look forward to long periods of silence and stillness. You can know peace. You can *be* peace. But Buddhists, of course, are human, enlightened or not.

Mortal Teachers

Even if someone experiences enlightenment it does not make that person an otherworldly, superhuman being. Enlightened teachers sometimes retain many of their more human foibles and defects. In the twelfth century in Japan a rebellious group of Zen practitioners evolved. They decided it was a good idea to drink and womanize and so they did. Not all Buddhists will live all of the precepts and you will find enlightened alcoholics and enlightened people who commit sexual indiscretions.

Chögyan Trungpa Rinpoche was loved by many; he was largely regarded as an excellent teacher and a highly enlightened man. However, he was also an active alcoholic and his drinking eventually contributed to his early death. Sometimes enlightened people can compartmentalize their enlightenment so that it does not apply to their life at large. There are many stories of wonderful teachers who were ill-tempered outside of the temple settings, smoked, drank, were sexually permissive, and could not apply what they knew in enlightened mind to their larger life. Humans will still be humans, enlightenment or not. Some of the bigger Buddhist centers in the United States have been rocked by scandal and will most likely continue to be rocked by scandals in the future. Buddhism is not exempt from the same troubles that have dogged other great religions.

FACT

In 1983 the San Francisco Zen Center experienced a huge upheaval when the roshi, Richard Baker, was forced to resign. It was discovered that Baker, who was married at the time, had been having an affair with another married member of the sangha.

When looking for a teacher it is always advisable to see if you want what the teacher has, and if you respect the way the teacher practices in all parts of her or his life. Some enlightened teachers are wonderful examples of compassion while living the precepts in all ways.

Here and Now

Buddha told us we should discover the nature of reality for ourselves. Questioning things is a good place to start. Many Western people do not stumble onto the practices of Buddhism because everything is just terrific and nothing could make them happier than if nothing were to change. Many of the people who end up in a *zendo* staring at a teacher in a robe are in pain and are looking for answers to some pretty big questions in life. Buddhism encourages that beginner's mind. If we can keep that open, questioning mind, we will do well in life. It is when we close down and stop searching for answers that things get particularly dark.

Buddhism encourages us to ask questions and to live now. So many of us are waiting until vacation to live, or until retirement, or until we get our Ph.D. or our children go to college. Life will begin sometime down the road when we are done with all those things we have to do that make us feel that we are only half-alive. Buddhism tells you to live *now*. Life happens now. It happens while you wash the dishes, scoop the litter, change a diaper, drive to work, blow your nose, mow the grass, and watch television. If we practice mindfulness we can wake up to life. Just remember what the Buddha said: "If you live your whole heart from morning to night, then you have truly had an auspicious day."

Appendices

Appendix A

Glossary

Appendix B

Resources

Appendix C

Buddhist Monasteries and Practice Centers in the United States

Glossary

Anatman: No-soul, no-self.

Arhat: "Worthy one" in Sanskrit. An arhat is one who has attained enlightened mind and is free of desires and cravings.

Ascetic: One who believes that spiritual growth can be obtained through extreme self-denial and the renunciation of worldly pleasures—ascetics often practice poverty, starvation, and self-mortification.

Bhikkunis: Buddhist nuns.

Bhikkus: Buddhist monks.

Bodhi Tree: Tree of Wisdom; a fig tree.

Bodhisattva: A person who had already attained enlightenment, or is ready to attain enlightened, but puts off his or her own final enlightenment in order to re-enter the cycle of samsara and save all sentient beings.

Brahmin: The priests and the highest class of the hereditary caste system of India. The Brahmins were those motivated by knowledge.

Buddha: The Fully Awakened One. From the Sanskrit *budh,* which means "to awaken."

Buddha-nature: Our true nature, our original nature before we became who we are today. Buddha-nature is that which is within us that gives us the ability to attain enlightenment.

Ch'an: Literally, meditation. A school of Buddhism started in China in the sixth century by Bodhidharma. Known in Japan as Zen.

Daikensho: Enlightenment.

Dana: Acts of generosity.

Dharma: The Path, the teachings of the Buddha. What is, and what should be. Dharma is everything: truth, the teachings, all things and states conditioned and unconditioned, nature, morality, ethics, and that which helps one achieve Nirvana, that which is virtuous and righteous.

Dharma Wheel: The wheel symbolizes the Buddhist cycle of birth and rebirth. The wheel often has eight spokes, symbolizing the Eightfold Path.

Dokusan: A private encounter with a Zen teacher.

Duhkha: Dissatisfaction, suffering, disease, or anguish caused by attachment and desire.

Eightfold Path: The path to enlightenment: right understanding, right thought, right speech, right action, right livelihood, right effort, right mindfulness, and right concentration.

Five Precepts: Buddhist guidelines for conduct and ethical living: 1. Do Not Destroy Life, 2. Do Not Steal, 3. Do Not Commit Sexual Misconduct, 4. Do Not Lie, and 5. Do Not Take Intoxicating Drinks.

Gassho: To place two palms together.

Kalpa: A unit of time for measuring the existence of worlds. One eon is said to be the amount of time it would take a seven-mile high mountain of granite to erode if it were brushed by a soft cloth every 100 years.

Karma: The force generated by action and intention that affects one's quality of life in the next life. Good intention can lead to a good life in the next life via karmic implication. Negative intention can lead to a harder life in the next life via karmic implication.

Kensho: Enlightenment, but not as strong as *daikensho* or *satori.*

Kinhin: Walking meditation in Zen practice.

Kshatriyas: According to the caste system of Hinduism and ancient India, Kshatriyas were rulers and warriors.

Lotus Position: A position used for meditation practice. Lotus position entails sitting cross-legged with the top of your left foot on your right thigh and the top of your right foot on your left thigh.

Metta: Loving-kindness.

Middle Way: The peaceful way between two extremes: neither excessive pleasure nor excessive pain. The Middle Way is the path to enlightenment.

Mindfulness: Being aware of things as they are and as they happen. Living in the moment.

Mu: No-thing, no, nothingness; the most famous Zen koan.

Nirvana: The cessation of suffering by the elimination of desire. Nirvana is not a place separate from us but lies in each of us; the very still center at the core of our beings.

Paranirvana: The attainment of Nirvana plus the total extinction of the physical self. When the Buddha died, he reached paranirvana.

Prajna: Wisdom.

Prana: Breath, life force.

Pretas: Hungry ghosts. Frequently Anglicized as *pretans*.

Roshi: A title given to a Zen master, under whom a student must study if he or she hopes to reach enlightened mind. In Japanese it means "venerable master."

Samadhi: A profound meditative state.

Samsara: The infinite repetitions of birth, death, and suffering caused by karma.

Sangha: Community of Buddhists. Traditionally could be seen as the community of monks, but any Buddhist community of followers.

Satori: Enlightenment.

Sesshin: A Zen meditation retreat where intensive zazen practice takes place.

Shikantaza: "Just sitting." Sitting without breath practice or any other directed concentration.

Shudras: According to the caste system of Hinduism and Ancient India, the Shudras were the unskilled laborers or the untouchables.

Shunyata: Emptiness

Son: Korean for Zen/Ch'an.

Stupa: Burial monument that stands for the Buddha and his enlightenment. In India, Tibet, and Southeast Asian countries, stupas are usually dome-shaped with a center spire. In China, Korea, and Japan they resemble a pagoda.

Sutra: The collection of teachings of the Buddha: discourses and dialogues.

Teisho: A presentation of insight from a teacher to students. Often the subject of a *teisho* will be a koan or koans.

Tanhakkhaya: Nirvana, the extinction of thirst.

Three Jewels: Buddha, dharma, sangha.

Tripitaka: The Pali canon, the Three Baskets.

Vaishyas: According to the caste system of Hinduism and ancient India, the Vaishyas were business people and artisans.

Zafu: A round cushion used for meditation.

Zazen: Seated meditation; total concentration of mind and body.

Zen: A school of Buddhism that emphasizes seated meditation and seeing directly into buddha-nature.

Appendix B

Resources

Books and Magazines

The American Journal of Jurisprudence Volume 41 (1996). P. 271–288, "A Buddhist Perspective on the Death Penalty of Compassion and Capital Punishment," by Damien P. Horigan.

Awakening to Zen, by Philip Kapleau, Scribner Books, NY, 1997.

The Book of Tea, by Okakura Kakuzo, Running Press, PA, 2002.

Breath Sweeps Mind, edited by Jean Smith, Riverhead Books, NY, 1998.

Buddha, by Karen Armstrong, Viking Press, NY, 2001.

Buddhadharma: The Pracitioner's Quarterly, Fall 2002 issue.

Buddhist Wisdom: The Diamond Sutra and the Heart Sutra, by Edward Conze, Vintage Paperbacks, NY, 1958.

Buddhism Without Beliefs, by Stephen Batchelor, Riverhead Books, NY, 1997.

The Buddhist Handbook, by John Snelling, Inner Traditions, VT, 1991; 1998.

The Eight Gates of Zen, by John Daido Loori, Dharma Communications, NY, 1992.

Essential Buddhism: A Complete Guide to Beliefs and Practices, by Jack Maguire, Pocket Books, NY, 2001.

Essential Tibetan Buddhism, by Robert A. F. Thurman, Harper Collins Books, NY, 1995.

Ethics for the New Millennium, by the Dalai Lama, Riverhead Books, NY, 1999.

Everyday Mind: 366 Reflections on the Buddhist Path, edited by Jean Smith, Riverhead Books, NY, 1997.

The Five Houses of Zen, by Thomas Cleary, Shambhala, Boston, MA, 1997.

How to Meditate: A Practical Guide, by Kathleen McDonald, Wisdom Publications, Somerville, MA, 1984.

An Introduction to Buddhism, by Peter Harvey, Cambridge University Press, Cambridge, England, 1990.

Living Buddha, Living Christ, by Thich Nhat Hahn, Riverhead Books, NY, 1995.

Meditations from Living Buddha, Living Christ, by Thich Nhat Hanh, Riverhead Books, NY.

The Miracle of Mindfulness, by Thich Nhat Hanh, Beacon Press, Boston, MA, 1976; 1999.

The New Buddhism, by James William Coleman, Oxford, NY, 2001.

One Dharma, by Joseph Goldstein, Harper, San Francisco, CA, 2002.

The Path to Tranquility, by the Dalai Lama, Viking Arkana, NY, 1998.

Racing Toward 2001, by Russell Chandler, Zondervan Publishing House, Grand Rapids, MI, 1992.

Radiant Mind, edited by Jean Smith, Riverhead Books, NY, 1999.

The Story of Buddhism: A Concise Guide to Its History and Teachings, by Donald S. Lopez, Jr., Harper San Francisco, CA, 2001.

Subtle Sounds: The Zen Teaching of Maurine Stuart, edited by Roko Sherry Chayat, Shambhala, MA, 1996.

Teach Yourself Buddhism: World Faiths, by Clive Erricker, Contemporary Books, Chicago, IL, 1995; 2001.

Thoughts Without a Thinker, by Mark Epstein, Basic Books, NY, 1995; 1997.

The Three Pillars of Zen, by Philip Kapleau, Anchor Books, NY, 1980; 1965; 1989; 2000.

The Tibetan Book of the Dead, translated by Robert A. F. Thurman, Bantam Books, NY, 1994.

Tricycle Magazine: The Buddhist Review.

Verses from the Center, by Stephen Batchelor, Riverhead Books, NY, 2000.

The Way of Zen, by Alan Watts, Vintage, NY, 1957; 1985; 1999.

What the Buddha Taught, by Walpola Rahula, Grove Press, NY, 1959; 1974; 1986.

What Would Buddha Do?, by Franz Metcalf, Ulysses Press, Berkeley, CA, 1999; 2002.

When the Iron Eagle Flies, by Ayya Khema, Wisdom Publications, NY, 2000.

When Things Fall Apart, by Pema Chödrön, Shambhala, Boston, MA, 1997; 2000.

Buddhism-Related Web Sites

Buddha 101: The History, Philosophy, and Practice of Buddhism ✍ www.buddha101.com

A worthwhile site devoted to discussion about: the Four Noble Truths; Dependant Origination; the Eightfold Path; the Three Characteristics of Existence; the Three Jewels and the Five Precepts; Karma and Intention; Rebirth and Nirvana; the History of Buddhism; the Practice of Buddhism. Site also includes books and Buddha shopping.

A Call for Reckoning: Religion and the Death Penalty
✍ http://pewforum.org/deathpenalty/resources/internetresources.php3

A Web site devoted to articles, books, and discussion on the stances various religions take on this topical issue.

Buddhapia ✍ www.buddhapia.com/eng

A Web site devoted to the study of Korean Buddhism.

BuddaMind ✍ www.buddhamind.info

A Web site dedicated to all things Buddhist.

BuddhaNet ✍ www.buddhanet.net/qanda.htm

"A cybersangha" designed to link up people so they can share information on their beliefs and practices.

Buddhism Today ✍ www.buddhismtoday.com

A Web site devoted to the study of Buddhism.

Buddhist Door ✍ www.buddhistdoor.com

A bimonthly magazine sponsored by Tung Lin Kok Yuen.

Colorado State University: The Edicts of King Ashoka
✍ www.cs.colostate.edu/~malaiya/ashoka.html

Written by the Venerable S. Dhammika, this paper discusses in depth the edicts of King Ashoka of the third century B.C.E.

Dalai Lama ✍ *www.dalailama.com*

A Web site dedicated to the life and voice of the current Dalai Lama.

Dharma Haven ✍ *www.dharma-haven.org*

A Harbor from the Storms of Panic and Confusion.

DharmaNet ✍ *www.dharmanet.org*

Among other things, DharmaNet is a wonderful place to find socially engaged Buddhist resources.

The Government of Tibet in Exile ✍ *www.tibet.com*

A Web site dedicated to the current political situation in Tibet, as well as history and teachings on all things Tibetan.

The Greyston Bakery ✍ *www.buycake.com*

A Web site about Bernarnd Tetsugen Glassman and the Greyston Foundation.

In the Footsteps of the Buddha: Traveling in India and Nepal ✍ *www.buddhapath.com*

A travel guide to pilgrimage destinations in India and Nepal.

Nalandabodhi *www.nalandabodhi.org*

A Web site devoted to the study of Buddhism.

Sakyadhita: The International Association of Buddhist Women ✍ *www.sakyadhita.org*

Sakyadhita means "Daughters of the Buddha." The objectives of Sakyadhita are: to promote world peace through the practice of the Buddha's teachings, to create a network for Buddhist women, to promote harmony and understanding among Buddhist traditions, to encourage and help educate women as teachers of Buddhism, to provide improved facilities for women to study and practice, and to help establish a community of ordained nuns where one does not currently exist.

Saigon.com ✍ *www.saigon.com*

An information site on all things Vietnamese.

The Simple Living Network ✍ *www.simpleliving.net*

A Web site focused on creating an international network of like-minded individuals who enjoy sharing their ideas and insights about simple living, or voluntary simplicity.

Tricycle Magazine ✍ *www.tricycle.com*

Founded in 1991, Tricycle is a nonprofit Buddhist magazine.

Voluntary Simple Living: A Dual Social Movement and Indicator of Changing Cultural Values ✍ *www3.telus.net/mapletree/voluntary_simple_living.htm*

An interesting paper providing evidence that: voluntary simple living is both a reform movement and an alternative movement, both movements are in the coalescence stage of development, and voluntary simple living is an expression of changing cultural values.

WAiB (Women Active in Buddhism) ✍ *http://members.tripod.com/~Lhamo/13famou.htm*

A Web site devoted to Buddhist women in society.

The Zoo Fence: A Commentary on the Spiritual Life ✍ *www.zoofence.com*

An independent commentary on matters pertaining to those seeking a spiritual life.

Appendix C

Buddhist Monasteries and Practice Centers in the United States

Alabama

Green Mountain Zen Center
Soto Zen
Huntsville, AL
jag@hiwaay.net

The Fairhope Tibetan Society
Gelugpa Tradition of Tibetan
Buddhism
Fairhope, AL
www.angelfire.com/yt/fairtibet

Zen Center of Huntsville
Zen
Huntsville, AL

Alaska

Anchorage Zen Center
Zen
Anchorage, AK

Anchorage Zen Community
Zen
Anchorage, AK
www.alaska.net/~zen

Juneau Shambhala Center
Shambhala
Juneau, AK
www.shambhala.org/centers/Juneau

Arizona

Bodhi Heart
Tibetan Buddhism
Phoenix, AZ
bodhiheart_info@bodhiheart.org
www.rivetdesign.com/bodhiheart/
default.asp

Desert Lotus Zen Sangha
Zen
Chandler, AZ
www.vuu.org/zen

The Garchen Buddhist Institute
Tibetan Buddhism
Chino Valley, AZ
www.garchen.com

Karma Thegsum Chöling
Tibetan Buddhism
Tempe, AZ
www.kagyu.org/centers/usa/usa-pho.html

Tucson Shambhala Meditation Group
Shambhala
Tucson, AZ
www.azstarnet.com/nonprofit/shambhala

Zen Desert Sangha
Zen
Tucson, AZ

Arkansas

The Ecumenical Buddhist Society of Little Rock Nyingma Practice
Vajrayana Buddhism
Little Rock, AR
www.ebslr.org/nyingma.htm

The Ecumenical Buddhist Society of Little Rock Sakya Practice
Tibetan Buddhism
Little Rock, AR
www.ebslr.org/Sakya.htm

California

BodhiPath Buddhist Center
Tibetan Buddhism
Santa Barbara, CA
www.bodhipath-santabarbara.org

Chagdud Gonpa
Tibetan Buddhism
Various locations
www.snowcrest.net/chagdud

Chico Dharma Study Group
Chico, CA
www.ecst.csuchico.edu/~dsantina

City of Ten Thousand Buddhas
Zen
Talmage, CA
www.drba.org

Community of Mindful Living
Zen
Berkeley, CA
www.iamhome.org

Dechen Ling
Tibetan Buddhist
Hornbrook, CA
http://dechenling.org

Dewikoti Center
Dharma Center of Mahayana
Buddhism
Marin, CA
www.kadampas.org/kbba_pgs/marin.html

Dharma Zen Center
Zen
Los Angeles, CA
www.dharmazen.com

Diamond Way Buddhism
Vajrayana Buddhism
Los Angeles, CA
www.diamondway.org/la

Drikung Kyobpa Chöling
Vajrayana Buddhism
Escondido, CA
www.sanghaweb.com/dkc

Duldzin Dragpa Buddhist Center
Mahayana Buddhism
San Jose, CA
www.kadampas.org/kbba_pgs/sj.html

Dzogchen Community
Tibetan Buddhism
Berkeley, CA
www.dzogchencommunitywest.org

Empty Gate Zen Center
Zen
Berkeley, CA
www.emptygatezen.com

Gyalwa Gyatso Buddhist Center
Mahayana Buddhism
San Jose, CA
www.gyalwagyatso.org

Harbor Sangha
Zen
San Francisco, CA
www.zendo.com/~hs/harbor.html

Hazy Moon Sangha
Zen
Los Angeles, CA
www.hazymoon.com

Healing Buddha Foundation
Tibetan Buddhism
Sebastopol, CA
www.healingbuddha.org

Jikoji Zen Mountain Retreat Center
Zen
Los Gatos, CA
www.zendo.com/~jikoji/jikoji.html

Kagyu Droden Kunchab
Mahayana and Vajrayana Buddhism
San Francisco, CA
www.kdk.org

Karma Mahasiddha Ling
(a.k.a. Idyllwild Dharma Center)
Tibetan Buddhism
Idyllwild, CA (in the San Jacinto Mountains)
www.rinpoche.com/kml.html

Karma Thegsum Chöling
Tibetan Buddhism
Los Angeles, CA; San Diego, CA
Santa Cruz, CA
www.kagyu.org/centers/usa/usa-los.html
www.kagyu.org/centers/usa/usa-sand.html
www.kagyu.org/centers/usa/usa-santc.html

Kannon Do Zen Center
Zen
Mountain View CA
www.howardwade.com/kannon_do/kdo.html

Land of Compassion Buddha
Tibetan Buddhist
West Covina, CA
www.compassionbuddha.org

Mahayana Zengong
Zen
El Monte, CA
www.zengong.org

Mother Tara Sakya Center
Tibetan Buddhism
Los Angeles, CA
www.TaraLing.com

Mt. Baldy Zen Center
Zen
Mt. Baldy, CA
www.mbzc.org

Nyingma Institute
Tibetan Buddhism
Various locations
Berkeley, CA
www.nyingmaInstitute.com

Nyingma in the West
Tibetan Buddhism
Various locations
www.nyingma.org

Odiyan Buddhist Retreat Center
Tibetan Buddhism
Berkeley, CA
www.odiyan.org

Palyul International
Tibetan Buddhism
Mill Valley, CA and various locations
www.palyul.org

Rigpa North America
Vajrayana
Santa Cruz, CA
www.rigpa.org/Courses/RetreatCenters.html

Sakya Dechen Ling
Tibetan Buddhism
Oakland, CA
www.sakyadechenling.org

San Francisco Diamond Way Buddhist Center
Karma Kagyu, Tibetan Buddhism

San Francisco, CA
www.diamondway.org/sf

San Francisco Zen Center
Zen
San Francisco, CA
www.sfzc.com

Saraha Buddhist Center
Mahayana Buddhism
San Francisco, CA
www.kadampas.org/kbba_pgs/sf.html

Shambhala Center
Shambhala
Los Angeles, CA
http://isd.usc.edu/~czachary/ShCen.html

Shambhala Center
Shambala
San Francisco, CA
www.shambhala.org/centers/san-francisco

Shambhala Meditation Center
Shambhala
Berkeley, CA
www.shambhala.org/centers/Berkeley

Shasta Abbey
Zen
Mount Shasta, CA
www.shastaabbey.org

Sonoma Mountain Zen Center
Zen
Sonoma, CA
www.smzc.net

Spirit Rock Meditation Center
Vipashyana
Woodacre, CA
www.spiritrock.org

Thubten Dhargye Ling
Tibetan Buddhism
Long Beach, CA
www.tdling.com

Vajrapani Institute
Tibetan Buddhism
Boulder Creek, CA
www.vajrapani.org

Vajrayana Foundation
Vajrayana Buddhism
Corralitos, CA
www.vajrayana.org

Waken Ray Tseng Temple
El Monte, CA
http://world.tbsn.org/us/waken

Zen Center of Los Angeles
Zen
Los Angeles, CA
www.zencenter.org

Colorado

Boulder Shambhala Meditation Center
Shambhala
Boulder, CO
www.indra.com/jewels/sc

Colorado Ratnashri Sangha
Tibetan Buddhism
Boulder, CO
www.kagyu-medialab.org/ratnashri

Crestone: Karma Thegsum Tashi Gomang
Karma Kagyu Tibetan Buddhist
Crestone, CO
www.kagyu.org/centers/usa/usa-cre.html

Denver Zen Center
Zen
Denver, CO
www.zencenterofdenver.org

Dorje Khyung Dzong
Shambhala
Gardner, CO
www.shambhala.org/centers/dkd

Great Mountain Zen Center
Zen
Boulder, CO
www.gmzc.org

Fort Collins Shambhala Meditation Center
Shambhala
Fort Collins, CO
www.fortcollins.shambhala.org

Nalandabodhi Boulder
Tibetan Buddhist
Boulder, CO
www.nalandabodhi.org/boulder.html

Shambhala Mountain Center
Shambhala Center
Red Feather Lakes, CO
www.rmsc.shambhala.org

Shambhala Meditation Center
Shambhala
Denver, CO
www.shambhala.org/centers/denver

Spring Mountain Sangha
Zen
Colorado Springs, CO
www.pcisys.net/~sms.zen

Tara Mandala Retreat Center
Tibetan Buddhist
Four Corners area, CO
www.taramandala.com

Thubten Shedrup Ling
Tibetan Buddhism
Colorado Springs, CO
www.tsling.com

Connecticut

The Center for Dzogchen Studies
Tibetan Buddhism
New Haven, CT
http://pages.cthome.net/tibetan-buddhism

Chenrezig Tibetan Buddhist Center
Nonsectarian
Middletown, CT
http://dharma-haven.org/cherezig/index.htm

Diamond Way Buddhist Center
Tibetan Buddhist
Naugatuck, CT
http://dharma-haven.org/kagyu

Godstow Retreat Center
Redding, CT
www.world-view.org/godstow/index.html

Hartford Shambhala Meditation Group
Shambhala
Hartford, CT
www.shambhala.org/centers/hartford

Karma Thegsum Chöling
Tibetan Buddhism
Hartford, CT
www.kagyu.org/centers/usa/usa-har.html

Karma Thegsum Chöling
Tibetan Buddhism
New Milford, CT
www.kagyu.org/centers/usa/usa-new.html

Shambhala Center
Shambhala and Tibetan Buddhism
New Haven, CT
http://dharma-haven.org/shambhala

Delaware

Wilmington Menlha Buddhist Center
Tibetan Buddhism
Wilmington, DE
www.geocities.com/menlhaorg/calendar.html

Florida

Cypress Tree Zen Group
Zen
Tallahassee, FL
www.tfn.net/~cypress

Karma Kagyu Study Group
Tibetan Buddhist Center
St. Augustine, FL
www.kagyu.org/centers/usa/usa-sta.html

Karma Thegsum Chöling
Tibetan Buddhist
Gainesville, FL
www.kagyu.org/centers/usa/usa-gai.html

Karma Thegsum Chöling
Tibetan Buddhism
Jacksonville, FL
www.ktcjax.org

Palm Beach Dharma Center
Tibetan Buddhism

Palm Beach, FL
www.pbdc.net

Southern Palm Zen Center
Zen
Boca Raton, FL
www.floridazen.com

Tampa Bay Karma Thegsum Chöling
Tibetan Buddhism
Tampa Bay, FL
www.tampaktc.org

Tubten Kunga Center
Tibetan Buddhist
Palm Beach, Broward, and Dade Counties, FL
www.tubtenkunga.org

Georgia

Atlanta Soto Zen Center
Zen
Atlanta, GA
www.aszc.org

Drepung Loseling Institute
Tibetan Buddhism
Atlanta, GA
www.drepung.org

Shambhala Meditation Center
Shambhala
Atlanta, GA
www.atlantashambhalacenter.org

Hawaii

Diamond Sangha
Zen
Honolulu, HI
www.ciolek.com/WWWVLPages/ZenPages/DiamondSangha.html

Vajrayana Foundation Hawaii
These are Western Buddhists following the Nyingma tradition from Tibet. As teachers of Dzogchen, they offer classes, retreats, and death and dying support.
www.vajrayanahawaii.org

Idaho

Golden Blue Lotus Tara Tibetan Buddhist Meditation Center
Tibetan Buddhism
Moscow, ID
http://community.palouse.net/lotus

Illinois

Chicago Karma Thegsum Chöling
Tibetan Buddhism
Chicago, IL
http://home.attbi.com/~evam/new ktcsite

Jewel Heart Chicago
Tibetan Buddhism
Chicago, IL
www.jewelheart.org/chapters/chicago.html

Rimé Foundation
Tibetan Buddhism
Chicago, IL
www.geocities.com/RimeFoundation

Shambhala Meditation Center
Shambhala
Chicago, IL
www.shambhala.org/centers/chicago

Indiana

Dagom Gaden Tensung Ling Buddhist Monastery
Tibetan Buddhism
Bloomington, IN
www.ganden.org

Indianapolis Zen Center
Zen
Indianapolis, IN
www.ameritech.net/users/indyzen/izg.html

Tibetan Cultural Center
Tibetan Buddhism
Bloomington, IN
www.tibetancc.com

Zen Center of Bloomington
Zen
Bloomington, IN
www.bloomingtonzen.org

Iowa

Ames Karma Kagyu Study Group
Tibetan Buddhism
Gilbert, IA
www.kagyu.org/centers/usa/usa-ames.html

Cedar Rapids Zen Center
Zen
Cedar Rapids, IA
http://avalon.net/~crzc

Kansas

Karma Kagyu Study Group
Tibetan Buddhism
Wichita, KS
www.kagyu.org/centers/usa/usa-wic.html

Shambhala Meditation Center
Shambhala
Kansas City, KS
www.toto.net/community/churchs/kcshambhala/center.htm

Kentucky

Shambhala Center
Shambhala
Lexington, KY
www.shambhala.org/centers/Lexington

Louisiana

The American Zen Association
Zen
New Orleans, LA
http://home.gnofn.org/~aza

Blue Iris Sangha
Zen
New Orleans, LA
http://home.bellsouth.net/p/s/community.dll?ep=16&groupid=45151&ck=

Dhongak Tharling Dharma Center
Tibetan Buddhism
New Orleans, LA
http://quietmountain.com/dharmacenters/dhongak_tharling/dhongak1.htm

Maine

Brunswick Shambhala Center
Shambhala/Tibetan Buddhism
Brunswick and Portland, ME
www.shambhalabp.org

The Morgan Bay Zendo
Zen, Ch'an and *Vipashyana*
Surrey, ME
www.morganbayzendo.org

Maryland

Bodhi Path Buddhist Center
Tibetan Buddhism
Potomac, MD
www.bodhipath.org

The Baltimore Shambhala Meditation Center
General
Baltimore, MD
www.baltimoreshambhala.org

Sakya Phuntsok Ling
Tibetan Buddhism
Silver Spring, MD
http://users.erols.com/sakya

Tibetan Meditation Center
Tibetan Buddhism
Frederick, MD
www.drikungtmc.org

Massachusetts

Boston Shambhala Center
Shambhala
Brookline, MA
www.primordialdot.org

Cambridge Zen Center
Zen
Cambridge, MA
www.cambridgezen.com

Dzogchen Center Cambridge
Tibetan Buddhism
Cambridge, MA
www.cambridgedzogchen.org

Insight Meditation Center
Vipashyana
Barre, MA
www.dharma.org/ims/index.htm

Kurukulla Center for Tibetan Buddhist Studies
Tibetan Buddhism
Boston, MA
www.kurukulla.org

Lama Yeshe Wisdom Archive
Tibetan Buddhism
Weston, MA
www.lamayeshe.com

Manjushri Temple
Tibetan Buddhism
Shrewsbury, MA
http://home.earthlink.net/~ sakyacenter.htm

Rangrig Yeshe Center
Tibetan Buddhism
Stockbridge, MA
www.tibetan-buddhist.org

Sakya Institute
Abhidharma, Madhyamika, and Mind-Training
Cambridge, MA
www.fas.harvard.edu/~pluralsm/ 98wrb/bu_saky.htm

Sakya Retreat Center
Lama Migmar teaches Abhidharma, Madhyamika, and Mind-Training
Barre, MA
http://home.earthlink.net/~ sakyacenter

Single Flower Sangha
Zen
Cambridge, MA
www.singleflowersangha.org

Michigan

Buddhist Society for Compassionate Wisdom
Zen
Ann Arbor, MI
www.zenbuddhisttemple.org

Heart Center: Karma Thegsum Chöling
Tibetan Buddhism
Big Rapids, MI
www.kagyu.org/centers/usa/usa-hea.html

Jewel Heart
Tibetan Buddhism
Ann Arbor, MI
www.jewelheart.org/chapters/anna rbor.html

Karma Thegsum Chöling
Tibetan Buddhism
Ann Arbor, MI
www.kagyu.org/centers/usa/usa-ann.html

Lama Tsong Khapa Center
Tibetan Buddhist
Kalamazoo, MI
http://vajra.us

Michiana Shambhala Meditation Group
Shambhala
Portage, MI
http://hometown.aol.com/ dharmagroup/shambhala.htm

Minnesota

Compassionate Ocean Dharma Center
Zen
Minneapolis, MN
www.oceandharma.org

Clouds in Water Zen Center
Zen
St. Paul, MN
www.cloudsinwater.org

Karma Thegsum Chöling
Tibetan Buddhism
Minneapolis, MN
www.kagyu.org/centers/usa/usa-min.html

Missouri

Boonville One Drop Zendo (formerly Columbia Zen Center)
Zen
Boonville, MO
http://zen.columbia.missouri.org

Rime Buddhist Center
General
Kansas City, MO
www.rimecenter.org

Montana

Osel Shen Phen Ling Tibetan Buddhist Center
Mahayana Tradition
Missoula, MT
www.fpmt-osel.org

Nebraska

Nebraska Zen Center
Zen
Omaha, NE
www.prairiewindzen.org/index2.html

Shen Phen Ling Tibeten Buddhist Center
Tibetan Buddhism
Lincoln, NE
www.fpmt-osel.org

Nevada

Sierra Friends of Tibet
Tibetan Buddhism
www.sierrafriendsoftibet.org

New Hampshire

Dzogchen Sangha
Tibetan Buddhism
Concord, NH
www.geocities.com/concorddzogchen

Shambhala Meditation Group
Shambhala
Hanover, NH
www.shambhala.org/centers/hanover

New Jersey

Olna Gazur
Tibetan Buddhism
Howell, NJ
www.olnagazur.org

Tibetan Buddhist Learning Center
Tibetan Buddhism
Washington, NJ
www.baus.org/misc/tblc.html

The Zen Society
Zen
Cinnaminson, NJ
www.jizo-an.org

New Mexico

Albuquerque Zen Center
Zen
Albuquerque, NM
www.azc.org/azc

Dharma Sangha
Zen
Crestone Mountain, NM

Karma Thegsum Chöling
Tibetan Buddhism
Albuquerque, NM
www.kagyu.org/centers/usa/usa-albu.html

Mountain Cloud Zen Center
Zen
Sante Fe, NM
http://members.tripod.com/~mczc/index.html

New York

Columbia County Karma Kagyu Study Group
Tibetan Buddhism
Ghent, NY
www.kagyu.org/centers/usa/usa-cty.html

Dharma Drum Mountain
Zen
Elmhurst, NY
www.chan1.org

Empty Hand Zendo
Zen
Rye, NY
www.emptyhandzen.org

Jewel Heart Center
Tibetan Buddhism
New York, NY
www.jewelheart.org/chapters/newyork.html

Kagyu Thubten Chöling
Tibetan Buddhism
Wappingers Falls, NY
www.kagyu.com

Karma Thegsum Chöling
Tibetan Buddhism
Albany, NY
www.timesunion.com/communities/albanyktc

Karma Thegsum Chöling
Tibetan Buddhism
New York, NY
www.kagyu.org/centers/usa/usa-nyc.html

Karma Triyana Dharmachakra
Tibetan Buddhism
Woodstock, NY
www.kagyu.org

Namgyal Monastery
Tibetan Buddhism
Ithaca, NY
www.namgyal.org

New York Diamond Way Buddhist Center
Vajrayana Buddhism
New York, NY
http://diamondway.12pt.com

Padmasambhava Buddhist Center
Tibetan Buddhism
Various locations
http://padmasambhava.org

Palyul Ling New York
Tibetan Buddhist
McDonough, NY
www.palyul.org/center_ny/

Pine Hill Zendo
Zen
Katonah, NY
www.pinehillzendo.org

Rangrig Yeshe Center
Tibetan Buddhism
Syracuse, NY
www.tibetan-buddhist.org

Rochester Zen Center
Zen
Rochester, NY
www.rzc.org

The Shambhala Meditation Center of New York
Shambhala
New York City, NY
http://ny.shambhala.org

Shambhala Meditation Group
Shambhala
Albany, NY
www.angelfire.com/ny2/albanyshambhala

Zen Center of New York City/ Fire Lotus Temple
Zen
New York, NY
www.mro.org/zcnyc/firelotus.shtml

North Carolina

Chapel Hill Zen Center
Zen
Chapel Hill, NC
www.intrex.net/chzg

Charlotte Community of Mindfulness
Zen
Charlotte, NC
www.coe.uncc.edu/~billchu/sangha

Kadampa Center
Mahayana Buddhism
Raleigh, NC
www.kadampa-center.org

Karma Thegsum Chöling
Tibetan Buddhism
Durham, NC
www.mindspring.com/~strategix/DurhamKTC

Karma Thegsum Chöling
Tibetan Buddhism
Greenville, NC
www.kagyu.org/centers/usa/usa-gre.html

Shambhala Center
Shambhala
Durham, NC
www.shambhala.org/centers/Durham

Southern Dharma Retreat Center
Variety of paths
Near Asheville and Hot Springs, NC
www.southerndharma.org

Ohio

Cloud Water Zendo
Zen
Cleveland, OH
www.cloudwater.org

Jewel Heart Chapter
Tibetan Buddhism
Cleveland, OH
www.jewelheart.org/chapters/cleveland.html

Shambhala Meditation Group
Shambhala/Tibetan
Cleveland, OH
www.parasamgate.com/shambhala

Shambhala Meditation Group
Shambhala
Columbus, OH
www.shambhala.org/centers/columbus

Oklahoma

Mind Essence Zen Center
Zen
Oklahoma City, OK
www.geocities.com/Paris/Metro/1494

Oregon

Dharma Rain Zen Center
Zen
Portland, OR
www.dharma-rain.org

Diamond Way Buddhist Group
Tibetan Buddhism
Portland, OR
www.diamondway.org/Portland

Kagyu Changchub Chuling
Vajrayana Buddhism
Portland, OR
www.kcc.org

Karma Kagyu Study Group
Tibetan Buddhism
Portland, OR
www.kagyu.org/centers/usa/usa-por.html

Shambhala Meditation Center
Shambhala
Portland, OR
www.portlandcenter.net

Zen Community of Oregon
Zen
Portland, OR
www.zendust.org

Pennsylvania

Karma Kagyu Study Group
Tibetan Buddhism
Perkiomenville, PA
www.kagyu.org/centers/usa/usa-per.html

The Philadelphia Meditation Center
Tibetan Buddhism
Havertown, PA
http://philadelphiameditation.org

Shambhala Meditation Center
Tibetan Buddhism, Shambhala
Philadelphia, PA
www.philashambhala.org

Three Rivers Dharma Center/ Buddhist Society of Pittsburgh
Pittsburgh, PA
http://trfn.clpgh.org/bsp/trdcgroup.html

Tibetan Buddhist Center
Nonsectarian
Philadelphia, PA
www.libertynet.org/~tibetan

Rhode Island

The Kwan Um School of Zen
Korean Zen
Cumberland, RI
www.kwanumzen.com/kusz-body.shtml

Providence Zen Center
Zen
Cumberland, RI
www.kwanumzen.com/pzc

South Carolina

Charleston Zen Center
Zen
Charleston, SC
www.geocities.com/chaszencenter

Shambhala Center
Tibetan Buddhism
Columbia, SC
http://members.tripod.com/~ColumbiaSC_Shambhala

The Skyflower Dharma Center
Tibetan Buddhism
Outside of Columbia, SC
www.geocities.com/Athens/Acropolis/1943

South Carolina Buddhist Dharma Group
Tibetan Buddhism
Columbia, SC
www.scdharmagroup.org

Tennessee

Losel Shedrup Ling
Tibetan Buddhism
Knoxville, TN
www.korrnet.org/lslk

The Nashville Tibetan Buddhist Group
Tibetan Buddhism
Nashville, TN
www.nashvilletibetbuddhism.com

Nashville Zen Center
Zen
Nashville, TN
www.nashvillezencenter.org

Shambhala Memphis
Shambhala
Memphis, TN
www.dharmamemphis.com/dm/shambhala/shambhala.html

Texas

Dallas Shambhala Center
Shambhala
Dallas, TX
www.shambhala.org/centers/dallas

Dawn Mountain
Tibetan Buddhism
Houston, TX
www.dawnmountain.org

Diamond Way Buddhist Center
Vajrayana Buddhism
Austin, TX
http://uts.cc.utexas.edu/~diamond

Diamond Way Buddhist Centers
Tibetan Buddhism
Houston and Clear Lake, TX
*http://members.tripod.com/~
diamondway/kagyu.html*

Karma Kagyu Study Group
Tibetan Buddhism
Midland, TX
*www.kagyu.org/centers/usa/usa-
mid.html*

Karma Thegsum Chöling
Tibetan Buddhism
Dallas, TX
www.ktcdallas.org

Maria Kannon Zen Center
Zen
Dallas, TX
www.mkzc.org

**Nalandabodhi Texas
Study Groups**
Tibetan Buddhism
Various locations
www.nalandabodhi.org/texas.html

Shambhala Center
Shambhala
San Antonio, TX
www.sashambhala.org

Shambhala Meditation Center
Shambhala
Austin, TX
www.shambhala.org/centers/austin

Shambhala Meditation Center
Shambhala
Houston, TX
*http://web2.iadfw.net/dharma/inde
x.html*

Utah

Kanzeon Zen Center
Zen
Salt Lake City, UT
www.zencenterutah.org

Vermont

Anadaire Celtic Buddhist Center
Celtic Buddhism
Putney, VT
www.celticbuddhism.org

**Karmê-Chöling Buddhist
Meditation Center**
Tibetan Buddhism and Shambhala
Barnet, VT
www.kcl.shambhala.org

Shambhala Center
Shambhala
Burlington, VT
*www.shambhala.org/centers/Burlin
gton*

Shambhala Meditation Center
Shambhala
St. Johnsbury, VT
www.stjshambhala.org

Virginia

Ekoji Buddhist Sangha
Pure Land, Zen, and Tibetan
Buddhism
Richmond, VA
www.ekojirichmond.org

Washington

Chagdud Gonpa Amrita
Tibetan Buddhism
Seattle, WA
www.cmc.net/~amrita

Cloud Mountain Zen Center
Zen
Castle Rock, WA
www.cloudmountain.org

Dai Bai Zan Cho Bo Zen Temple
Zen
Seattle, WA
www.choboji.org

Dharma Friendship Foundation
Tibetan Buddhism
Seattle, WA
http://dharmafriendship.org

Dharma Sound Zen Center
Zen
Seattle, WA
www.dharmasound.org

Nalandabodhi
Tibetan Buddhism
Seattle, WA
www.nbseattle.org

**Sakya Kachod Chöling
Retreat Center**
Tibetan Buddhism
San Juan Island, WA
www.rockisland.com/~thrinley

**Sakya Monastery of
Tibetan Buddhism**
Tibetan Buddhism
Seattle, WA
www.sakya.org

**Seattle Karma
Kagvu Study Group**
Tibetan Buddhism
Seattle, WA
*http://members.aol.com/seakksg/se
akksg*

Washington, D.C.

Washington Mindfulness Community
Zen
Washington, D.C.
www.mindfulnessdc.org

Wisconsin

Deer Park Buddhist Center
Tibetan Buddhism
Oregon, WI
www.deerparkcenter.org

Diamond Way Buddhism
Vajrayana Buddhism
La Crosse, WI
www.diamondway.org/lacrosse

Diamond Way Buddhist Center
Vajrayana Buddhism
Madison, WI
www.diamondway.org/Madison

Dragon Flower Ch'an Temple
Zen
Rhinelander, WI
www.dragonflower.org

Karma Kagyu Study Group
Tibetan Buddhism
Hay River, WI
www.kagyu.org/centers/usa/usa-hay.html

Mahayana Dharma Center
Mahayana Dharma
Spring Green, WI
http://dharmacenter.globalview-intl.com

Milwaukee Shambhala Center
Shambhala
Milwaukee, WI
www.shambhalacenter.org/home0.html

Oshkosh Zen Group
Zen
Oshkosh, WI
http://personalpages.tds.net/~ozg

Index

A

Abhidhyan Yoga Institute, 172
actions
    and karma, 7, 33, 78–82, 93, 94
    and rebirth, 83–84
    right action, 38, 42, 44, 46–47
aggregates, 32–34
Ajatasattu, King, 104, 226
American Buddhism, 248–51, 255
Ananda, 104, 108, 113, 222
anatman, 35
animals, 86, 92, 94–97
architecture, 226–28
arhats, 108, 117–18, 191, 192, 193
Aristotle, 10
Armstrong, Karen, 105, 194
art, 225–36
Art of Happiness, 244
asceticism, 20, 55
ascetics, 17, 20–21
Ashoka, King, 9, 109–11, 113, 130,
    135, 201, 226–27
Ashokan Pillar, 201, 202
Atisha, 150–51, 153
attachment, 29, 32–34, 37, 86, 98
Avalokiteshvara, 88, 121, 125, 153,
    154, 180

B

Baker, Richard, 261
Basho, 232, 233
Batchelor, Stephen, 244
Beck, Charlotte Joko, 222
beginner's mind, 71, 72, 160–63, 261
Being Peace, 68
Bercholz, Samuel, 196
Bertolucci, Bernardo, 246
Bessette, Carolyn, 80
bhikkunis, 132, 222
bhikkus, 28, 59–60
Bodhgaya, 200, 202
Bodhi Tree, 22–23, 68, 131, 202
bodhicitta, 121, 180, 193
Bodhidharma, 137–38, 159, 165, 197
bodhisattvas, 59, 88, 119–21, 170,
    192–93
Bön, 124, 147–49
Book of Tea, The, 205
Book of the Kindred Saying, The,
    190
Borobudur Temple, *135*, 227
Bound by Command school, 148,
    150–51
bowing, 162
Brahmins, 14, 15, 98, 99
breath, concentration on, 50,
    162–63, 176–77
Buddha, 105, 194
Buddha
    birth of, 14, 200
    death of, 13, 105–6, 226–27
    early life of, 15–26
    ethics of, 51–63
    eyes of, *259*
    as first jewel, 66, 68–69
    as Fully Awakened One, 22, 25,
       66
    gold Buddha, *18*
    history of, *xi*
    laughing Buddha, *229*, 231
    life of, 13, 104–5
    living Buddha, 69, 75, 147
    meditating Buddha, *11*, *93*
    quotes by, 6, 81, 104, 196, 201
    reclining Buddha, *173*, 229
    son of, 18, 215
    statues of, *70*, *88*, 228–29, *245*
    teachings of, 2–3, 27–39, 70
    see also Gautama, Siddhartha
buddha-nature, 62, 120, 138–39, 162,
    260
Buddha of Infinite Light, 138
Buddhaghosa, 131
Buddhism
    awareness of, 146
    beginnings of, 2
    choosing, 256–57
    diversification of, 111, 114, 116–17
    first evidence of, 9
    holy sites of, 200
    practicing, 4, 253–61
    resources on, 75, 266–70
    schools of, 109
    spread of, 109, 113–14, 127,
       129–43

traditions of, *xi*
understanding of, *xi*, 1–3
vehicles of, 111, 115–27
in the West, 237–51, 255–56
Buddhist centers, 74, 271–81
Buddhist community, 65–75, 257
Buddhist cosmos, 85, 86, 91–102
Buddhist Handbook, The, 94, 189
Buddhist Temple, 99, *113*, 201, *217*
Buddhists, number of, 2, 5, 74
Burma, 111, 113, 131–33

C

calendars, 209–10
calligraphy, 233–35, 260
Cambodia, 111, 113, 133, 134, 142
Catholicism, 241, 242
cave temples, 228
celebrations, 199–212
celibacy, 220
Ch'an Buddhism, 136–39, 152, 159.
    See also Zen Buddhism
Chan, Jackie, 245
Chandler, Russell, 2
change
    and death, 223
    and five aggregates, 32–34
    and karma, 79, 82, 84
    and suffering, 35, 140
Channa, 17, 18
Chanoyu, 205
chashitsu, 206
children, 214–15
Chin-wu, Chiang, 155
China, 2, 8, 12, 111, 113, 133,
    136–38, 142, 146, 156
Chödrön, Pema, 179, 222, 244
Christianity, 1, 2, 11, 60–61, 102, 194,
    225, 240, 241
Clarke, Richard B., 254
Coleman, James William, 215, 242
community, 65–75, 257
compassion
    bodhisattva of, 88, 153–54, 180

of Buddha, 24–25
and mindfulness, 49
principles of, 44, 45, 53, 61–62,
    82, 120–21
compassionate meditation, 179–80
*Complete Idiot's Guide to
    Understanding Buddhism, The*,
    179, 216
concentration, 38, 42, 44, 49–50, 57,
    121, 180
Confucianism, 8, 12, 216
consciousness, 33–34, 56, 86, 100
Cooper, David A., 196
cosmos. *See* Buddhist cosmos
craving, 52–53, 66–67, 82, 85–86, 98,
    186

D

daikensho, 192, 194
Dakpo Kagyu school, 152
Dalai Lama
    first lamas, 154, 155
    meaning of, 153
    popularity of, *xii*, 124, 143, 145,
        244
    and practice, 39
    of present day, 125, 146, 149, 154,
        181, 242
    quotes by, 22, 25, 154, 196
dana, 210
death, coping, 25–26, 61–62, 83,
    223–24, 251
death, symbolism of, 86
demons, 23–24, *24*, 95–96
denizens, 94, 95, 98
desire
    as cause of suffering, 36–37, 67
    elimination of, 4, 186
    and Nirvana, 194–95
    problem with, 6, 45
    as sickness, 30
    symbolism of, 86, 98
Desire, Realm of, 94–98
Devanampiyatissa, King, 130–31

Dhammapada, 70, 112, 118, 187,
    192, 219
dharma, 27, 29, 66, 70–71, 110
dharma body, 120
Dharma Communications, 248
Dharma Wheel, 28, 44, 202
dharmakaya, 120
Dharmek Stupa, 202
diamond Sutra, 112
Dogen, 139, 160, 165, 197, 226
dokusan, 164, 166, 167
duhkha, 19, 22, 30–36
Dzogchen, 149, 152

E

Earth Sangha, 204
Edicts of King Ashoka, 110
education, 216–17
effort, 22, 38, 42, 44, 48, 57
ego, 23, 35, 45, 85, 258
Eight Gates of Zen, The, 248
Eightfold Path
    actions of, 38, 42
    categories of, 42–43
    as cure for sickness, 30
    and karma, 89
    as key to Nirvana, 127, 185, 186
    practicing, 44, 57, 70
    and rebirth, 83–84
    steps toward, 38–39, 41
Ekai, Mumon, 197
Elements of Buddhism, The, 189
emptiness, 121, 137, 259–60
Engaged Buddhism, 204, 249, 251
enlightenment
    attaining, 2, 5–6, 37, 71, 96, 101,
        120, 124–25, 193, 197
    benefits of, 6–8
    enjoying, 165
    moment of, 30
    stages of, 191–92
    understanding, 196–97
    see also Nirvana
enso, 234

Entering the Stream, 196
Epstein, Mark, 247, 248, 258
Essential Buddhism, 124, 191
ethics, 8, 51–63, 180

F

Fields, Rick, 239
Fire Sermon, 37, 195
First Council, 107–8, 117
First Sermon, 202
Five Ascetics, 20–21, 26, 28
Five Hindrances, 57–58
Five Precepts, 51, 52, 57, 83–84
form, 86, 122
Form, Realm of, 99–100
Four Great Kings, 100
Four Great Vows, 170
Four Noble Truths, 29–39, 45, 89,
    117, 121, 127, 186
Fourth Council, 110–11, 112
Freud, Sigmund, 247
Fruit teachings, 151
fukusa, 206, 207
Fully Awakened One, 22, 25, 66
furo, 206, 207

G

Gach, Gary, 179, 216, 259
Gambo, Songtsen, 140, 146
Gampopa, 152
Ganden Monastery, 153
gantha-dhura, 118
gassho, 162, 208
gatha, 170
Gautama, Siddhartha
    and ascetics, 20
    birth of, 14, 200
    death of, 13, 105–6, 226–27
    early life of, 15–26
    encounters of, 5–6, 17, 21
    marriage of, 16
    son of, 18, 215
    see also Buddha

Gelug tradition, 148, 153
generosity, 53, 54, 82, 180, 210
Gere, Richard, 145
ghosts, 86, 94, 95, 97–98
Ginsberg, Allen, 238, 244, 256
Glassman, Bernard Tetsugen, 244,
    249–50
God, 194–95, 240–41
gods, 85, 92, 94, 95
Golden Rule, *xi*, 8
Goldstein, Joseph, 244, 255, 256
Great Translator, The, 131
*Greater Discourse on the
    Foundations of Mindfulness,
    The*, 182
greed, 52–53, 66–67, 82, 85–86,
    98, 186
group practice, 164–65, 255, 257
guru, 125, 127, 154
Gyatso, Tenzin, 156
Gyelpo, Khön Könchok, 151

H

Haiku, 232–33
half lotus position, 161, 176
Halifax, Joan Jiko, 251
Hanh, Thich Nhat, 3, 49, 68, 169,
    194, 203, 239–41, 244
hara, 176
Harvey, Peter, 83
hatred, 45, 52, 53, 57–58, 66–67,
    82, 85, 98, 186
Heart Sutra, 112, 122, 170
hell, 86, 92, 94–95, 98, 195
Hill of Sanchi, 227
Himalayan Mountains, 14, 124, 140
Hinayana Buddhism, 111, 116
Hinduism, 1, 8, 11–12, 98
holidays, 209–12
Holmes, Sandra, 250
How to Meditate, 179
Howe, Julia Ward, 238
Hsüan-tsang, 203

humans, 85, 94, 95, 96–97
hungry ghosts, 86, 94, 95, 97–98

I

ignorance, 52, 66–67, 83, 85–86,
    96, 186
ikebana, 235
Ikkyu, 220
illusions, 4, 34, 35, 172, 189
impermanence, 22, 26, 32, 84–85,
    172, 194, 223
India, 2, 8, 9, 11–15, 23, 103–14,
    130, 146, 202–3
insight meditation, 118
Insight Meditation School, 255
interconnectedness, 22, 41
intoxicants, 56–57
Introduction to Buddhism, An, 83
Isipatana, 26, 28
Islam, 1, 11, 225

J

James, William, 247, 248
Japan, 71, 72, 111, 113, 136, 139–40,
    142
Jataka tales, 112, 228
Jayavarman, King, VII, 134
Jesus, 9, 239–40
*Jewel Ornament of Liberation,
    The*, 152
Jones, Ernest, 247
Judaism, 11
Jung, Carl, 247
Jushin, Joshu, 167

K

Kagyu tradition, 148, 152
Kakuzo, Okakura, 206
kalpas, 92, 95
Kamad, 148, 150–51
Kanishka, King, 110–11, 228
Kapleau, Philip, 244, 256

Kapor, Mitch, 48
karma
    basis of, 33
    misconceptions of, 78–81
    negative karma, 80–82, 88–89
    positive karma, 80–82, 88–89
    and rebirth, 83–88
    understanding, 6–7, 77–79, 93, 94
    Vedic doctrines of, 12
Karma Kagyu school, 152
kashi, 206, 207
Katagiri, Dainin, 73
Kennedy, John F., 79–80
Kennedy, John F., Jr., 79–80
Kennedy, Robert, 79–80
kensho, 192
Kerouac, Jack, 238, 244
Khema, Ayya, 58, 244
Khön school, 151
kindness, 45, 48, 53, 56.
    See also loving-kindness
King, Martin Luther, Jr., 239
kinhin, 163, 167, 181
koans, 164, 166–68
Kondanna, 14, 20, 30
Korea, 111, 113, 136
Korean Buddhism, 141–42, 239
Kornfield, Jack, 184, 244, 255, 256
Kung Fu, 138
Kushinagara, 200, 201

L

Lam-dre, 151
lama, 125, 153, 154
*Lamp for the Path of
    Enlightenment*, 150, 151
Lao-tzu, 8, 12, 140–41
Laos, 111, 113, 133–35, 142
laughing Buddha, *229*, 231
Leggett, Trevor, 183
Levitt, Peter, 244
Lion Capital, 202, 226
Little Buddha, 246

livelihood, 38, 42, 44, 47–48
living Buddha, 69, 75, 147
Living Buddha, Living Christ, 239
Loori, John Daido, 172, 244, 248–49
Lopez, Donald S., Jr., 52
lotus position, 161, 175–76
Lotus Sutra, 39, 112, 140, 170
love, 24, 56
loving-kindness, 44, 49, 61, 82–83,
    179–80
Low, Albert, 61, 244
Lumbini, 200
Lumbini Garden, 201, 226
Lust for Enlightenment, 220

M

Macau, 142
Macy, Joanna, 244
Madhyamika, 123
magic, 118, 124, 125, 127, 147
Maguire, Jack, 124, 191, 244
Mahabodhi Temple, 202
Mahamudra, 152
Mahayana Buddhism, 109, 111,
    115–23, 134–36, 142, 192–93, 238,
    256
Mahayana canon, 111, 112, 140
Mahinda, 130–31, 132
Mainyu, Aura, 10–11
Maitreya, 122, 192, 231
mandalas, 125, *169*, 230
Mani wheels, 125–26
Manjushri, 119, 121
mantras, 125, 154, 175, 180–81, *211*
Mara, 23–24, 58, 69
Marpa, 152
marriage, 218–20
masks, *141*
Matrix, The, 189, 245
Matthiessen, Peter, 244
Maya, Queen, 14, 16, 200–201
Mazda, Ahura, 10–11
McClure, Michael, 244
McDonald, Kathleen, 179

meditating Buddha, *11, 93*
meditation
    benefits of, 172
    breathing, 50, 162–63, 176–77
    length of, 162
    mental discipline of, 45
    one-pointed meditation, 50
    posture for, 161, 175–76, 179
    practicing, 20, 58, 121, 138,
        160–69, 171–84
    reasons for, 4, 172
    supplies for, 161, 173–74
    techniques for, 164–69, 177–81
    types of, 149, 152, 160–63, 171
    Vedic doctrines of, 12
meditation cushions, 161, 173, 174
mendicant monks, 18, 47, 104, 130
mental discipline, 43, 45, 50, 156
Merton, Thomas, 241–42
metta, 179, 257
Middle Way, 30, 38, 41, 44, 212
Middle Way, The, 189
Milarepa, 152
mindfulness
    of Buddha, 21–23
    and children, 214–15
    practicing, 58, 160, 163, 168–69,
        182–84, 261–62
    right mindfulness, 38, 42, 44,
        49, 57
    understanding, 3–5
Miracle of Mindfulness, The, 169,
    194, 244
moment, living in, 3–5, 21–23, 49,
    169, 246, 261–62
moment, staying in, 45, 160, 163,
    168–69, 182–84
"Monkey Temple," *202*
monks, 17–19, 28, *31*, 47, *54*, 59–60
morality, 4, 43, 44, 63, 121
"Mother of Buddhism," 16
Mount Meru, 95, 96, 100
Mount Tremper, 172, 248
Mountains and Rivers, 248–49

Mu, 167–68
mudra, 127
Mulagandhakuti Vihara, 202
mustard seed, 25–26
Myanmar, 131, 133, 142

N

Nalanda University, 82, 203, 216, 217
Naropa, 152
Naropa Institute, 87, 222
Naropa University, 157, 216
Nepal, 14, 23, 110, 111, 113, 142, 200–201
New Buddhism, The, 215, 242, 243
nibbana, 7. *See also* Nirvana
Nichiren Buddhism, 140, 239
Nine Schools of Son, 142
nirmanakaya, 120
Nirvana, 185–97
    after death, 193–94
    attaining, 4, 6, 172, 191, 197
    definition of, 4, 186
    versus Heaven, 194–95
    and paranirvana, 105
    path to, 28–30, 38–39
    teachers on, 195–97
    see also enlightenment
Nirvana Temple, 201
no-body, 194–95
No-Form, Realm of, 100–101
no-soul, 35
no-thing, 167, 258–60
Norbu, Thubten Jigme, 154
nothingness, 4–5, 100, 258
Nung, Shen, 208
nuns, 16, 58, 132, 222
Nyingma tradition, 148, 149

O

O'Halloran, Maureen "Soshin," 222
ox-herding pictures, 233–34

P

Padmasambhava, 124, 147–48, 149, 224
pagoda, *106, 150*
Pali canon, 112, 117, 122, 131
paramitas, 180
paranirvana, 105, 193
past lives, 92, 97
Path teachings, 151
Path to Purity, 131
Path to Tranquility, The, 196
Path with Heart, A, 184
peace, 2, 38, 48, 204, 260
Peace Is Every Step, 203
pilgrimages, 200–203
Plato, 10
poetry, 232–33
Prajapati, 16, 221
prajna. *See* wisdom
Prajna-paramita Sutra, 119
prayer wheels, *43*, 125–26
precepts, 51, 52, 57, 59–61, 108–9
psychotherapy, 247–48
Pure Land Buddhism, 116, 123, 136, 138–39, 142

R

Racing Toward 2001, 2
Radiant Mind, 196
Rahula, 18, 215
Rahula, Walpola, 45, 196
Ramkhamhaeng, King, 134
Rank, Otto, 247
reality, 4, 28, 45, 172
Realm of Desire, 94–98
Realm of Form, 99–100
Realm of No-Form, 100–101
realms of existence, 93–101, 181
rebirth
    cycle of, 7, 18, 20, 57, 84–88, 92
    freedom from, 96, 101
    results of, 78, 83, 193
refuge, 6, 67–69

reincarnation, 6, 12
Rexroth, Kenneth, 238, 244
right action, 38, 42, 44, 46–47
right concentration, 38, 42, 44, 49–50, 57
right effort, 38, 42, 44, 48
right livelihood, 38, 42, 44, 47–48
right mindfulness, 38, 42, 44, 49, 57
right speech, 38, 42, 44, 46
right thought, 38, 42, 43, 45–46
right understanding, 38, 42, 43, 44–45
Rinpoche, Chögyam Trungpa, 84, 87, 256, 260–61
Rinpoche, Dilgo Khyentse, 102
Rinpoche, Gen, 180, 181
Rinpoche, Samdhong, 156
Rinpoche, Taktser, 154
Rinzai school, 139–40
rites of passage, 215–16
Robles, Al, 244
Roosevelt, Franklin D., 257
roshi, 71, 164
Roshi, Hakuyu Taizan Maezumi, 248
Roshi, Suzuki, 71, 196, 244

S

"Sage of the Shakya Clan," 17, 22
Saijo, Albert, 244
Sakya tradition, 148, 151
Sakyadhita, 58
Salzberg, Sharon, 222, 244, 255, 256
samadhi, 43, 50, 166
sambhogakaya, 120
samsara
    cycle of, 7, 18, 20, 57, 84–88, 92
    escaping, 96, 101
    results of, 78, 83, 193
sand paintings, 230
sangha, 66, 68, 74, 164, 257
Sanghamitta, 131, 132
Sarnath, 200, 202, 203, 226
satori, 192, 194, 196
"School of the Elders," 117

schools of thought, 111, 115–27
Second Council, 108–9, 114, 116, 119
seiza, 161
Sengstan, 254, 255
sesshin, 34, 167, 170
Seven Years in Tibet, 245
sexual misconduct, 55–56, 221, 260–61
Shaku, Soyen, 238
Shakya, 14, 17
Shakyamuni, 17, 22
Shakyamuni Buddha, 146
shamanism, 141, 147
shamatha, 177
Shantideva, 78, 82
Shaolin Temple, 138
shastras, 112
shikantaza, 165
shila, 4, 43, 44, 63, 121
Shion, Kakuan, 234
shoshin, 71, 72
shunyata, 122
Silence, Simplicity, and Solitude, 196
Six Perfections, 121
Six Symbolic Worlds, 85–86
Six Yogas of Naropa, 152
Snelling, John, 94, 189
Snyder, Gary, 238, 244
Socrates, 10
Son Buddhism, 142
Soto school, 139–40
soul, 35–36, 194–95
speech, 38, 42, 44, 46
Spirit Rock Meditation Center, 255, 256
spiritual world, 125–26
Sri Lanka, *xii*, 2, 22, 58, 111–13, 130–32, 142, 200
Star Wars, 246
statues, *70*, *88*, 228–29, *245*
Stevens, John, 220
Stone, Sharon, 243
Story of Buddhism, The, 52

Stuart, Maurine, 222, 244
stupas, 106, 107, 201, 226–28, *250*
Suddhodhana, King, 14–16, 201
suffering
    causes of, 4, 11, 22, 30–37, 67, 84–85
    cessation of, 4, 19, 30, 37–39, 58, 63, 94, 186, 187, 190
    letting go of, 20, 29
sutras, 70, 112, 170
Suzuki, D. T., 196, 238, 239, 241, 244
Suzuki, Shunryu, 72, 160, 244

T

T'an-ching in the Way of Zen, 197
tantras, 112, 123
Tantric Buddhism, 116, 124, 135, 149. *See also* Vajrayana Buddhism
tantric practices, 152, 154, 221
Taoism, 8, 12
Te Tao Ching, 12
tea ceremonies, 205–9, 233
teachers, 72, 75, 84, 87, 164, 166, 195–97, 216, 260–61
teisho, 164, 165, 167
Temple of the Tooth, 131, 132
Ten Commandments, 60, 82
Ten Precepts, 59, 61, 108–9
Ten Stages, 248, 249
Tendzin, Osel, 222
Thailand, 111, 113, 131, 133–34, 142
thangkas, *207*, 230
therapy, 247–48
Theravada Buddhism, 109, 111–12, 115–18, 121–23, 133–35, 142, 191, 193, 255
Third Council, 109–10, 114
Thoughts Without a Thinker, 248, 258
Three Body Doctrine, 120–21
Three Jewels, 51, 66
Three Poisons, 66–67, 85, 186

Thurman, Robert, 244
Tibet, *xii*, 2, 111, 113, 123–24, 140–43, 154–57
Tibetan Book of the Dead, 70, 83, 93, 223, 224
Tibetan Buddhism, 116, 145–57, 239, 256
Tibetan Buddhism from the Ground Up, 196
Tilopa, 152
titans, 86, 92, 94, 95–96
tonglen, 179–80
Toshoji Temple, 222
Transmitted Command school, 148, 152
Tricycle: The Buddhist Review, 242
Tripitaka, 131
Trungpa, Chögyam, 157, 222
truth, 3, 29–39, 120
Truth of Dhukha, 30–36
Truth of the Cause of Suffering, 30, 36–37
Truth of the Cessation of Suffering, 30, 37–38
Truth of the Path That Leads to Nirvana, 30, 38–39
Tsongkhapa, 153
Tworkov, Helen, 242

U

Ultimate Reality, 28, 37
Ultimate Truth, 29, 45
unborn, 189, 190, 191
unconditioned, 189, 190, 191
understanding, 38, 42, 43, 44–45
United States, Buddhism in, 118, 143, 157, 238–39, 248–51, 255–56
unmade, 189, 190, 191
unoriginated, 189, 190, 191
Upali, 107, 108
Upanishads, 8, 11–12
Upaya Study Center, 250, 251

V

Vacchagotta, 72
Vaishyas, 15
vajras, 127
Vajrayana Buddhism, 115, 116, 123–27, 133, 192
Varanasi, 26, 28
Vedic doctrines, 11–12
vegetarians, 47, 212
vehicles of Buddhism, 111, 115–27
"Verses on the Faith-Mind," 254, 255
Vietnam, 111, 113, 133, 142
Vietnam War, *xii*, 239
violence, 24, 45, 48, 83
vipashyana, 177, 178, 184, 255–57
vipashyana-dhura, 118
Virtuous school, 148, 153
Visuddhimagga, 131
"Voice of Enlightenment," 131
vows, taking, 52, 139, 170

W

Waldman, Anne, 238, 244
walking meditation, 163, 181
Wallace, B. Alan, 196
war, 48, 86, 96
Wat Pho, 229
Watts, Alan, 197, 244

Wei, Wang, 174
Welch, Lew, 244
Western Buddhism, 237–51
Whalen, Philip, 244
What the Buddha Taught, 196
Wheel of Life, The, 84–88, *188*
When the Iron Eagle Flies, 58
When Things Fall Apart, 179
wisdom, *x*, 43, 44, 118–21, 180
women, 221–23
Wu, Emperor, 137–38

Y

yanas, 117. *See also* vehicles of Buddhism
Yasodhara, 16, 18, 222
yoga, *xi*, 12, 20
Yogacara, 116, 123

Z

Zabat-Zinn, John, 232
zabuton, 161, 174
zafus, 161, 174
zazen, 160–64, 167, 168, 170, 172, 177
Zen and the Birds of Appetite, 241
Zen and the Ways, 183
Zen art, 233–36

Zen Buddhism, 159–70
  beginner's mind, 160–63
  group practice, 164–65
  koan practice, 166–68
  meditation, 160–63
  origins of, 136–39, 159
  popularity of, 123, 245–46
  schools of, 116, 139–40
  teachers of, 72, 164
  in the West, 238
  work practice, 168–69
  see also Ch'an Buddhism
Zen master, 71
Zen Mind, Beginner's Mind, 160, 244
Zen Mountain Monastery, 172, 248–49
Zen Teachings of Bodhidharma, The, 197
zendo, 164, 168, 257
zenga, 234
Zenji, Dogen, 248
Zoroaster, 10–11

THE EVERYTHING SERIES!

BUSINESS

Everything® Business Planning Book
Everything® Coaching and Mentoring Book
Everything® Fundraising Book
Everything® Home-Based Business Book
Everything® Landlording Book
Everything® Leadership Book
Everything® Managing People Book
Everything® Negotiating Book
Everything® Online Business Book
Everything® Project Management Book
Everything® Robert's Rules Book, $7.95
Everything® Selling Book
Everything® Start Your Own Business Book
Everything® Time Management Book

COMPUTERS

Everything® Computer Book

COOKBOOKS

Everything® Barbecue Cookbook
Everything® Bartender's Book, $9.95
Everything® Chinese Cookbook
Everything® Chocolate Cookbook
Everything® Cookbook
Everything® Dessert Cookbook
Everything® Diabetes Cookbook
Everything® Fondue Cookbook
Everything® Grilling Cookbook
Everything® Holiday Cookbook
Everything® Indian Cookbook
Everything® Low-Carb Cookbook
Everything® Low-Fat High-Flavor Cookbook
Everything® Low-Salt Cookbook
Everything® Mediterranean Cookbook
Everything® Mexican Cookbook
Everything® One-Pot Cookbook
Everything® Pasta Cookbook
Everything® Quick Meals Cookbook
Everything® Slow Cooker Cookbook
Everything® Soup Cookbook

Everything® Thai Cookbook
Everything® Vegetarian Cookbook
Everything® Wine Book

HEALTH

Everything® Alzheimer's Book
Everything® Anti-Aging Book
Everything® Diabetes Book
Everything® Dieting Book
Everything® Hypnosis Book
Everything® Low Cholesterol Book
Everything® Massage Book
Everything® Menopause Book
Everything® Nutrition Book
Everything® Reflexology Book
Everything® Reiki Book
Everything® Stress Management Book
Everything® Vitamins, Minerals, and
    Nutritional Supplements Book

HISTORY

Everything® American Government Book
Everything® American History Book
Everything® Civil War Book
Everything® Irish History & Heritage Book
Everything® Mafia Book
Everything® Middle East Book

HOBBIES & GAMES

Everything® Bridge Book
Everything® Candlemaking Book
Everything® Card Games Book
Everything® Cartooning Book
Everything® Casino Gambling Book, 2nd Ed.
Everything® Chess Basics Book
Everything® Crossword and Puzzle Book
Everything® Crossword Challenge Book
Everything® Drawing Book
Everything® Digital Photography Book
Everything® Easy Crosswords Book
Everything® Family Tree Book

Everything® Games Book
Everything® Knitting Book
Everything® Magic Book
Everything® Motorcycle Book
Everything® Online Genealogy Book
Everything® Photography Book
Everything® Poker Strategy Book
Everything® Pool & Billiards Book
Everything® Quilting Book
Everything® Scrapbooking Book
Everything® Sewing Book
Everything® Soapmaking Book

HOME IMPROVEMENT

Everything® Feng Shui Book
Everything® Feng Shui Decluttering Book, $9.95
Everything® Fix-It Book
Everything® Homebuilding Book
Everything® Home Decorating Book
Everything® Landscaping Book
Everything® Lawn Care Book
Everything® Organize Your Home Book

EVERYTHING® KIDS' BOOKS

All titles are $6.95

Everything® Kids' Baseball Book, 3rd Ed.
Everything® Kids' Bible Trivia Book
Everything® Kids' Bugs Book
Everything® Kids' Christmas Puzzle
    & Activity Book
Everything® Kids' Cookbook
Everything® Kids' Halloween Puzzle
    & Activity Book
Everything® Kids' Hidden Pictures Book
    Everything® Kids' Joke Book
Everything® Kids' Knock Knock Book
Everything® Kids' Math Puzzles Book
Everything® Kids' Mazes Book
Everything® Kids' Money Book

All Everything® books are priced at $12.95 or $14.95, unless otherwise stated. Prices subject to change without notice.

Everything® Kids' Monsters Book
Everything® Kids' Nature Book
Everything® Kids' Puzzle Book
Everything® Kids' Riddles & Brain Teasers Book
Everything® Kids' Science Experiments Book
Everything® Kids' Soccer Book
Everything® Kids' Travel Activity Book

KIDS' STORY BOOKS

Everything® Bedtime Story Book
Everything® Bible Stories Book
Everything® Fairy Tales Book

LANGUAGE

Everything® Conversational Japanese Book
  (with CD), $19.95
Everything® Inglés Book
Everything® French Phrase Book, $9.95
Everything® Learning French Book
Everything® Learning German Book
Everything® Learning Italian Book
Everything® Learning Latin Book
Everything® Learning Spanish Book
Everything® Sign Language Book
Everything® Spanish Phrase Book, $9.95
Everything® Spanish Verb Book, $9.95

MUSIC

Everything® Drums Book (with CD), $19.95
Everything® Guitar Book
Everything® Home Recording Book
Everything® Playing Piano and Keyboards Book
Everything® Rock & Blues Guitar Book
  (with CD), $19.95
Everything® Songwriting Book

NEW AGE

Everything® Astrology Book
Everything® Dreams Book
Everything® Ghost Book
Everything® Love Signs Book, $9.95
Everything® Meditation Book
Everything® Numerology Book
Everything® Paganism Book
Everything® Palmistry Book
Everything® Psychic Book
Everything® Spells & Charms Book
Everything® Tarot Book
Everything® Wicca and Witchcraft Book

PARENTING

Everything® Baby Names Book
Everything® Baby Shower Book
Everything® Baby's First Food Book
Everything® Baby's First Year Book
Everything® Birthing Book
Everything® Breastfeeding Book
Everything® Father-to-Be Book
Everything® Get Ready for Baby Book
Everything® Getting Pregnant Book
Everything® Homeschooling Book
Everything® Parent's Guide to Children
  with Asperger's Syndrome
Everything® Parent's Guide to Children
  with Autism
Everything® Parent's Guide to Children
  with Dyslexia
Everything® Parent's Guide to Positive Discipline
Everything® Parent's Guide to Raising a
  Successful Child
Everything® Parenting a Teenager Book
Everything® Potty Training Book, $9.95
Everything® Pregnancy Book, 2nd Ed.
Everything® Pregnancy Fitness Book
Everything® Pregnancy Nutrition Book
Everything® Pregnancy Organizer, $15.00
Everything® Toddler Book
Everything® Tween Book

PERSONAL FINANCE

Everything® Budgeting Book
Everything® Get Out of Debt Book
Everything® Homebuying Book, 2nd Ed.
Everything® Homeselling Book
Everything® Investing Book
Everything® Online Business Book
Everything® Personal Finance Book
Everything® Personal Finance in Your
  20s & 30s Book
Everything® Real Estate Investing Book
Everything® Wills & Estate Planning Book

PETS

Everything® Cat Book
Everything® Dog Book
Everything® Dog Training and Tricks Book
Everything® Golden Retriever Book
Everything® Horse Book
Everything® Labrador Retriever Book
Everything® Poodle Book

Everything® Puppy Book
Everything® Rottweiler Book
Everything® Tropical Fish Book

REFERENCE

Everything® Car Care Book
Everything® Classical Mythology Book
Everything® Einstein Book
Everything® Etiquette Book
Everything® Great Thinkers Book
Everything® Philosophy Book
Everything® Psychology Book
Everything® Shakespeare Book
Everything® Toasts Book

RELIGION

Everything® Angels Book
Everything® Bible Book
Everything® Buddhism Book
Everything® Catholicism Book
Everything® Christianity Book
Everything® Jewish History & Heritage Book
Everything® Judaism Book
Everything® Koran Book
Everything® Prayer Book
Everything® Saints Book
Everything® Understanding Islam Book
Everything® World's Religions Book
Everything® Zen Book

SCHOOL & CAREERS

Everything® After College Book
Everything® Alternative Careers Book
Everything® College Survival Book
Everything® Cover Letter Book
Everything® Get-a-Job Book
Everything® Job Interview Book
Everything® New Teacher Book
Everything® Online Job Search Book
Everything® Personal Finance Book
Everything® Practice Interview Book
Everything® Resume Book, 2nd Ed.
Everything® Study Book

SELF-HELP/ RELATIONSHIPS

Everything® Dating Book
Everything® Divorce Book
Everything® Great Sex Book

All Everything® books are priced at $12.95 or $14.95, unless otherwise stated. Prices subject to change without notice.

Everything® Kama Sutra Book
Everything® Self-Esteem Book

SPORTS & FITNESS

Everything® Body Shaping Book
Everything® Fishing Book
Everything® Fly-Fishing Book
Everything® Golf Book
Everything® Golf Instruction Book
Everything® Knots Book
Everything® Pilates Book
Everything® Running Book
Everything® T'ai Chi and QiGong Book
Everything® Total Fitness Book
Everything® Weight Training Book
Everything® Yoga Book

TRAVEL

Everything® Family Guide to Hawaii
Everything® Family Guide to New York City,
   2nd Ed.

Everything® Family Guide to Washington D.C.,
   2nd Ed.
Everything® Family Guide to the Walt Disney
   World Resort®, Universal Studios®,
   and Greater Orlando, 4th Ed.
Everything® Guide to Las Vegas
Everything® Guide to New England
Everything® Travel Guide to the Disneyland
   Resort®, California Adventure®,
   Universal Studios®, and the
   Anaheim Area

WEDDINGS

Everything® Bachelorette Party Book, $9.95
Everything® Bridesmaid Book, $9.95
Everything® Creative Wedding Ideas Book
Everything® Elopement Book, $9.95
Everything® Father of the Bride Book, $9.95
Everything® Groom Book, $9.95
Everything® Jewish Wedding Book
Everything® Mother of the Bride Book, $9.95
Everything® Wedding Book, 3rd Ed.

Everything® Wedding Checklist, $7.95
Everything® Wedding Etiquette Book, $7.95
Everything® Wedding Organizer, $15.00
Everything® Wedding Shower Book, $7.95
Everything® Wedding Vows Book, $7.95
Everything® Weddings on a Budget Book, $9.95

WRITING

Everything® Creative Writing Book
Everything® Get Published Book
Everything® Grammar and Style Book
Everything® Grant Writing Book
Everything® Guide to Writing a Novel
Everything® Guide to Writing Children's Books
Everything® Screenwriting Book
Everything® Writing Well Book